MARKETS WITH LIMITS

In *Markets with Limits* James Stacey Taylor argues that current debates over the moral limits of markets have derailed. He argues that they focus on a market-critical position that almost nobody holds: That certain goods and services can be freely given away but should never be bought or sold. And he argues that they focus on a type of argument for this position that there is reason to believe that *nobody* holds: That trade in certain goods or services is wrongful solely because of what it would communicate.

Taylor puts the debates over the moral limits of markets back on track. He develops a taxonomy of the positions that are actually held by critics of markets, and clarifies the role played in current moral and political philosophy by arguments that justify (or condemn) certain actions owing in part to what they communicate. Taylor argues that the debates have derailed because they were conducted in accord with market, rather than academic, norms—and that this demonstrates that market thinking should not govern academic research. *Markets with Limits* concludes with suggestions as to how to encourage academics to conduct research in accord with academic norms and hence improve its quality.

Key features

- Provides original suggestions concerning how to improve the exegetical quality of academic research
- Systematically identifies the primary exegetical errors—and the ways in which these errors have adversely influenced current debates—that Jason Brennan and Peter Jaworski made in their influential book, *Markets Without Limits*

- Argues that despite the current, widespread view that semiotic objections to markets are widespread in the literature, they are in actuality rare to non-existent
- Offers an up-to-date taxonomy of the current arguments in the various debates over both the ontological and the moral limits of markets
- Provides an extensive overview of mistaken claims that have been made and propagated in various academic literatures

James Stacey Taylor is Professor of Philosophy at The College of New Jersey, USA. He is the author of *Death, Posthumous Harm, and Bioethics* (2012), *Practical Autonomy and Bioethics* (2009), and *Stakes and Kidneys: Why Markets in Human Body Parts Are Morally Imperative* (2005), and is the editor of *The Metaphysics and Ethics of Death* (2013) and *Personal Autonomy: New Essays on Personal Autonomy and Its Role in Contemporary Moral Philosophy* (2005).

MARKETS WITH LIMITS

How the Commodification of
Academia Derails Debate

James Stacey Taylor

NEW YORK AND LONDON

Cover image: Off the Rails: Night of Disaster. The crash of the express service at Preston on 15 August 1896. By Graham Coton. Original artwork from Look and Learn no. 478 (13 March 1971). Also used in Look and Learn Book 1986. Credit: © Look and Learn

First published 2022
by Routledge
605 Third Avenue, New York, NY 10158

and by Routledge
2 Park Square, Milton Park, Abingdon, Oxon OX14 4RN

Routledge is an imprint of the Taylor & Francis Group, an informa business

© 2022 Taylor & Francis

The right of James Stacey Taylor to be identified as author of this work has been asserted in accordance with sections 77 and 78 of the Copyright, Designs and Patents Act 1988.

All rights reserved. No part of this book may be reprinted or reproduced or utilised in any form or by any electronic, mechanical, or other means, now known or hereafter invented, including photocopying and recording, or in any information storage or retrieval system, without permission in writing from the publishers.

Trademark notice: Product or corporate names may be trademarks or registered trademarks, and are used only for identification and explanation without intent to infringe.

Library of Congress Cataloging-in-Publication Data
A catalog record for this title has been requested

ISBN: 978-1-032-17149-4 (hbk)
ISBN: 978-1-032-17148-7 (pbk)
ISBN: 978-1-003-25199-6 (ebk)

DOI: 10.4324/9781003251996

Typeset in Bembo
by Taylor & Francis Books

For Octavia, who always checks her references

CONTENTS

Acknowledgments   xii

    Introduction   1

    A Debate in Dire Need of Rescue 1
    Markets, Morals, Mischaracterizations, and Mute Inglorious
       Miltons 3
    Positive Contributions to the Debates 4
    A Map of the Cat 4

PART I
How the Debates Over the Moral Limits of Markets
Became Derailed   9

 1 The Magical Asymmetry Thesis   11

    Introduction 11
    Sandel and Satz Do Not Endorse the Asymmetry Thesis 11
        Sandel and the Asymmetry Thesis 12
        Satz and the Asymmetry Thesis 15
    Anderson: Sex, Surrogacy—and Symmetry 19
        Sex and Sphere Differentiation 20
        Surrogacy and Symmetry 23
    Walzer and Archard Are Not Anticommodification Theorists,
       Either 25

Walzer on Markets and Justice 25
Archard on Blood 27
Conclusion 28

2 Semiotic Objections to Markets   35

Introduction 35
Brennan and Jaworski's Critique of Semiotic Objections to
   Commodification 37
Essentialist Semiotics 39
Contingent Semiotics 40
Conclusion 42

3 Sandel, Semiotics, and Money-Based Exchange   48

Introduction 48
Sandel's Putative Semiotic Objections to Markets 48
Markets in Children and Information Markets in Terrorism and
   Death 50
Inappropriate Gifts? Gift Certificates and Cash 51
Money and the Norms of Friendship 52
Intrinsic Value, Instrumental Value, and Yosemite 56
Conclusion 57

4 Sex, Surrogacy, Semiotics, and Spheres: Anderson on Market
    Exchange   61

Introduction 61
Brennan and Jaworski Attribute Essentialist Semiotic Objections to
   Anderson 61
Anderson Rejects Semiotic Essentialism 63
Anderson Supports Revising Costly Norms 64
Anderson Does Not Offer Semiotic Arguments Against Commodified
   Sex or Surrogacy 66
Conclusion 71

5 Walzer, Satz, Archard, and Semiotics   75

Introduction 75
Michael Walzer's Spheres of Justice 75
Debra Satz and Stanford's Student Newspaper 79
   Satz and the Meaning of Friendship, Love, and Prizes 80
   Satz, Semiotics, Surrogacy, and Sex 81

David Archard's Dominoes 83
Conclusion 86

PART II
Getting the Debates Back on Track   91

6 Expressivist Arguments   93

Introduction 93
Not All Expressivist Arguments Are Semiotic Arguments 93
Expressivist Arguments 95
Descriptive Expressivism 96
Consequentialist Prescriptive Expressivist Arguments 97
Non-consequentialist Prescriptive Expressivist Arguments 99
 Non-consequentialist Prescriptive Expressivist Justifications of Individual Action 99
 Non-consequentialist Prescriptive Expressivist Justifications of Law and Policy 101
New Expressivist Arguments in the Debate Over the Moral Limits of Markets 103
 Booth's Argument 103
 Sparks' Argument 106
 Responses to Booth's and Sparks' Arguments 107
Implications of These Responses 110
Conclusion 111

7 What We Talk About When We Talk About the Limits of Markets   118

Introduction 118
Inherent Moral Limits on Markets 119
Ontological Limits of Markets 120
 Goods and Services that Cannot Be Bought and Sold 120
 Market Transformation 122
 The Importance of Ontological Clarity 124
Contingent Objections to Markets 124
Market Economy vs. Market Society 127
 Pluralistic Value and the Adoption of Norms 128
 Understanding Relationships 128
 Norms and Assessing Competing Conceptions of Relationships 129

Moving Forward to Improve Society 133
Conclusion 133

PART III
From Market Norms to Academic Norms   139

8 Why Good Academics Produce Bad Research: Academic Incentives, Woozles, and Hoaxes   141

Introduction 141
Why Good Academics Produce Bad Research: The Perversity of Current Academic Incentives 141
Propagating Woozles 146
Academic Incentives, Market Norms, and Academic Excellence 149
    A Note on Norms 149
    Norms in Academia 150
Conclusion 151

9 Market Norms and Academic Norms   159

Introduction 159
A Clarification: Markets Norms as Academic Admixture 160
A Market-Based Defense of the Status Quo 161
Academic Errors and a Defense of Market Norms 162
    Reference Errors 163
    Substantial Errors and Market Norms 164
    Factual Errors 164
    Quotation Errors 169
Do Substantial Errors Matter? Continuing the Defense of Market Norms 169
    The Benefits of Error 170
Defending the Primacy of Academic Norms 172
Conclusion 174

10 The Theory and Practice of Changing Norms   182

Introduction 182
Changing Norms in Theory 182
Changing Norms in Practice 185
    Encourage Referees to Become Bounty Hunters 186
    Shifting Incentives for Academic Researchers 188

Revising Other Academic Incentives to Reinforce
    Academic Norms 190
Plagiarism, Negligence, and Academic Norms 191
Conclusion 195

Conclusion					199

Bibliography				*204*
Index					*215*

ACKNOWLEDGMENTS

This project was completed during a semester-long sabbatical from The College of New Jersey. I thank the College for providing me with this time to write. I also thank all of the staff of the R. Barbara Gitenstein Library at The College of New Jersey for their tireless work in fulfilling my many Interlibrary Loan requests.

During the Spring of 2018, James Spence taught a class at Adrian College on my work on "Wrongful Contracts." This involved several synchronous online discussions of my work in progress, including a draft of a paper that contained the early ancestors of some of the arguments in Chapters 2–5. I thank both Spence and his excellent students—Noah Brueckner, Dana Dowd, Clarence Kennedy, Michael Phillips, and Madison Tluczek—for their helpful comments on that early manuscript. I am similarly very grateful to the Institute for Humane Studies for hosting a workshop in 2020 on another work in progress ("Bloody Morality") that at that time included a draft of a chapter that was an early ancestor of some of the discussion on semiotic arguments that appears in this volume. I thank Stewart Robertson and Adrienne DePrisco for organizing the workshop, and all of those who participated in it—Andrew I. Cohen, David Dick, Iskra Fileva, Bill Glod, Michael Huemer, Peter Jaworski, Nancy Jecker, Chris MacDonald, Vida Panitch, Travis Timmerman, Christopher Tollefsen, Jeppe von Platz, and Steven Weimer—for their very helpful comments and suggestions.

I thank Jason Grinnell, Tom May, James Spence, and Paul Tudico for their helpful suggestions on the Introduction to this volume, and David McMillan for discussions that helped me to clarify my views. I thank Mark J. Cherry and Margaret Taylor-Ulizio for theological advice in the context of my discussion of the Asymmetry Thesis. I also thank Ben Bridges, the Editor-in-Chief of *Folklore Forum*, for his help in tracking down what might be the first published use of the term "scholarshit," and Sarah Fee for helpful correspondence on the customs of the Tandroy of Madagascar.

Very early ancestors of some sections of Chapter 3 first appeared as "Sandel, Semiotics, and Money-Based Exchange: What We Can Learn from Brennan and Jaworski's Failed Critique," *Public Affairs Quarterly* 33, 2 (2019): 159–176. I thank Nicholas Rescher, the Executive Editor, for his gracious permission to include here whatever might have survived from that early effort. Similarly, early ancestors of some parts of my discussion of Debra Satz's work in Chapter 5 first appeared as "Satz and Semiotics: Brennan and Jaworski's Misplaced Criticisms," *International Journal of Applied Philosophy*, 33, 2 (2019): 243–257. I thank Elliot D. Cohen, the Editor, for his gracious permission to include here whatever might have survived the extensive rewriting of that earlier paper. I also thank the anonymous referees for both *Public Affairs Quarterly* and the *International Journal of Applied Philosophy* for their helpful comments on (even earlier versions) of these papers.

I thank Andrew Beck and Marc Stratton at Routledge for their support and encouragement during the writing and completion of this volume. I am *especially* grateful to the three anonymous referees who reviewed the original manuscript of this volume for Routledge. Their extensive comments and suggestions helped me make this volume much better than it would otherwise have been. I am also extremely grateful to Susan Dunsmore for her meticulous copyediting of the manuscript which saved me from making more errors than I care to count!

The cover image of the paperback version of this volume is Graham Coton's "Off the Rails: Night of Disaster." I thank Reg and Geoff at The Book Palace Ltd for helping me identify the copyright holder, and Look and Learn Ltd. for their gracious permission to reproduce this image. I thank Dean Jane Wong for awarding me a Dean's Mini Grant to pay the reproduction fees.

INTRODUCTION

> So the train mov'd slowly along the Bridge of Tay,
> Until it was about midway,
> Then the central girders with a crash gave way,
> And down went the train and passengers into the Tay!
> The Storm Fiend did loudly bray,
> Because ninety lives had been taken away,
> On the last Sabbath day of 1879,
> Which will be remember'd for a very long time.
> —William McGonagall, "The Tay Bridge Disaster"

A Debate in Dire Need of Rescue

In recent years, much of the debate over the moral limits of markets has derailed. Many of its participants focus on a position on the morality of commodifying certain goods and services that there is no good reason to believe that anyone holds. And they address arguments for this position that there is good reason to believe that *nobody* holds.

These claims might appear implausible. After all, how could it have gone (largely) unnoticed that many of the participants in one of the most flourishing debates in moral philosophy have for the last few years simply been tilting at windmills? I argue in this volume that the answer to this question lies in the incentives that academics are faced with in their professional lives. An academic's professional success is largely judged by the number and quality of her publications, with the usual proxy for the latter being the reputation of the venue in which they appeared (for articles) or their publisher (for books). Academic work that is published after undergoing peer review is supposed to have thereby received an imprimatur of quality. But while academics have an incentive to publish, they have little incentive to serve as peer reviewers—and even *less* incentive to engage in the time-consuming work of checking submitted manuscripts to ensure that they are exegetically accurate. It is thus only to be expected that exegetically inaccurate work will enter the academic literature. And just as academics have little incentive to check the exegetical accuracy of the work that they referee, so too do they have little incentive to check the exegetical accuracy of published work. Once an exegetical error has been introduced in print, it might come to be accepted at face value—and then repeated by others, becoming entrenched in the literature into which it entered. If the error that becomes thus entrenched is a misrepresentation of a prominent position in a debate, it could result in the derailing of that debate. And the greater the number of such errors that become entrenched in a debate, the more it will veer off track.

This is what has happened in the debates over the moral limits of markets.

Many of the participants in the current debates over the moral limits of markets accept that "the action" within them focuses on the question of whether there are any goods or services that exhibit a certain asymmetry in the means by which they can be legitimately distributed: They can be given away freely but they should not (morally) be bought or sold.[1] (I will call the thesis that there are such goods or services the "Asymmetry Thesis.") Many of the participants in these debates also believe that the claim that there are such goods or services is commonly supported by appeal to "semiotic" objections to markets.[2] (A semiotic objection is, roughly, that the sale of certain goods or services is wrongful because such sale would necessarily communicate a wrongful attitude, either toward the goods or services in question or toward something that they are associated with.) This focus on the Asymmetry Thesis and on the semiotic arguments that are supposedly widely offered in its support is the direct result of the widespread influence of Jason Brennan and Peter M. Jaworski's work on the moral limits of markets.[3] Brennan and Jaworski ascribe these views to those they identify as "critics of markets" (such as Michael J. Sandel, Elizabeth Anderson, Debra Satz, Michael Walzer, and David Archard). They then proceed to offer trenchant criticisms of them. On the face of it, these criticisms are utterly compelling. They appear to demonstrate clearly (and humorously!) that most (if not all) of the objections to markets that can be found in the contemporary literature are unsound. As a result, their work has received significant critical acclaim. Their book, *Markets Without Limits*, has been described as "a tour de force of philosophical argument that leaves the opponents' camp routed and the ground strewn with gauntlets thrown down in challenge."[4] Their critiques of those they take to be critics of markets have been widely cited in philosophical debates, ranging from those where this could be anticipated (e.g., concerning the morality of prostitution),[5] to those where it might be surprising (e.g., concerning the morality of designing artificially intelligent agents to be servants to humans).[6] The influence of their work has also extended outside philosophy. It has been cited and discussed in economics,[7] sociology,[8] and law.[9] It has even (unusually for work in philosophy) garnered positive attention from national news media, including *The Washington Post* in the United States and the *National Post* in Canada.[10]

Unfortunately, very few of the participants in these discussions have noticed that Brennan and Jaworski have systematically (if inadvertently) misrepresented the views of the critics of the market whose work they address.[11] None of these critics endorse the Asymmetry Thesis. And none endorse the semiotic arguments that Brennan and Jaworski claim are commonly offered in support of it.

Markets, Morals, Mischaracterizations, and Mute Inglorious Miltons

That Brennan and Jaworski's work is both highly influential and deeply misleading is problematic. If it is widely accepted *both* that the most prominent critics of markets in philosophy markets support their endorsement of the Asymmetry Thesis with semiotic arguments *and* that Brennan and Jaworski have successfully shown both that the Asymmetry Thesis is false and that semiotic arguments are unsound, then it will also be likely that it will be widely accepted that the arguments of the critics of markets will have been "routed."[12] The widespread acceptance of Brennan and Jaworski's (mis)characterization of the debate will thus lead to an inaccurate view of the current state of the debate. It will be widely (but erroneously) believed that the debate over the moral limits of markets is a debate over whether or not the Asymmetry Thesis is true, with the critics of markets univocally holding that it is and the defenders of markets holding that it is not. It will be widely (but erroneously) believed that the primary arguments offered against markets in "contested commodities" are semiotic.[13] And it will be widely (but erroneously) believed that the major moral objections to "markets" in (e.g.) sex, votes, kidneys, surrogate pregnancy, and other "contested commodities" that have been offered by the critics of markets have all been met.

But the propagation of these false views of the state of play in the debates over the moral limits of markets are not problematic merely because it is bad for people to have false views. They are problematic because their widespread acceptance could derail these debates. Persons who accept the above mischaracterization of the debates over the moral limits of markets might decide not to engage in them as they believe (falsely) that the issues they addressed are now settled. Their potential contributions to these debates could thus be lost. Persons who do not think that the issues are settled but who accept the above mischaracterization of the debate might not engage with the work of the critics of markets whose work Brennan and Jaworski criticized as they believe it to be a dead end. The productive discussion of those critics' work that they could have contributed could thus be lost. And the widespread acceptance of the above mischaracterizations of the debates could lead people to engage in defending or criticizing positions that were (largely or entirely) absent from the original debates. If these positions were originally absent because they are untenable, then discussion of them would both fail to advance the debate and quickly peter out. And if this state of affairs is combined with the possibility that robust objections to markets could be neglected, out of the mistaken belief that they have been "routed," it could lead to persons prematurely concluding their discussions after having either arrived at the wrong conclusions, or (perhaps) the right conclusions for the wrong reasons. None of these are desirable situations.

Positive Contributions to the Debates

Although this volume begins with a discussion of how Brennan and Jaworski have mischaracterized the debates over the appropriate limits of markets, its primary aims are all positive rather than negative. Correcting the relevant errors in their work will improve the quality of the debates over the proper limits of markets by clearing away the misconceptions it has introduced into them.[14] This will clarify both the positions that are actually held by the critics of markets and the arguments that they have actually advanced in favor of them. These clarifications will enable the debate over the criticisms of markets to be more productive. Similarly, clarifying the relationship that holds between semiotic arguments of the sort criticized by Brennan and Jaworski and similar (non-semiotic) arguments that condemn or justify certain practices on the basis of what they express will enable the debates over these arguments to be more productive. It will enable both the critics and defenders of the latter sort of (non-semiotic) argument to focus on them rather than on distinct (semiotic) arguments that merely resemble them. Finally, this volume will develop an explanation of how systematic error could enter the academic literature, escape detection, and even be propagated.[15] This explanation will provide the basis for the final positive contribution that this volume will make to the debate over where the appropriate limits of markets should lie: An argument that the norms of the academy—and *not* the norms of the market—should direct academic research.

A Map of the Cat

I have some made some bold claims above. I will now outline how I will support them.

This volume is divided into three Parts. In Part I, I will demonstrate that Brennan and Jaworski have mischaracterized the views of those critics of markets whose work they address. I will argue in Chapter 1 that none of the critics of markets whose work they address endorses the Asymmetry Thesis that they attribute to them. I will then argue in Chapter 2 that while Brennan and Jaworski's criticisms of semiotic objections to markets are sound, not only do none of the critics of markets whose work they address offer such objections, but there is good reason to believe that *no-one* offers them. I will reinforce the arguments of Chapter 2 in Chapters 3, 4, and 5. In those chapters I will examine more carefully Brennan and Jaworski's attribution of semiotic objections to markets to Sandel, Anderson, Walzer, Satz, and Archard. In each case I will demonstrate how Brennan and Jaworski have both misunderstood their (varied) critiques of markets and have misrepresented the arguments that they provide for them. Again, the aim of this critique is positive rather than negative: It is to clear the way to get the debates over the moral limits of markets back on track.

Having identified in Part I how the debates over the moral limits of markets have become derailed, I turn in Part II to rerailing them. In Chapter 6, I will build upon Chapters 2–5 by providing an account of the relationship between semiotic arguments and expressivist arguments. (An expressivist argument is one that appeals to the expressive functions of acts or practices, either to identify them as a particular type of act or practice, or to justify or condemn them, where the expressive function of an act or practice could either be what it is taken to express or its effects on what other acts or practices are taken to express.) In brief, I will argue that while all semiotic arguments are expressivist arguments, not all expressivist arguments are semiotic arguments. A failure to appreciate this relationship between semiotic arguments and expressivist arguments has taken hold in the literature on the moral limits of markets. It is also starting to creep into other discussions in moral and political philosophy. This is leading to confusion in debates where expressivist arguments play a role. The taxonomy of expressivist arguments that I will outline in Chapter 6 will thus play a positive role within these debates by clarifying the nature of various types of expressivist arguments. In so doing, I will demonstrate that they are immune to the objections that Brennan and Jaworski have leveled against semiotic arguments. Chapter 7 will play a similarly positive role by clarifying the nature of the debates—plural—concerning the limits of markets. This chapter will reinforce the arguments of Chapter 1 that "the action" in these debates is very far from the Asymmetry Thesis. It will also clarify the relationships (and, in some cases, the *lack* of relationship) between the various concerns that different theorists have regarding both the expansion of markets themselves as well as the concerns that some express regarding the expansion of market norms.

Having rerailed the debates over the appropriate limits of markets—and market thinking—in Part II, I turn in Part III to contribute to the latter debate by developing a market-critical position: That academic research should be primarily governed by academic, and not market, norms. I lay the foundation for this argument in Chapter 8, in which I explain that the various misconceptions that I identify in Chapters 1–5 might be the result of—and subsequently escaped detection owing to—the incentive structure of contemporary academia. (In this chapter I will also provide further examples of errors—some amusing!—that have entered various academic literatures and that have been subsequently propagated within them.) In this chapter, I elaborate the above outline of how the incentive structure of contemporary academia motivates academics to conform to the norms of the market rather than the norms of the academy. Rather than motivating them primarily to produce work that furthers understanding of their subject, it instead motivates them primarily to produce work that will serve as a "product" to secure extrinsic rewards, such as merit raises, paid speaking engagements, or grants. This redirection of academic efforts toward market success rather than academic achievement leads to academic research being produced in conformity with the norms of the market rather than those of the academy. This, in turn, will (likely) result in the production of academic work that is exegetically inaccurate. Since such exegetical accuracy could involve misrepresenting others' views, it could inhibit rather than advance understanding of the subject that it addresses. There thus appears to be good reason to resist the intrusion of market norms into academic work. I continue my discussion of this issue in Chapter 9, where I consider various ways in which the use of market norms as the primary guides for academic research could be defended. I argue that all of these defenses are flawed and that academic, and not market, norms should be those to which academic researchers should primarily adhere.

Having argued that market thinking should not dominate academic research, I turn in Chapter 10 to suggest ways to discourage the production of academic work in accord with market norms and foster its production in accord with academic norms. I outline ways in which the incentives that academics face could be reorientated to encourage the production of academic work in conformity with the norms of the academy rather than those of the market. This requires motivating referees to identify and document exegetical errors in the manuscripts that they referee, whether these be trivial (e.g., misspelling an author's name, or providing an inaccurate citation) or more serious (e.g., attributing a view to an author that she has explicitly denied holding). It also requires that authors similarly be motivated to ensure that their work is exegetically accurate. And it involves refocusing academic rewards away from the financial and toward the intellectual. I also argue in Chapter 10 that accepting that academic norms should guide academic research will lead to the surprising conclusion that academic plagiarism is not as great an academic sin as it is widely believed to be.

I draw on Chapters 9 and 10 to note in the Conclusion that while this volume is located in the middle of the shared research project that concerns the appropriate limits of markets, its arguments also stand at the start of another: The question concerning both the nature and scope of market norms within the academy. I note that many of the questions that surround what is sometimes referred to as the "commodification" of academic research are empirically testable and provide some initial suggestions as to how to formulate and then test hypotheses in this area. Just as sweetness can come forth from strength, so too can new research projects in the social sciences emerge from philosophical questions.

One final point: Please read the notes and check my references! I outline why this is necessary in Chapters 8 and 9. To encourage this, I have hidden Easter

Eggs among the notes—some of which can only be discovered by checking the references provided.

Let the games begin!

Notes

1 The phrase "the action" as used in this context is owed to Jason Brennan and Peter M. Jaworski, *Markets Without Limits: Moral Virtues and Commercial Interests* (New York: Routledge, 2016), 15. I document the recent widespread acceptance of this view in Chapter 1, note 2.
2 See Chapter 6, note 2.
3 This is primarily contained in Jason Brennan and Peter M. Jaworski, "Markets Without Symbolic Limits," *Ethics* 125, 4 (2015): 1053–1077, and Brennan and Jaworski, *Markets Without Limits*.
4 George Leef, "What's Really Disgusting?," *Regulation* (Spring 2016), 63.
5 Hannah Carnegy-Arbuthnott, "On a Promise or on the Game: What's Wrong with Selling Consent?," *Journal of Applied Philosophy* 37, 3 (2020), 409.
6 Bartek Chomanski, "What's Wrong with Designing People to Serve?," *Ethical Theory and Moral Practice* 22, 4 (2019), 998.
7 See, for example, Geoffrey M. Hodgson, "On the Limits of Markets," *Journal of Institutional Economics* 17, 1 (2021): 153–170.
8 See, for example, Nick Cowen and Rachela Colosi "Sex Work and Online Platforms: What Should Regulation Do?," *Journal of Entrepreneurship and Public Policy* 10, 2 (2021), 288.
9 See, for example, Ram Rivlin, "The Puzzle of Intra-Familial Commodification," *University of Toronto Law Review* 67, 1 (2017), 82, note 51.
10 Ilya Somin, "Opinion: Brennan and Jaworski's 'Markets Without Limits'," *The Washington Post* (November 13, 2015). Available at: www.washingtonpost.com/news/volokh-conspiracy/wp/2015/11/13/brennan-and-jaworskis-markets-without-limits/.
Jesse Kline, "Read Any Good Books Lately? Post Editors and Columnists Submit Their Picks for Your Holiday Reading: *Markets Without Limits*," *National Post* (December 26, 2016). Available at: https://nationalpost.com/opinion/read-any-good-books-lately-post-editors-and-columnists-submit-their-picks-for-your-holiday-reading
11 A notable exception is Julian J. Koplin, "Commodification and Human Interests," *Journal of Bioethical Inquiry* 15, 3 (2018): 429–440.
12 Leef, "What's Really Disgusting?," 63.
13 The phrase "contested commodities" is owed to Margaret Jane Radin, *Contested Commodities: The Trouble with Trade in Sex, Children, Body Parts, and Other Things* (Cambridge, MA: Harvard University Press, 1996).
14 One of Routledge's referees for this volume observed that I had performed the useful task of identifying all of the errors in *Markets Without Limits*. Alas, I have not. I have only identified (some of) the errors associated with those aspects of it that I address directly.
15 And how these errors could even appear in highly selective academic outlets—as Brennan and Jaworski take care to remind us, their work on the moral limits of markets has been published by "top venues" such as *Ethics* and Routledge. Brennan and Jaworski, *Markets Without Limits*, 227, note 3.

PART I
How the Debates Over the Moral Limits of Markets Became Derailed

1
THE MAGICAL ASYMMETRY THESIS

Introduction

In the Introduction to this volume I noted that none of the "anti-commodification theorists" to whom Brennan and Jaworski ascribed the Asymmetry Thesis endorsed it. This is not surprising: The Asymmetry Thesis is a highly implausible view. According to this Thesis, there are certain goods or services that persons can legitimately both possess (occupy, perform, etc.) and give away but which it would necessarily be wrongful for them to buy or sell. On the Asymmetry Thesis what makes a purchase or sale of the goods or services to which it applies wrongful is the mere fact that the good or service in question was purchased or sold. According to the Asymmetry Thesis, then, the wrong of buying or selling a good that the proponents of the Thesis have determined can be given away but not bought or sold is what W.D. Ross called a "bare wrong"—an act that is wrong independently of anything other than the fact that it is wrong.[1] Indeed, the Asymmetry Thesis is not only highly implausible—it is almost a magical view. It holds that the mere performance of a particular set of actions alone will (independently of anything apart from their performance) generate wrongness where none was before. Given that the Asymmetry Thesis is so implausible, it is not surprising that few (if any) critics of markets accept it. But despite the obvious implausibility of the Asymmetry Thesis, Brennan and Jaworski's attribution of it to Sandel, Satz, Anderson, Walzer, and Archard has been widely (and uncritically) accepted.[2]

Sandel and Satz Do Not Endorse the Asymmetry Thesis

Brennan and Jaworski explicitly (and wrongly) attribute the Asymmetry Thesis to both Sandel and Satz. They write:

DOI: 10.4324/9781003251996-3

When critics of the market, such as Sandel or Satz, write books about what should not be for sale, what they intend to do is to identify things that are normally permissible for adults to possess, own, have, occupy, provide, or use, but which are not permissible for those adults to trade, sell, and/or buy. They intend to discuss cases where markets really do transform otherwise permissible activities into wrongful actions. They intend to identify cases where the wrongness of buying and selling an object originates in the buying and selling, not in the object itself.[3]

Sandel and the Asymmetry Thesis

Writing of Sandel's views, they state that:

> Sandel of course thinks it is permissible for you to stand in line at Disney World. He even thinks it is permissible for you to hold a spot in line for your kids, only to jump out at the last minute so they can ride the roller coaster in your place. But he doesn't want people to sell line-standing services. You can hold the line for free, but you can't sell your spot.[4]

This is not Sandel's view.

Sandel's discussion of line-standing services occurs in "Jumping the Queue," the first chapter of his insightful book *What Money Can't Buy: The Moral Limits of Markets*. Sandel begins this chapter by outlining various different ways in which people can buy their way out of standing in line. One can, for example, pay extra to board an airplane before other passengers, buy a pass at Universal Studios to skip waiting in line for rides, or pay someone to wait in line for you to gain one of the free tickets that New York City's Public Theatre offers to see outdoor performances of Shakespeare in Central Park.[5]

Sandel notes that the increasing opportunities that people have to pay to avoid waiting in line for a good or service that they desire show that "the ethic of the queue—'first come, first-served'—is being displaced by the ethic of the market—'you get what you pay for'."[6]

Sandel notes that two arguments are commonly offered to support the use of markets over queues to allocate goods and services. The first he terms "libertarian"—"that people should be free to buy and sell whatever they please, as long as they don't violate anyone's rights."[7] Sandel is more interested in the second, utilitarian, argument: That market exchanges make (*ex ante*) both parties to them better off, and so improve social utility.[8] Sandel notes that this utilitarian argument can be buttressed with a second: That the people who most value the good or service on offer would be those who would be most willing to pay to secure it. Thus, to ensure that tickets to (e.g.) Shakespeare in the Park go to those who most value them—and hence whose receipt of them would maximize social utility—they should be distributed by market means rather than by queuing.[9]

In response to this second argument, Sandel holds that "[e]ven if your goal is to maximize social utility, free markets may not do so more reliably than queues."[10] Market prices reflect not just willingness to pay for a good but the ability to do so. It is thus possible that the market distribution of goods and services could allocate them to persons who value them less than others who were unable to pay the market price for them but who would have been willing to wait in line to receive them. As such, Sandel concludes, while it is possible that the market distribution of some goods and services would maximize social utility, it is also possible that, for other goods and services, social utility would be maximized by distributing them through queuing. Whether markets or queues would work better to maximize the social utility that is generated by the distribution of any given good or service is hence an empirical question.[11] Since he accepts this, Sandel does not hold the view that while it is permissible to "hold the line for free," it is always impermissible to "sell your spot," as Brennan and Jaworski claim. Indeed, if the market distribution of a particular good or service would maximize social utility, but this good or service was being distributed through queuing, Sandel might *support* rather than oppose the sale of line-standing services. Conversely, if the distribution of a good or service by queuing would maximize social utility, Sandel might oppose the sale of line-standing services. But this would only be an incidental—not a necessary—limit on this market.

It is not surprising that Sandel does not endorse the Asymmetry Thesis with respect to line-standing services for he does not defend this Thesis at all. He is not concerned with identifying goods and services that could be legitimately possessed (or performed) and given away free but not bought or sold.[12] Instead, he addresses the question of whether in addition to being a market *economy* (in which productive activity is organized by the market), the contemporary United States should also be a market *society* (in which all human interactions are governed by the norms of money-based market exchange).[13] Sandel's interest in queuing thus stems from his interest in the question of whether certain goods or services should be distributed in accordance with non-market rather than market *norms*. His initial answer to this question was noted above—that if social utility were to be maximized by the non-market distribution of certain goods and services (e.g., through queuing), we should oppose their distribution in accordance with market norms. But Sandel also provides an alternative (but related) answer to this question.

Sandel observes that in some cases "[h]ow a good is allocated may be part of what makes it the kind of good it is."[14] Sandel illustrates this by holding that if tickets to Shakespeare in the Park were distributed by the market rather than by queues, its performances would no longer be public festivals open to all but would instead become privatized for-profit events. Similarly, he argues, allowing access to Congress to be distributed by market means would transform it into a business "rather than an institution of representative government."[15] On this view, certain goods can only be distributed by non-market means; attempts to distribute them by market means will transform them into similar but distinct goods.[16] If the versions of the goods in question that would exist when they are distributed by non-market means are superior to those that would exist when they are distributed by market means, then this would provide reason to oppose the introduction of the market-based version of the good in question. Sandel considers the "public festival" version of Shakespeare in the Park to be superior to the for-profit event version, and the version of Congress where it is an institution of representative government to be superior to its business-orientated version. Since he believes that access to the superior version of these goods would be more likely to maximize social utility, Sandel opposes these goods being distributed in accordance with market norms.[17]

In holding that the distribution of certain goods or services in accord with market norms would transform them into similar but distinct versions of the goods they would have been had they been distributed in accordance with non-market norms, Sandel is not committed to holding that the goods or services in question should only be given away and never sold. He is only committed to the (weaker) claim that such goods should not be distributed *in accord with market norms*.[18] Consider two further examples that Sandel offers: the scalping of tickets both to campsites in Yosemite National Park and to Bruce Springsteen concerts. Sandel notes that there was public outrage when it was discovered that ticket scalpers were selling reservations at Yosemite campsites for up to $150 a night—reservations that they had acquired from the National Park Service at the original nominal cost of $20 a night.[19] He also observed that when in 2009 Springsteen played two concerts in his home state of New Jersey, he deliberately charged less than market price for his tickets as "a way of keeping faith with his working-class fans."[20] Sandel approved of the terms of sale that existed in the primary market for these goods—campsites priced at a nominal $20, Springsteen tickets priced below market value.[21] He objected to the subsequent re-sale of these goods at the market price.[22] Sandel would thus not object were tickets to Shakespeare in the Park or to Congress sold at a nominal cost. This would be compatible with their being distributed by the non-market means that preserved the existence of the superior non-market versions of these goods. There is thus no reason to ascribe the Asymmetry Thesis to him.

I noted above that Sandel's concern is with the various questions that arise from considering the extent to which market norms should govern social behavior. While for the purposes of the above discussion (establishing that Sandel does not endorse the Asymmetry Thesis), these questions did not need to be clearly differentiated, it would be useful to offer a brief taxonomy of them. The first of these questions (which Sandel addresses in his initial discussion of queuing) is the empirical question of whether the use of markets or non-market forms of distribution would be most likely to maximize social utility. The second concerns the issue of which method of distribution would be best used to allocate goods and services whose nature would differ, depending on whether they were distributed by market or non-market means. Sandel raises this question through the examples of paying line-standers to Congress and the below-market pricing of Springsteen tickets. To address it, it will first need to be established that the nature of the good in question will change depending on its method of distribution. Then, if it is determined that the good that is allocated by market means is distinct from the similar good that is allocated by non-market means, it will need to be determined which of these goods would be preferable given the situation in which its distribution will take place. This determination will require considering a variety of factors. These will include the perceived relative value of these goods to their recipients, the numbers of persons that would receive each version of the goods at issue (if this would differ) and whether preserving a set of non-market goods would further any morally salient ends (and whether the non-market version of this good should be included in that set).[23]

The third question that Sandel raises is whether there are any goods that should not be distributed in accord with market norms because to allocate them in this way would (given the prevailing understanding of the social symbolism of market distribution) be wrongfully to treat them as having mere instrumental (rather than intrinsic) value. (This is the issue that he addresses when he objects to the market distribution of campsites at Yosemite.) Finally, Sandel questions whether the acceptance of a particular set of norms (e.g., market norms, or non-market norms) to govern interactions between persons in particular relationships (e.g., friendships) would evince a particular understanding of the nature of the type of relationship in question. From this, he raises the question of whether the adoption of market norms to govern the interactions of the persons in the relationship in question (e.g., friends trying to maximize each other's preference satisfaction) would indicate that the persons in question understood their relationship in a way that would be less likely to lead to their flourishing than would an alternative understanding of it. These third and fourth questions (and the subsidiary questions that arise from the latter) appear to be concerned primarily with semiotic issues rather than with the Asymmetry Thesis. I will accordingly consider them in Chapter 3 in the context of discussing Brennan and Jaworski's erroneous attribution to Sandel of essentialist semiotic objections to markets.

Satz and the Asymmetry Thesis

Brennan and Jaworski initially attribute to Satz what could be termed the "anti-expansion" criticism of markets. They write that she has "argued that certain things should not be for sale" as she opposes "putting something up for sale that was not previously the kind of thing people tended to buy and sell."[24] The view that the only goods and services that should be available for sale are those that are "the kind of thing" that people "previously ... tended to buy and sell" is distinct from the Asymmetry Thesis.[25] Instead of holding that there are certain goods or services that can be given away freely but not bought and sold, the anti-expansion criticism of markets opposes *initiating* the buying and selling of goods and services that were not previously bought and sold. Unlike the Asymmetry Thesis, it does not hold that there are certain goods or services that it would be *inherently* wrongful to buy or sell. Instead, it holds that the buying or selling of certain goods or services would be wrongful in *particular situations* where this kind of good or service had not been bought or sold previously. It is thus a contingent, not an essentialist, objection to certain markets.[26]

Brennan and Jaworski go on to clarify that they understand Satz's aim in her book, *Why Some Things Should Not Be for Sale*, to "identify things that are normally permissible for adults to possess, own, have, occupy, provide, or use, but which are not permissible for those adults to trade, sell, and/or buy."[27] At no point when they outline what they take to be Satz's views do Brennan and Jaworski refer to her work to justify their attribution of these positions to her. This is unfortunate. Had they attempted to cite her work to support their reading of it, they would have discovered that Satz is committed to neither of the views—the anti-expansion criticism of markets or the Asymmetry Thesis—that they attribute to her.[28]

Satz does not offer an anti-expansion objection to markets. She does not argue for the conservative position that some things that have not previously been "the kind of thing that people tended to buy and sell" should remain market inalienable.[29] Instead, she develops a complex theory of what would make a market in a good or service noxious in a particular situation. On this theory, potentially wrongful markets should be assessed in terms of four parameters: (1) vulnerability, (2) weak agency, (3) extremely harmful outcomes for individuals, and (4) extremely harmful outcomes for society.[30] This approach *could* lead to the condemnation of "putting something up for sale that was not previously the kind of thing people tended to buy and sell"; Satz criticizes newly-emerging markets in women's reproductive labor as these operate within contemporary American society.[31] But it could also justify the moral acceptance of newly emerging markets. Satz is, for example, open to the possibility that futures markets in human kidneys could be morally acceptable.[32] And, of course, Satz's approach could lead to the condemnation of markets in certain goods and services that have existed for centuries: She opposes bonded labor, the employment of children as prostitutes or soldiers, and female adult prostitution when this perpetuates inequality between men and women.[33]

As I noted in the Introduction to this volume, the target of Brennan and Jaworski's critique of "anti-commodification" theorists is the Asymmetry Thesis. They do not directly address the anti-expansion criticisms of markets.[34] It thus does not matter to their arguments that this is not Satz's view. But what does matter to their arguments is that Satz is not committed to the Asymmetry Thesis that captures the anti-commodification position that they criticize.

I noted above that Satz's "theory of what makes particular markets noxious" rests on assessing them both against the quality of the agency exhibited by those who participate in them and against their effects. On the first dimension of assessment we need to determine whether persons involved in the market in question would accept "any terms of exchange that are offered" (i.e., they are vulnerable) and whether they either have "poor information about the goods they are exchanging" or "depend on others' decisions."[35] On the second dimension of assessment we need to determine if the markets in question would have extremely harmful outcomes, either for individuals or for society (e.g., by undermining "the framework needed for a society of equals").[36] Satz holds that "[h]igh scores along any one of these dimensions, or several of them together, can make any market appear 'noxious' to us."[37] She is also clear that how a particular market scores on these dimensions will depend on the particular circumstances against which that market operates, "so that markets that are currently noxious may emerge under other conditions as perfectly acceptable (or the reverse)."[38]

Satz thus endorses a view that is very similar to that of Brennan and Jaworski.[39] Brennan and Jaworski believe that if selling a good or service is wrong, the wrongness stems from the time, place, and manner in which the good or service is sold, not from the fact that it is that good or service that is being sold.[40] To illustrate a case of "bad timing," they state that it would be morally problematic to sell life insurance at a friend's funeral. This, they hold, is not because it is morally wrong to sell life insurance but because it is morally wrong to sell life insurance at a funeral.[41] To show that markets can sometimes have wrong locations, they note that there is no moral obligation incumbent upon homeowners to host others' Tupperware parties. But this is not because the sale of Tupperware is morally wrong. It is just because it would be morally wrong for Tupperware salespersons to force themselves into others' homes to sell their wares. The homes of unwilling hosts are not the place to sell Tupperware.[42] Finally, Brennan and Jaworski observe that the manner in which market transactions occur matters morally. To illustrate this, they compare markets to guitar amplifiers. They note that "[j]ust as guitar amps have various knobs (gain, volume, bass, midrange, treble…) so markets might have a range of variables that can be put to different settings."[43] Brennan and Jaworski identify "seven dimensions of market manner":

1. who the participants in the market are;
2. what the means of exchange is (e.g., money, barter, giftcards);
3. what the price of the good or service is;
4. how much value each party to the transactions gets from it;
5. what the mode of exchange is (e.g., whether it is an auction, a lottery, a bazaar, etc.);
6. what the mode of payment is (e.g., a salary, a tip, a scholarship, etc.);
7. what the motive for exchange is (e.g., whether it is for profit, for the public benefit, for charity, etc.).[44]

Brennan and Jaworski hold that "even if selling certain goods and services a certain way might be bad, there is always a different time, place, and manner for selling those goods and services that would remove those objections."[45] Thus, while it might be morally impermissible to purchase a kidney from a desperate seller for $5, it might not be morally impermissible to purchase a kidney from a wealthy person for $500,000. The (apparent) wrongness of the first transaction does not stem from the wrongness of markets in kidneys but from the wrongful manner in which this trade was conducted. But while this approach to assessing the morality of particular markets differs in detail from Satz's, it does not differ in kind.[46] Like Brennan and Jaworski, Satz believes that markets in certain goods or services that are noxious in particular circumstances could be rendered palatable by altering the "manner" of the market in morally relevant ways. She writes that a noxious market might be rendered palatable by "legislating a safety net, or by educational policies designed to increase information, or by mechanisms aimed at increasing accountability, or by tax-and-transfer schemes to reduce inequality."[47] But this implies that, like Brennan and Jaworski, Satz could accept that there is no good or service whose nature requires that it only be given away free and never sold. There are only goods and services whose sale would be contingently wrongful under certain conditions. She is thus not committed to the Asymmetry Thesis as Brennan and Jaworski believe.

But while there is nothing in Satz's theory of what renders a market noxious that commits her to the Asymmetry Thesis, at times she comes close to writing as though she endorses it with respect to certain goods or services. Satz believes that a market in a good or service that would undermine the equality of citizens within a democracy would inflict an extreme harm upon society and hence be noxious.[48] Thus, if markets in "political, regulatory, judicial, and legal decision mechanisms" would undermine citizen equality by allowing the rich to gain disproportionate power over their fellow citizens, this would provide a reason to block them.[49] Alternatively, she notes, if one adopted a republican (rather than a regulative) conception of government, one would view votes as "acts of political co-deliberation."[50] Adopting this view of democracy would lead one to hold markets in votes to be wrongful on the grounds that voting is not a process to aggregate private interests but "an act undertaken only after collectively deliberating about what is in the common good."[51] Votes (as well as judicial and legislative offices) should thus not be sold, as to do so would be to abdicate one's political responsibility as a co-deliberator. Similar concerns with citizen equality would also prohibit markets in voluntary slaves.[52]

Yet Satz's apparent willingness to support prohibiting these markets is compatible with her rejecting the Asymmetry Thesis.[53] The first and most general point to be made is that Satz analyzes these markets "in terms of general social practices and not acts."[54] She recognizes that the possible problems that might result from widespread sales of these goods and services might not arise if transactions in them were very limited in number.[55] Her (possible) condemnation of allowing markets in these goods and services (where the term "market" implies a widespread social practice of buying and selling a particular good or service) thus does not commit her to the view that under no circumstances could these goods or services be bought or sold.[56]

Second, one could reject the Asymmetry Thesis even if one endorsed either the regulative or republican ideal of democracy, as these are outlined by Satz. The regulative ideal of democracy would lead one to oppose markets in votes, judicial offices, and legislative offices on the grounds that such markets must be prohibited to prevent the rich from securing a disproportionate amount of power over others. But this reasoning should also lead one to prohibit the holders of votes or these offices being free to reallocate them "for free" at their own discretion. Allowing such discretionary reallocation would enable popular people or members of political dynasties to secure a disproportionate amount of power over others. An adherent of the regulative ideal of democracy would thus not hold that while it would be always acceptable to give these goods or services away "for free," they could never be bought or sold. She would thus not endorse the Asymmetry Thesis with respect to them. Similar points can be made with respect to the republican ideal of democracy. On this ideal, votes and offices should only be allocated as part of a collective deliberative procedure about what is in the common good. Allocating them on the basis of other criteria or through other processes would be thus wrongful. It would, for example, be wrong to give one's vote away to someone else as this would be to abdicate one's responsibility to participate in collective deliberation. And it would be wrongful for an officeholder to give her office away to someone else independently of the collective deliberative process that should determine their allocation.[57] The Asymmetry Thesis thus does not apply to votes or offices under the republican ideal of democracy as, under this ideal, they should neither be given away nor sold.

Third, the opposition to markets in votes voiced by a proponent of the regulative ideal of democracy is really an incidental objection to vote markets, not an objection that vote markets are inherently wrong. This objection is based on the view that such a market would give the rich disproportionate power over others. It thus only has weight in societies where wealth is unequally distributed.[58]

Finally, that the proponents of both the regulative and the republican ideals of democracy would condemn markets in voluntary slaves does not commit them to the Asymmetry Thesis. Their opposition to voluntary slavery stems from the unequal status of the slaves, not from the fact that the slaves sold themselves into slavery. They would thus oppose voluntary slavery independently of whether the slaves sold themselves into slavery or entered into it for free. (This view has an affinity with Anderson's view of surrogacy, as discussed below.) Thus, even if Satz did join with the proponents of either of these views of democracy in opposing markets in votes, offices, and voluntary slaves, this would not commit her to endorsing the Asymmetry Thesis.

Anderson: Sex, Surrogacy—and Symmetry

Just as Brennan and Jaworski explicitly (but erroneously) attributed the Asymmetry Thesis to Sandel and Satz, so too do they explicitly (but erroneously) attribute it to Anderson. They write that

Elizabeth Anderson has no problem with you having casual sex or with you serving, for free, as a pregnancy surrogate for your infertile sister. But she doesn't want people to sell sex or surrogacy. For her, you can give it away, but you can't sell it—and others shouldn't buy it.[59]

As with their discussion of Satz's views, Brennan and Jaworski provide no citations for this account of Anderson's views concerning commercial sex and surrogate pregnancy.[60] But this is not surprising since Anderson does not endorse the Asymmetry Thesis with respect to commercial sex and surrogate pregnancy.

Sex and Sphere Differentiation

To understand why Anderson rejects the Asymmetry Thesis, her views concerning commercial sex and surrogate pregnancy should be placed within the context of her wider ethical theory. Anderson's view that the use of market norms to structure social relations should be limited "is based on a pluralistic theory of the social conditions for freedom and autonomy."[61] She believes that a person is free if she "has access to a wide range of significant options through which she can express her diverse valuations."[62] Drawing on this pluralistic theory of value, Anderson holds that persons can only develop and express certain evaluations if these are recognized and supported by the norms that exist in their social milieu. For example, a person "cannot honor someone outside a social context in which certain actions, gestures, and manners of speaking are commonly understood to express honor."[63] Even when these communicative performances are understood to express honor, this expression will not be adequate unless others recognize it as being appropriate.[64] A person is thus not free to honor another unless she is in a social context in which there are norms governing both how honor is to be expressed and when it is appropriate to do this. For a person to be free to express her diverse valuations of different goods, then, she must have access to differing social spheres in which these different norms of evaluation (e.g., honor) are recognized and supported. For Anderson, then, freedom requires "*multiple sphere differentiation*" with (permeable) boundaries separating differing social environments.[65] This differentiation between social spheres ensures that the norms that are upheld in one sphere as properly governing the way in which persons value the goods associated with it do not dominate other spheres, thereby reducing the number of different sets of norms that persons can draw upon to evaluate goods in different ways.[66]

This is a complex view. To illustrate it, consider the differences between the norms that structure how persons interact with each other and value goods in a market setting and those that structure how they interact with each other in a professional setting.[67] Anderson notes that market norms "have five features that express the attitudes surrounding use [of economic goods] and embody the economic ideal of freedom: they are impersonal, egoistic, exclusive, want-regarding, and orientated to 'exit' rather than 'voice'."[68] She notes that "[e]ach party to a market transaction views his relationship to the other as merely a means to the satisfaction of ends defined independently of the relationship and of the other party's ends."[69] The parties to market transactions are "free to switch trading partners at any time," and a person's access to money is the only determinant of her access to the goods and services traded on the market.[70] Each is "free to pursue their individual interests without considering others' interests" and each is "expected to take care of herself."[71] By contrast, professional norms determine the actions that it would be appropriate for those governed by them to perform in accordance with "the standards of goods internal to the practice rather than by external instrumental criteria such as profitability."[72] A lawyer, for example, is bound by professional norms that enjoin her both to uphold justice and to work in the best interests of her clients. Her excellence as a lawyer is not defined by how profitable her practice is but by how well she represents her clients and serves justice. A lawyer thus should not view her relationships with her clients as merely a means to satisfy ends that are defined independently of those relationships but should view them as satisfying ends that are defined by the lawyer-client relationship itself. She is also not free to cease representing her clients at will—she can only do so if there are external circumstances that would justify this. And she is not free to pursue her own interests without considering those of her client. She is not, for example, free to prolong a probate case even if this would earn her more fees unless this would serve her client's interests. If the social milieu in which a lawyer practiced was governed by none of these norms but only by those of the market, she would not be free to practice *as a lawyer* as this profession is understood when governed by these norms. There would be nothing to differentiate the kind of activity that a professional engages in from the kind of activity that a market actor engages in. In this sense, there would be nothing to distinguish a lawyer's practice from that of a store clerk.

The norms that govern market transactions and the norms that govern professional behavior can thus conflict. But, Anderson notes, this does not entail that professionals should avoid participating in the market. The freedom to be governed by different sets of evaluative norms requires only that the spheres in which they operate be *differentiated* not that they be *segregated*.[73] It is possible for professionals—such as lawyers—to sell their services while continuing to adhere to professional norms. This partial commodification of the goods internal to their professions (e.g., legal services) is not morally problematic. Indeed, Anderson notes, it could promote both equality of opportunity (opening up professions to persons who are not independently wealthy) and personal autonomy (by securing them "voice" over their own activities by freeing them from being dependent on wealthy benefactors).[74] Yet while Anderson accepts that some permeability between different spheres of normativity could enhance their occupants' autonomy, she cautions against allowing market norms to "wholly govern exchanges of money for professional products or services."[75] To preserve their autonomy, professionals should not relinquish their adherence to professional norms in exchange for money. Lawyers should not merely act as "hired guns" for their clients, "harassing those against whom their clients have no genuine legal case" and doctors should not perform "profitable but medically unwarranted services on ignorant or demanding patients."[76] To give up their adherence to the norms internal to their professions in this way would, for Anderson, reduce professionals to the status of mere employees. Their actions would no longer be directed by the values that they had reflectively endorsed but by the desires of others who had both the ability and willingness to pay them to act at their behest. To the extent that this is so, their autonomy with respect to those actions would be diminished.

Anderson observes that there are other ways in which unfettered commodification could adversely affect the autonomy of some of those who participate in them. Allowing the sale of addictive drugs could compromise the autonomy of persons who would be susceptible to having their autonomy compromised through drug abuse. Similarly, within certain social contexts, allowing the sale of certain goods (e.g., votes) could lead to the autonomy of certain classes of persons being compromised. If, for example, votes were commodified in a society in which there was widespread economic inequality, this could lead to the poor being *de facto* disenfranchised which could, in turn, compromise their autonomy.[77]

Anderson thus agrees with Brennan and Jaworski that there are "some things that people inherently should not have" and so in consequence there are some things that "people should not buy or sell."[78] (For Anderson, this class would include addictive drugs, while Brennan and Jaworski hold that people should not have child pornography or nuclear weapons.[79]) And she agrees with them that the reason that such goods should not be commodified is because they would be likely to adversely affect people—it is the goods themselves that are morally problematic and not their means of distribution. She also agrees with Brennan and Jaworski that markets are subject to incidental limits—that at certain times and places certain goods or services should not be exchanged for money, while at other times or in other places such exchanges would be morally unproblematic.[80]

But Anderson's primary concern is neither with the question of which goods or services should never be commodified nor with the question of which goods and services could legitimately be commodified in a particular circumstance. Instead, she is concerned with the separate question of which norms should govern the distribution of certain goods and services. In particular, she is concerned with the question of which goods and services should be governed (and hence distributed) according to the norms of the market (i.e., which should be commodified) and which should be governed by other norms (i.e., which should not be commodified even if they are exchanged for cash).[81] Most importantly, for Anderson, the moral concern with freedom and autonomy requires that the distribution of goods embodied in the person ("such as freedom of action and the powers of productive and reproductive labor") are not governed solely by the norms of the market.[82] To illustrate this, consider Anderson's distinction between the sale of sex when this is governed by market norms (i.e., prostitution) and when this is governed by professional norms (e.g., sex therapy). For Anderson, the commodification of sex occurs when it is sold according to the norms of the marketplace. In this situation, each party to the transaction values the other only instrumentally;[83] each views their "relationship to the other as merely a means to the satisfaction of ends defined independently of the relationship and the other party's ends."[84] But while the customer's cash payment is "impersonal and fully alienable," the prostitute yields to him power over her person.[85] In selling her sexuality in accordance with market norms, she relinquishes her claim to exercise voice over how it is manifested, retaining only the ability to exit the deal.[86] Through thus subjecting herself to the domination of another, her autonomy is compromised and she is correspondingly degraded. By contrast, argues Anderson, when the sale of sex is not governed by market norms, the sellers' autonomy could be inviolate. To show this, she considers "a worthwhile practice of professional sex therapy aimed at helping people liberate themselves from perverse, patriarchal forms of sexuality."[87] The sale of sex in this milieu would be governed by professional, rather than market, norms. As such, the sellers of sex would not alienate control over their actions by selling them, but, instead, would retain their voice through the period of the therapist-client relationship. They would thus neither be degraded through selling sex, nor would their autonomy be compromised by this. The sale of sex by such therapists would be more akin to the sale of legal services by lawyers (when these are governed by the norms reflectively endorsed by the legal profession) than to the sale of (commodified) sex by prostitutes. Anderson is thus clear that she believes that the provision of sexual services for payment is permissible provided that the transaction is governed by the appropriate (professional) norms rather than those of the market. (She would thus agree with Brennan and Jaworski that her objections to the sale of sex are objections to particular ways in which sex is sold rather than objections to the sale of sex as such.[88]) She thus does not hold that it is never permissible to sell sex, as Brennan and Jaworski assert.

Surrogacy and Symmetry

Brennan and Jaworski are similarly mistaken to claim that Anderson believes that while it is permissible for someone to serve as a pregnancy surrogate "for free," she believes that it is impermissible "to sell ... surrogacy." Anderson believes that it is impermissible to serve as a pregnancy surrogate simpliciter independently of whether one is paid to do so or not.

Anderson argues that not all contracts that persons freely enter into will "express and uphold" their autonomy.[89] She holds that "some rights in one's person are so essential to dignity and autonomy that they must be held inalienable."[90] She is clear that "[t]his is not a paternalistic claim"; it is not the claim that some persons (i.e., those who would contract themselves into slavery) should be protected "from their own bad judgement."[91] Rather, it is the claim "that there are some ways of treating people that are morally objectionable, even if they consent to being treated those ways."[92] Even if a woman autonomously consented to a surrogacy contract, it might still be wrongful if its terms required her to submit to treatment that failed to respect her autonomy. For Anderson, then, to establish that a surrogacy contract is permissible, one cannot merely determine that both parties consented to it. One must also "examine the details of such contracts to see whether they treat inalienable rights as if they were alienable commodities."[93] Anderson does not mean that individual surrogacy contracts should be examined to determine whether they treat the women party to them in impermissible ways. She acknowledges that in some cases the contracting agency and the commissioning parents would treat the mother with respect. But she notes that even if this were always the case, this could not be used to defend surrogacy contracts against her charge that they are wrongful. Anderson argues that surrogacy contracts are in important respects similar to slavery contracts. It would, she holds, be mistaken to argue in favor of the moral permissibility of voluntary slavery contracts on the grounds that "there is nothing inherent in a slave contract that violates the dignity and autonomy of the slave" because "many slave owners treat their slaves decently and permit them a wide range of freedoms."[94] This defense of slavery contracts is, she holds, mistaken because such contracts give the slave owners "a license to disrespect their slaves."[95] This alone "is enough to render the slave contract an objectionable form of commodification, because it treats the slave's inalienable rights as alienable."[96] Similarly, she argues, a surrogacy contract treats "the mother's inalienable right to love her child, and to express that love by asserting a claim to custody in its own best interests, as if it were alienable in a market transaction."[97] Just as a slave contract inherently fails to respect the autonomy of the slave by treating it as alienable, so too, for Anderson, does a surrogacy contract fail to respect the autonomy of the surrogate mother. This is because, she argues, a mother's right to love her child is not grounded in the mother's interests but in the obligations that she has to her child. Drawing on Kant's conception of autonomy, Anderson then holds that persons do not express their autonomy by pursuing their "optional personal projects" but by fulfilling their duties.[98] A surrogacy contract, however, will require a mother emotionally to distance herself from her child. The surrogacy contract thus requires the mother to fail to fulfil her duty to the child and hence requires her to refrain from expressing her autonomy in this way. Thus, for Anderson, just as a slavery contract is wrongful because it inherently fails to respect the autonomy of the slave, so too is a surrogacy contract wrongful because it inherently fails to respect the autonomy of the mother.[99]

Anderson's account of why slavery contracts and surrogacy contracts are wrong rests on the claim that they treat certain inalienable rights of personhood whose possession is essential to (Kantian) dignity and autonomy as if they were alienable commodities. A slavery contract wrongs the slave as its acceptance constitutes a rejection of the view that the slave is an end in himself. A surrogacy contract wrongs the mother as it constitutes a rejection of the view that her autonomy is intrinsically valuable by requiring her to refrain from its exercise in fulfilling her obligations to her child. For Anderson, then, it is the *content* of the contract that renders it wrongful—*not* the reason for which the (prospective) slave or surrogate mother agreed to it. The wrongfulness of such contracts thus does not lie in the (prospective) slave or mother being paid to enter into them. They would be just as wrongful if the (prospective) slave or surrogate mother entered into them without being paid to do so—if, for example, they did so altruistically, merely to please his prospective owner or the couple for whom she would carry a child. Anderson, then, holds that slavery contracts and surrogacy contracts are wrongful independently of whether the (prospective) slave or surrogate mother is paid to enter into them. She is thus not committed to the view that money introduces wrongness into a surrogacy transaction where none was before, as she does not believe that it would be permissible to enter into these contracts without payment but impermissible to do so in exchange for money.[100] She thus does not endorse the Asymmetry Thesis with respect to surrogacy.

Anderson is thus not an anti-commodification theorist with respect to surrogacy or sex as Brennan and Jaworski define this position. Instead, she (like Brennan and Jaworski) believes that there are some goods or services that should neither be given away freely nor sold for money.[101]

Walzer and Archard Are Not Anticommodification Theorists, Either

Brennan and Jaworski also attribute the Asymmetry Thesis to Michael Walzer and David Archard. They write that Walzer believes that "certain things cannot be for sale" and that Archard argues that blood should not be bought and sold.[102]

Walzer on Markets and Justice

That Walzer does not endorse the Asymmetry Thesis becomes clear when his views concerning commodification are placed within the context of his theory of justice. Walzer believes that most theories of distributive justice begin with the view that "*People distribute goods to (other) people.*"[103] But he holds that this is too simplistic. Instead, theories of distributive justice should recognize that "*People conceive and create goods, which they then distribute among themselves.*"[104] The conceptions of certain goods will determine how they are to be distributed. Walzer expresses this idea by writing:

> it is the meaning of goods that determines their movement. Distributive criteria and arrangements are intrinsic not to the good-in-itself but to the

social good ... All distributions are just or unjust *relative to the social meanings of the goods at stake.* [105]

(I will argue in Chapter 5 that Walzer's views on the importance of the social meanings of goods and services do not lead him to endorse a semiotic objection to the commodification of certain goods and services, as Brennan and Jaworski believe.) The medieval Christian understanding of ecclesiastical office, for example, required that such office be distributed to persons on the basis of "their knowledge and piety and not for their wealth."[106] When different goods are understood such that they are to be distributed according to different criteria (offices should go to the meritorious, for example, while luxury goods could be purchased by anyone with the means to do so), the distributions of these goods must be autonomous. Each good occupies a distinct "distributive sphere within which only certain criteria and arrangements are appropriate."[107] Thus, on the medieval Christian understanding, "[m]oney is inappropriate in the sphere of ecclesiastical office; it is an intrusion from another sphere. And piety should make for no advantage in the marketplace, as the marketplace has commonly been understood."[108]

Walzer notes that the autonomy of these different spheres of distribution is often violated and in most societies, "one good or one set of goods is dominant and determinative of value in all the spheres of distribution."[109] When a group is able to own or control such a dominant good to exploit its dominance, they will become the ruling class with a (partial) monopoly over the good in question.[110] Walzer observes that it is common among political philosophers to hold that such monopoly is unjust and to attempt to rectify it by redistributing the dominant good to achieve "simple" equality—equity (or relative equity) in possession of the dominant good. Walzer, however, argues that rather than focusing upon the monopolistic use of the dominant good (whether this is money, political power, or something else), theories of distributive justice should instead focus on securing "complex" equality by reducing dominance. That is, they should focus not on eliminating monopoly but on precluding one good from dominating the others. In a society that exhibited such complex equality, some goods might be monopolistically held—the entrepreneurial class might have the bulk of the wealth, for instance, while charismatic people might monopolize political office—but no one good could be readily converted into a good from another distributive sphere. For example, the wealthy would not be able to buy political office. This approach to distributive justice, argues Walzer, would support the distributive principle that *"No social good* x *should be distributed to men and women who possess some other good* y *merely because they possess* y *and without regard to the meaning of* x," where the "social meaning" of goods is to be understood as outlined above.[111] Accordingly, argues Walzer, in any given society, goods should be distributed according to different allocative mechanisms that are appropriate to the social understanding of the nature of that good in that society. This approach would preclude money from becoming the dominant allocative mechanism in any society and this would, in turn, lead a more just (as more horizontal) distribution of different goods.[112]

Placing Walzer's arguments concerning the legitimate scope of markets in the context of his theory of justice makes it clear that he does not endorse the Asymmetry Thesis. Walzer's argument is not that the "meaning" of certain goods and services necessarily precludes their being distributed for money. Instead, he believes that within a particular society the social meaning of certain goods and services could preclude their distribution in this way. Walzer could thus endorse a *contingent* form of the Asymmetry Thesis: That for any given society it is possible that certain goods and services should only be distributed "for free" and not "for money." But this contingent version of the Asymmetry Thesis does not support the view that there are inherent limits to markets. Walzer is thus not an anti-commodification theorist as Brennan and Jaworski define this position. He does not endorse the essentialist version of the Asymmetry Thesis that they attribute to him and to which they object.[113]

Archard on Blood

Archard is also not an anti-commodification theorist as Brennan and Jaworski define this position. Archard defends Richard Titmuss' objections to the commodification of blood (and Peter Singer's defense of Titmuss' objections) against "orthodox philosophical criticism."[114] He outlines what Margaret Jane Radin has termed a "domino argument" against allowing markets in certain goods and services.[115] He observes that domino arguments begin with the premise that "it is important for a non-market regime to exist or that such a regime is morally preferable to the market regime."[116] They then continue with the premise that "the market and non-market regimes cannot co-exist, the former driving out the latter."[117] Archard notes that there are two distinct versions of any domino argument: The "Contamination of Meaning" version and the "Erosion of Motivation" version.[118] Brennan and Jaworski focus on the "Contamination of Meaning" version of domino arguments because they believe that it is an essentialist semiotic argument against the commodification of blood. They conclude that Archard's use of it is subject to their criticisms of such arguments. I will argue in Chapter 5 that this is not a semiotic argument. Here, however, I will focus on showing that Archard does not utilize this argument to defend the view that blood should always be given away "for free" and never bought or sold.

The "Contamination of Meaning" argument begins with the premise that "With respect to some good, P, one must think of P in either exclusively monetary terms (P is priced) or exclusively non-monetary terms (P is priceless, without price, beyond price)."[119] The second premise is that "the effect of a market in P ... is that P comes to be thought of in dominantly if not exclusively monetary terms."[120] Thus, the proponents of this argument conclude, "the market in *P* comes to dominate in the sense that there is no opportunity for a pure 'gift' of *P*, the donation of *P* being equivalent to the transfer of its monetary value."[121] Archard explains that, on this view, the monetary value associated with the sale of blood will also become associated with blood that is donated, changing the meaning of the donation from one that was previously "priceless" to one that was the equivalent of a monetary donation. The meaning of donations would thus become "contaminated" by the presence of the market.[122]

This argument is based on the claim that the introduction of a market for blood would preclude persons from donating blood in a situation where their donations could not be construed as the donation of a good with a specific cash value. Its focus is on protecting a "space" in which persons can give "pure" gifts of blood.[123] But protecting this "space" for pure gifts of blood is not valuable in itself. Rather, argues Archard, it is valuable both to sustain a sense of community between the persons who live in the society in which such "pure" gifts of blood could take place and for its consequent effect in fostering pro-social behavior within that society.[124] This argument is thus concerned with the effects that a market in blood might have upon community solidarity and pro-social behavior.

Archard's claim concerning the effects that the commodification of blood would have on the meaning of those acts involved in its non-market provision should thus be understood as a contingent claim that might (or might not) be borne out in practice. Rather than holding that the introduction of payment for blood would *necessarily* change the meaning of the non-market provision of blood, Archard is only committed to holding that *if* it did, then it will have restricted the freedom of some providers to donate blood in a situation where such donations held a particular meaning.

This reading of the "Contamination of Meaning" argument shows that Archard is not defending the Asymmetry Thesis with respect to blood. He is not defending the claim that markets in blood are inherently wrong but the weaker conditional claim that if the effect of a market in blood is that donations of blood come "to be thought of in dominantly if not exclusively monetary terms," then this would be wrongful as it would have unjustly limited the freedom of some of the providers of blood. Archard is thus not defending the view that a market in blood is *inherently* wrongful but the view that such markets *could* (incidentally) be harmful in some social situations. He thus does not endorse the Asymmetry Thesis.

Conclusion

Brennan and Jaworski hold that the Asymmetry Thesis is where "the action" is in the commodification debates.[125] But they have provided no reason to believe that this is so. None of those that they identified as "anti-commodification theorists" endorse the Asymmetry Thesis.[126] Instead, they are all engaged in what Brennan and Jaworski describe as the "boring, trivial" debates over the incidental limits to markets, or the use of market norms to structure relationships, or whether there are any goods or services that persons should never either give away free or sell.[127] This is not to say that no theorists endorse the Asymmetry Thesis. Both Thomas Aquinas and Francisco Suárez argued that certain spiritual goods should never be bought and sold but should only be distributed without charge to those who merit them.[128] But medieval European discussions of simony are far from the mainstream of the contemporary debates over commodification and so Brennan and Jaworski have misidentified where the current "action" is. The critical focus of *Markets Without Limits* is thus aimed at a position that almost nobody holds.

Notes

1   The notion of a "bare wrong" was introduced by W.D. Ross in the context of his criticism of the utilitarian account of promissory obligation and his argument in favor of "the *intrinsic* rightness of a certain type of act." See *The Right and the Good*, (Ed.) Philip Stratton-Lake (Oxford: Clarendon Press, [1930] 2002), 37–39, 46–47.
2   See, for example, Luke Semrau, "Book Review: *Markets Without Limits*," *Economics and Philosophy* 33, 2 (2017), 326, citing Brennan and Jaworski in support of the view that Sandel, Anderson, and Satz hold this view; Richard Morrison, "Book Review: *Markets Without Limits: Moral Virtues and Commercial Interests*," *Cato Journal* 36, 3 (2016), 722, accepting Brennan and Jaworski's claim that many critics of markets view them as "inherently immoral"; Jeppe von Platz, "Person to Person: A Note on the Ethics of Commodification," *Journal of Value Inquiry* 51, 4 (2017), 649–650, implicitly accepting that Brennan and Jaworski's targets should be "anti-commodification theorists" as they understand this position; Lamont Rogers, "Book Review: Jason F. [sic] Brennan and Peter Jaworski, *Markets Without Limits: Moral virtues and commercial interests*," *Philosophy in Review* 37, 1 (2017), 8, accepting Brennan and Jaworski's attribution of the Asymmetry Thesis to the critics of markets; P. Konigs, "Two Types of Debunking Arguments," *Philosophical Psychology* 31, 3 (2018), 395, accepting Brennan and Jaworski's view that "critics of commodification" hold "the view that some goods should not be for sale"; Yew-Kwang Ng, *Markets and Morals: Justifying Kidney Sales and Legalizing Prostitution* (New York: Cambridge University Press, 2019), 110, following Brennan and Jaworski in holding that there should be no asymmetry between sales and gifts (i.e., if sales of a good are prohibited, then gifts should be also); Vida Panitch, "Liberalism, Commodification, and Justice," *Politics, Philosophy & Economics* 19, 1 (2020), 64, accepting that "the project of anticommodification theory … is precisely to explain and justify why certain goods bear the unique status of being tradable without being salable."
3   Jason Brennan and Peter M. Jaworski, *Markets Without Limits* (New York: Routledge, 2016), 12.
4   Ibid., 12. See also ibid., 7.
5   Michael J. Sandel, *What Money Can't Buy: The Moral Limits of Markets* (New York: Farrar, Straus and Giroux, 2012), 17–22.
6   Ibid., 28.
7   Ibid., 29.
8   Ibid., 29.
9   Ibid., 31.
10 Ibid., 31.

11 Ibid., 31–32.
12 Sandel is careless in identifying his theses for he writes that one of his concerns is with "the idea that some things should not be up for sale" (Sandel, *What Money Can't Buy*, 37). But that this is not his view is clear even from the discussion in which this claim takes place in which he does not object to the *sale* of Yosemite campsites but to their being exchanged for money *in accord with market norms*. This difference will be discussed further below, as well as in Chapters 3 and 4. Brennan and Jaworski are also careless in identifying their thesis; see James Stacey Taylor, "What Limits Should Markets Be Without?," *Business Ethics Journal Review* 4, 7 (2016): 41–46.
13 Sandel, *What Money Can't Buy*, 10–11.
14 Ibid., 33.
15 Ibid., 34.
16 See the discussion of this point in Chapters 3, 4, and 7.
17 Note that while Sandel did not elaborate this argument himself, it appears to be that which is developed in his discussion.
18 In this respect, Sandel's views resemble those of Anderson; see below and the discussion of Anderson's views in Chapter 4.
19 Sandel, *What Money Can't Buy*, 35–36.
20 Ibid., 38.
21 Sandel also states that Papal Masses are goods that should not be distributed according to market norms. Ibid., 37.
22 Ibid., 35–39.
23 While Sandel does not explicitly consider these issues, Michael Walzer addresses the last in *Spheres of Justice: A Defense of Pluralism and Equality* (New York: Basic Books, 1983). This will be discussed below.
24 Ibid., 7. Brennan and Jaworski also attribute this view to Ruth Grant, Michael Sandel, Robert Sidelsky, Margaret Jane Radin, Benjamin Barber, and George Ritzer. It appears that Brennan and Jaworski intended to articulate the Asymmetry Thesis when they wrote that some critics of markets believe that it is wrong to put "something up for sale that was not previously the kind of thing people tended to buy and sell" (ibid., 7). But, as I note below, this criticism of markets is distinct from the Asymmetry Thesis. Brennan and Jaworski are mistaken to attribute either of these views (the anti-expansion view or the Asymmetry Thesis) to any of these critics of markets. See the discussion of Sandel in both this chapter and Chapter 3, the discussion of Radin's views in Chapter 7, and the discussion of Grant, Sidelsky, Barber, and Ritzer's views in Chapter 8, note 33.
25 Brennan and Jaworski, *Markets Without Limits*, 7. This is not the only place where Brennan and Jaworski conflate distinct theses; similar confusion plagues their account of their own pro-commodification view. See Taylor, "What Limits Should Markets Be Without?," 41–46.
26 And on the face of it, it appears to be an absurd objection, committing its proponents to objecting to markets in any new good or service that is (in some sense) sufficiently different from goods or services (and so a new "kind") that are already bought or sold. Moreover, this objection could not be deployed against any existing market (e.g., for sex), no matter how contested the commodities within it might be.
27 Brennan and Jaworski, *Markets Without Limits*, 12.
28 I offer a possible explanation for their omission in Chapter 8.
29 Brennan and Jaworski, *Markets Without Limits*, 7.
30 Debra Satz, *Why Some Things Should Not Be for Sale: The Moral Limits of Markets* (Oxford: Oxford University Press, 2010), 9.
31 Ibid., 115. She notes that "[i]n the past several decades American society has begun to experiment with markets in women's reproductive labor … ."

32 Ibid., 202, 204. The most sustained defense of such markets has been offered by Lloyd Cohen, *Increasing the Supply of Transplant Organs: The Virtues of an Options Market* (Berlin: Springer, 1995).
33 Satz discusses adult female prostitution in *Why Some Things Should Not Be for Sale*, 153; the use of children as prostitutes or soldiers (ibid., 167) and bonded labor (ibid., 186–188).
34 This is a good thing, for it is unlikely that anyone holds it.
35 Satz, *Why Some Things Should Not Be for Sale*, 9.
36 Ibid., 9.
37 Ibid., 98.
38 Ibid., 112.
39 As Ginny Seung Choi and Virgil Henry Storr note, Brennan and Jaworski's position is "not fundamentally different" from that of Satz—although Brennan and Jaworski seem not to recognize this. *Do Markets Corrupt Our Morals?* (Basingstoke: Palgrave Macmillan, 2019), 237.
40 Brennan and Jaworski, *Markets Without Limits*, 30.
41 Ibid., 32. It is not obvious why it is morally wrong (rather than merely being rude) to sell life insurance at a funeral. But their point is clear even if their example is strange.
42 Ibid., 33. This is a sympathetic reconstruction of their argument which, as written, is very unclear.
43 Ibid., 39.
44 Ibid., 39.
45 Ibid., 29.
46 Strangely, Brennan and Jaworski recognize this and yet *still* attribute to Satz the Asymmetry Thesis that they reject. See ibid., 28, note 1.
47 Satz, *Why Some Things Should Not Be for Sale*, 111.
48 Ibid., 98, 102.
49 Ibid., 103
50 Ibid., 103; italics removed.
51 Ibid., 103.
52 Ibid., 103.
53 "Apparent" willingness, as a careful reading of Satz's discussion reveals that she does not commit herself to endorsing these prohibitions. She writes, for example, that "we *may* have reason to *block certain market exchanges altogether* if citizens are to be equals" (ibid., 102; initial emphasis added) without either committing herself to this view or to endorsing either the regulative or republican democratic ideals that could lead to this conclusion.
54 Ibid., 100.
55 Ibid., 100–101. It is thus possible that Satz would accept that votes could be bought and sold in a market that was regulated so as to preclude the possibility that its operation would influence electoral outcomes. See James Stacey Taylor, "Markets in Votes and the Tyranny of Wealth," *Res Publica* 23, 3 (2017): 313–328 and James Stacey Taylor, "Two (Weak) Cheers for Markets in Votes," *Philosophia* 46 (2018): 223–239. For a sound criticism of my argument in "Markets in Votes and the Tyranny of Wealth," see Alfred Archer, Bart Engelen, and Viktor Ivankovic, "Effective Vote Markets and the Tyranny of Wealth," *Res Publica* 25, 1 (2019): 39–54.
56 This raises the question of precisely what Brennan and Jaworski understand by "markets."
57 But what of the citizens as a body? Under a republican ideal of democracy, do they not "give away" offices to those whom they believe would best promote the common good through them? This raises the issue of what conditions must be met for someone to be said to "own" or "possess" something such that they could give it

away or sell it in the sense of these terms as they appear in the Asymmetry Thesis. While in some sense a judicial office "belongs" to the citizens of a democracy, as understood in accord with republican ideals, this sense of "belonging" clearly differs from the sense in which an office "belongs" to the office-holder. It is more akin to the sense in which the Nobel Prize "belongs" to the Swedish Academy as it is theirs to bestow upon a suitably qualified winner. Since the potential recipients of a Nobel Prize are circumscribed by the terms of award, just as the potential recipients of offices under a republican ideal of democracy are circumscribed by the requirement that they be identified after collective deliberation concerning the common good, it is not clear that either of these goods (Nobel Prizes, or offices) can be "given away" in the same sense that this phrase is used in the Asymmetry Thesis. Rather than their allocation being discretionary, it is prescribed; they are allotted to those who merit them rather than given away at their possessors' whims.

58 That this is the case in all known societies both past and present it is still merely a contingent fact—it is possible that there could be a democratic society where wealth was equally held and in that society this objection to markets in votes would not hold. The implications that this observation has for Brennan and Jaworski's argument will be outlined below.
59 Brennan and Jaworski, *Markets Without Limits*, 12.
60 Again, see Chapter 8 for a possible explanation of why this is so.
61 Elizabeth Anderson, *Value in Ethics and Economics* (Cambridge, MA: Harvard University Press, 1993), 141.
62 Ibid., 141.
63 Ibid., 12.
64 Ibid., 13.
65 Ibid., 141. Italics in original.
66 Boundaries must exist "not just between the state and the market, but between these institutions and other domains of self-expression, such as family, friendship, clubs, professions, art, science, religion, and charitable and ideal-based associations" (ibid., 141–142).
67 Since Anderson is explicit that norms are culturally contingent (see my discussion in Chapter 4), the following discussion is limited to the norms that (ideally) hold in the twenty-first-century West.
68 Anderson, *Value in Ethics and Economics*, 145.
69 Ibid., 145.
70 Ibid., 145.
71 Ibid., 145.
72 Ibid., 147. See too the discussion in Chapters 8 and 9 of the standards of excellence that would be internal to academic research governed by academic norms.
73 Ibid., 147.
74 Ibid., 147–148.
75 Ibid., 148.
76 Ibid., 148.
77 See, for example, James Stacey Taylor, "Autonomy, Vote Buying, and Constraining Options," *Journal of Applied Philosophy*, 34, 5 (2017): 711–723.
78 Brennan and Jaworski, *Markets Without Limits*, 15.
79 Anderson, *Value in Ethics and Economics*, 142; Brennan and Jaworski, *Markets Without Limits*, 11.
80 Ibid., 15. See the discussion, below, of Anderson's views concerning the exchange of money for sex.
81 Brennan and Jaworski's focus on the first two questions might have led them to misunderstand Anderson's view and hence to attribute to her positions that she does not hold. Note, too, that Brennan and Jaworski have misunderstood how Anderson

uses the term "commodification" and its cognates; this leads them to misunderstand aspects of her argument and in consequence some of their objections to her views misfire. See Chapter 4 for a fuller discussion of these points.
82 Anderson, *Value in Ethics and Economics*, 142.
83 Ibid., 154.
84 Ibid., 145.
85 Ibid., 154.
86 Ibid., 145.
87 Ibid., 156.
88 Brennan and Jaworski, *Markets Without Limits*, 35. Even though Brennan and Jaworski often write as though their approach to establishing the moral limits of markets is radically different from those whose views they criticize, it is not. Their belief that their position is heterodox simply stems from their misunderstanding the views that they criticize.
89 Elizabeth Anderson, "Why Commercial Surrogate Motherhood Unethically Commodifies Women and Children: Reply to McLachlan and Swales," *Health Care Analysis* 8 (2000), 22.
90 Ibid., 22–23.
91 Ibid., 23.
92 Ibid., 23.
93 Ibid., 23.
94 Ibid., 23.
95 Ibid., 23.
96 Ibid., 23. Brennan and Jaworski agree with Anderson's objections to slavery contracts, writing that such contracts violate the rights of the persons bought as slaves; *Markets Without Limits*, 48.
97 Anderson, "Why Commercial Surrogate Motherhood Unethically Commodifies Women and Children," 23.
98 Ibid., 23.
99 Ibid., 23–24.
100 Brennan and Jaworski recognize that Anderson's fundamental objection to commercial surrogacy contracts (that they require "women to undermine their natural bonds with the babies they carry") applies not only to commercial surrogacy but also to "unpaid surrogacy for one's family and friends" (*Markets Without Limits*, 155). It is thus puzzling as to why they assert (without supporting citation) that she believes that it would be permissible for a woman to serve as an unpaid surrogate for her sister (ibid., 12) and thus fail to recognize that Anderson rejects the Asymmetry Thesis with respect to surrogacy contracts.
101 Brennan and Jaworski disagree with Anderson as to which goods and services fall into this class. But since they focus on those market critics that they claim endorse the Asymmetry Thesis and provide no justification for precluding certain goods or services from the domain of the market, they have no theoretical resources to address those who dispute their account of where the boundaries of this class of monetarily-inalienable goods lie. This is a serious shortcoming. If few critics of markets endorse the Asymmetry Thesis, then the relevant debate over the moral limits of markets will be over where these boundaries are located. And it is precisely this debate with which Brennan and Jaworski have failed to engage.
102 Brennan and Jaworski, *Markets Without Limits*, 49. Brennan and Jaworski do not explicitly attribute the Asymmetry Thesis to Walzer and Archard. But they treat (what they take to be) their arguments to be offered in support of the Asymmetry Thesis: that while certain goods and services can be given away ("for free"), they cannot be bought and sold.

103 Walzer, *Spheres of Justice*, 6. Since Walzer's claims arise in the context of a political theory, it is not clear that they even count as *moral* concerns, and it is these that Brennan and Jaworski are concerned to address.
104 Ibid., 6.
105 Ibid., 8–9. Emphasis added.
106 Ibid., 9.
107 Ibid., 10.
108 Ibid., 10.
109 Ibid., 10.
110 Ibid., 10–13.
111 Ibid., 20.
112 Ibid., 3–63.
113 Ibid., 10.
114 David Archard, "Selling Yourself: Titmuss' Argument Against a Market in Blood," *The Journal of Ethics* 6, 1 (2002), 88.
115 Margaret Jane Radin, *Contested Commodities* (Cambridge, MA: Harvard University Press, 1996), 95–101.
116 Archard, "Selling Yourself," 93.
117 Ibid., 93.
118 Ibid., 93–94. The "Erosion of Motivation" argument begins with the observation that if there is a market in some good P, this would erode the motivation to donate P, and, from this concludes that the market in P will come to dominate in that "there will be little if any reason to retain the practice of non-monetary exchanges of P." Archard explains that Titmuss seemed to be concerned with the erosion of the motivation to donate blood as he believed that this would loosen the ties that existed between citizens. (Note that this concern with the erosion of motivation is a consequentialist concern rather than a concern with the possibility that a market in blood would express estrangement from one's fellow citizens and so is not a "Wrong Currency" objection to markets of the sort that will be discussed in Chapter 5.)
119 Ibid., 93.
120 Ibid., 94.
121 Ibid., 94.
122 Ibid., 95. The discussion that follows will have some affinity to the above discussion of Anderson's freedom-based argument against the legalization of prostitution.
123 Ibid., 194.
124 Ibid., 92–102. The argument that Archard develops is complex and he notes that it is not definitive but requires further support, both theoretical and empirical; ibid., 102–103.
125 Brennan and Jaworski, *Markets Without Limits*, 15. This is not true, as I will show in Chapter 7.
126 See also Chapter 8, note 33. Brennan and Jaworski also identify Margaret Jane Radin as an anti-commodification theorist; *Markets Without Limits*, 7. But, as I outline in Chapter 7, she does not defend the Asymmetry Thesis. (See, too, my comments in Chapter 8 on the conceptual confusion in the discussion at that point in *Markets Without Limits*.)
127 Ibid., 15.
128 Thomas Aquinas, *Summa Theologica*, II-II, q.100 a. 1c, in *The 'Summa Theologica' of St Thomas Aquinas Literally Translated by Fathers of the English Dominican Province* (Westminster, MA: Christian Classics, 1980); Francisco Suárez, "De virtute et statu religionis," in C. Berton (Ed.), *Opera Omnia* (Paris: Lodovicus Vives, 1859), vol. 11, lib. 4 (*De Simonia*) c.50 n. 1, 911.

2
SEMIOTIC OBJECTIONS TO MARKETS

Introduction

In Chapter 1, I argued that the critical focus of *Markets Without Limits* is misplaced. The anti-commodification view that is the target of Brennan and Jaworski's criticism—the Asymmetry Thesis—is only a marginal position in the debates over the moral limits of markets.[1] It is endorsed by very few people and then only with respect to a limited number of goods and services. A similar point can be made about the "argumentative core" of *Markets Without Limits*[2]—Brennan and Jaworski's criticism of what they term "semiotic objections" to markets in certain goods and services.[3]

A semiotic objection to a market is one that holds "that buying and selling certain goods and services is wrong because of what market exchange communicates or because it violates the meaning of certain goods, services, and relationships."[4] Brennan and Jaworski hold that the "*most common* class of objections against commodifying certain goods or services" are semiotic objections.[5] They believe that "[n]early every anti-commodification theorist at some point relies upon or advances a semiotic objection" to markets in certain goods or services.[6] As they are understood by Brennan and Jaworski, such arguments lead to the conclusion that (with respect to those goods and services that they focus on) the Asymmetry Thesis is correct. Since very few theorists endorse the Asymmetry Thesis, we might infer that semiotic objections to markets are equally rare. But this inference would be unjustified. It is possible that persons who do not endorse the Asymmetry Thesis but who are still critical of markets in certain goods and services (e.g., they either offer incidental objections to them or believe that they should not be distributed at all, whether by market or non-market means) have developed semiotic arguments of the sort criticized by Brennan and Jaworski in

DOI: 10.4324/9781003251996-4

support of their views. They would have been mistaken to have done so, for such arguments support a more extensive rejection of markets in the goods and services that they address than they wish to endorse. But that they would have been mistaken to have developed such arguments does not mean that they have not done so. And if they had done so, then Brennan and Jaworski's objections to essentialist semiotic objections would have bite.

I will argue in Chapters 3, 4 and 5 that none of the theorists to whom Brennan and Jaworski ascribe such objections have developed them. This is not surprising. Once the structure of the type of semiotic objections that Brennan and Jaworski address is made clear, it will become apparent that they are extremely implausible. This implausibility stems, in part, from their being based on a view of meaning that has been almost universally rejected by philosophers. This view is that certain actions or utterances necessarily communicate particular meanings, and which meanings they communicate can be known *a priori*. But while such semiotic essentialism has been widely rejected by philosophers, Brennan and Jaworski assert that this view is accepted by the theorists whose views they criticize.[7] Of course, that a view has been widely rejected by philosophers does not entail that it has not been endorsed by some philosophers (e.g., those whose arguments Brennan and Jaworski criticize). But as I will argue in the following chapters, this is not the case. *All* of the theorists whose views Brennan and Jaworski directly criticize *explicitly reject* the essentialist semiotics that they attribute to them.

But the essentialist semiotics of the semiotic arguments that Brennan and Jaworski attribute to those they criticize are not their only source of implausibility. As defined by Brennan and Jaworski, these arguments hold that particular actions (e.g., the sale of a certain good) would be wrong independently of any effect that they might have. (And this would be so whether the semiotics of the acts in question were essentialist or contingent, as I will discuss below.) They would also be wrong independently of any wrongfulness apart from the mere fact that they could be taken to communicate something wrongful. The wrong involved would be a "bare wrong"—the acts would be wrong simply because they were wrong.[8] This is implausible.

Just as the widespread rejection of essentialist semiotics does not entail that the theorists that Brennan and Jaworski criticize have also rejected this view, so too does the implausibility of semiotic arguments, as these are defined by Brennan and Jaworski, not entail that the theorists that they criticize have not offered them. I will thus spend time in the following chapters showing that not only do the theorists that Brennan and Jaworski criticize not offer *essentialist* semiotic objections to markets, they do not offer *semiotic* objections to markets at all.[9]

But before I turn to that task, I will outline Brennan and Jaworski's criticisms of the essentialist semiotic objections that they attribute to those they criticize. At first sight, their attribution of essentialist semiotic objections to the theorists that they criticize appears plausible. Since their objections to semiotic arguments are on target it is not surprising that it is widely believed that *Markets Without Limits* has dealt a serious blow to the arguments offered by the critics of markets. But this is not the case. Instead of furthering the debate over the moral limits of markets, *Markets Without Limits* has derailed it.

Brennan and Jaworski's Critique of Semiotic Objections to Commodification

Brennan and Jaworski define a semiotic objection as one that holds that

> to allow a market in some good or service X is a form of communication that expresses the wrong attitude towards X or expresses an attitude that is incompatible with the intrinsic dignity of X, or would show disrespect or irreverence for some practice, custom, belief, or relationship with which X is associated.[10]

They are clear that semiotic arguments are supposed to be "independent of worries about exploitation, misallocation, rights violations, self-destructive behavior, harm to others, or character corruption."[11] They hold that anti-commodification theorists deploy three types of semiotic objections to support the Asymmetry Thesis. The first is the "Mere Commodity objection." The proponents of this objection hold that "buying and selling certain goods or services shows that one regards them as having merely instrumental value."[12] The second is the "Wrong Signal objection." The proponents of this objection hold that "buying and selling certain goods and services communicates, independently of one's attitudes, disrespect for the objects in question."[13] The final semiotic objection that Brennan and Jaworski identify is the "Wrong Currency objection." The proponents of this objection hold that "inserting markets and money into certain kinds of relationships communicates estrangement and distance, and is objectionably impersonal."[14]

Brennan and Jaworski offer powerful objections to all three types of semiotic objection. In response to the Mere Commodity objection, they distinguish between something being a commodity and something being a mere commodity. A commodity is "simply anything with a price tag, anything that could be exchanged on a market."[15] A mere commodity, by contrast,

> is something with a price tag, exchanged on a market, that is properly viewed as having instrumental value, as something that may properly be used solely as a tool to satisfy the (non-moral) desires and preferences of the exchanging parties.[16]

Brennan and Jaworski rightly note that many items (such as pets or artwork) that have price tags and that are exchanged in markets are not treated as though they may be "properly be used solely as a tool to satisfy the (non-moral) desires and preferences of the exchanging parties" by those who trade in them. There is thus no necessary connection between exchanging a good or service for money and treating it as a mere commodity.[17] Furthermore, argue Brennan and Jaworski, if the defenders of the Mere Commodity objection respond by arguing that if persons buy and sell certain goods and services, then they will over time come to see them as mere commodities, thus, they will no longer be offering a *semiotic* objection to markets in those goods and services. Instead, they will be offering a *corruption* objection. They will be arguing that participating in markets for those goods and services would "tend to cause us to develop defective preferences or character traits."[18]

Brennan and Jaworski have an equally powerful response to the Wrong Signal and Wrong Currency objections. They begin by noting that proponents of these semiotic arguments hold "that some markets necessarily signal disrespect—that it is not a mere contingent social convention that such commodification signals disrespect."[19] In response to these "essentialist semiotic arguments" Brennan and Jaworski note that while there "are facts about what symbols, words, and actions" mean, these "vary from culture to culture."[20] In support of this claim they provide a wealth of historical and anthropological evidence. They note, for example, that while the ancient Greeks burned their dead to signal respect for them, the Callatians considered this barbaric, treating the dead like "mere trash."[21] The Callatians ate their dead to signal respect; a practice that the Greeks considered barbaric for this would be to treat them as "mere food."[22] Similarly, they note that while in contemporary Western culture a monetary gift "communicates a lack of concern," this is merely a Western view. For the Merina people of Madagascar, "monetary gifts carry no such stigma of being impersonal or thoughtless."[23] This, they claim, leads to a dilemma. We have "philosophical arguments from prominent theorists telling us that we can determine, a priori, that certain markets essentially signal disrespect."[24] But we also have "sociological and anthropological work that seems to show that extant markets in those very goods often have an entirely different meaning from what we Westerners attribute to them."[25]

Brennan and Jaworski hold that if we side with the philosophers, then we must conclude that people in other cultures are acting wrongly when they exchange certain goods and services for money, even if such exchanges do not signal anything wrongful in their culture. Alternatively, we could accept that since there are no wrongful meanings attached to those exchanges in other cultures, the people in those cultures do nothing wrong when they exchange the goods and services in question for money.[26] Brennan and Jaworski argue that we should accept that the meanings of symbols, words, and actions are merely contingent social constructs. They note that this opens up the possibility that people in the West *could* attribute different meanings to exchanges in certain goods and services than those that they currently attribute to them. This, in turn, opens up the possibility that they *should* attribute different meanings to them. Brennan and Jaworski argue that if a symbolic meaning that is attached to a practice either causes great harm or has high opportunity costs, then this provides strong *pro tanto* grounds for its revision. For example, "if a culture regards contraception as expressing contempt for life, then it will tend to perpetuate poverty and low status for women."[27] These results independently provide reason to revise the symbolic meaning that this culture attaches to contraception. More practically, they ask us to imagine that a market in human organs could exist without exploiting anyone or misallocating the organs. The sole objection to it is that in contemporary American culture the sale of body parts is understood to symbolically represent the commodification of life—and this is taken to be wrongful. Brennan and Jaworski argue that in this case the social meaning of the sale of body parts should be revised, not that organ sales should not occur. Moreover, even if this symbolism is intractable, they argue that Americans would be justified in participating in organ markets.[28]

Essentialist Semiotics

Brennan and Jaworski provide a wealth of evidence from the social sciences to show that "facts about what symbols, words, and actions signal ... vary from culture to culture."[29] But for this to play the central role in the debate over the moral limits of markets that they ascribe to it, they must establish that some theorists who oppose markets in certain goods and services have developed essentialist semiotic objections to them.

The view that the meanings of "symbols, words, and actions" are (often) conventional is both long-standing and widely held. As Brennan and Jaworski note, that the same actions might have different meanings in different cultures has long been recognized. Indeed, the story that they recount of the different ways by which the Greek and the Callatians showed respect to their dead fathers is one of the most famous in *The Histories* of Herodotus.[30] The view that meanings are only conventionally related to their signifiers is also widely held. As Brennan and Jaworski recognize, this is the dominant view in the social sciences. But it is also the dominant view in the humanities, ranging from linguistics,[31] to literary theory,[32] to art history.[33] Indeed, this conventionalist view of meaning is so widely accepted that it has been a feature of popular culture for decades. The British comedian Will Hay, for example, used it to humorous effect in a scene in the 1942 movie *The Goose Steps Out* when (as a British spy infiltrated into Nazi Germany), he teaches a group of Nazi students that the British two-finger V-sign is a mark of deep respect and encourages them to direct it toward a portrait of Hitler.[34] There have also been movements by subaltern groups to revise ("reclaim") the connotative meanings of terms used to derogate them.[35]

Given that conventionalism about meaning is a view that is both long-standing and widely held, it would be surprising if this position had been overlooked by the philosophers who oppose markets in certain goods and services. Of course, it might be the case that philosophy has followed a different trajectory that has led to the widespread philosophical acceptance of semiotic essentialism. But this is not so. Although Brennan and Jaworski claim that "philosophers see" particular actions as having "logically essential meaning," this claim has been routinely rejected by philosophers (including Sandel, Anderson, Satz, Walzer, and Archard, as I will argue in Chapters 3–5).[36] In recent decades, for example, J.L. Austin noted that the effect of performative utterances depends in part on convention,[37] while Ludwig Wittgenstein argued (roughly) that the meaning of a word is set by its use within a particular language-game.[38] H.P. Grice discussed the "non-natural" sense of meaning (roughly, that which that someone attempts to communicate through an action) in contrast to the "natural" sense of meaning (where "X means Y" should be understood—roughly—as "X indicates Y." or "X is a symptom of Y") where the former but not the latter rests on convention.[39] (John Skorupski drew on this distinction to untangle some conceptual confusions in sociological and anthropological work on the nature of symbols in ritual action, belying Brennan and Jaworski's implicit claim that social scientists have nothing to learn from philosophers concerning the nature of meaning.[40]) W.V.O. Quine argued for the indeterminacy of translation,[41] while David Lewis argued that linguistic meaning is generated by social convention.[42] Other prominent philosophers who recognize that meanings are not necessarily "logically essential" include Hilary Putnam,[43] Michael Dummett,[44] Simon Blackburn,[45] G.P. Baker and P.M.S. Hacker,[46] and Donald Davidson.[47] This view is not restricted to philosophers' work on philosophy of language. That the meanings of "symbols, words, and actions" are (often) conventional is also recognized in (for example) philosophical discussions that range from the question of whether the Confederate battle flag is a racist symbol,[48] to the question of what constitutes consent,[49] to questions that arise in legal theory as a result of linguistic indeterminacy.[50] It is also recognized in debates that address whether healthcare should be rationed according to person's perceived social usefulness,[51] and those that address questions concerning the "moral meaning of the body, sex, reproduction, kidneys, blood, semen, or genes."[52] And the list goes on.

Thus, while Brennan and Jaworski often write as though their conventionalist view of meaning is a radical departure from philosophical orthodoxy, precisely the opposite is true: This view has long been entrenched as the dominant view in philosophy.[53] This does not show that no philosopher endorses semiotic essentialism and has drawn on this to develop an objection to markets in certain goods and services.[54] But it does show that it is unlikely that a philosopher who is well-versed in her discipline would develop an essentialist semiotic objection to markets of the sort that is the target of Brennan and Jaworski's critique.[55]

Contingent Semiotics

However, Brennan and Jaworski's critique also applies to *contingent* semiotic objections to markets. A proponent of this type of semiotic objection holds that a particular transaction would be wrongful because of what it would communicate in the particular cultural milieu in which it took place, or because it would violate "the meaning[s] of certain goods, services, and relationships" that were accepted in that milieu.[56] Given the widespread acceptance of the view that the meanings of "symbols, words, and actions" are conventional, this type of semiotic objection is likely to be more common than essentialist ones. Recognizing this makes Brennan and Jaworski's critique stronger, for it would likely be applicable to a larger set of semiotic objections. But this increase in strength comes at the cost of the distinctiveness of their position. A theorist who offers a contingent semiotic objection to markets would not necessarily believe that there are any *inherent* limits to the market. She might only believe that there are *contingent* limits to markets. She might believe that, given the meanings of market exchanges in certain goods or services in a particular culture, they should not be bought and sold for money in that context. But this is compatible with her holding that it would be permissible to buy and sell them for money in another context where the meanings of such exchanges were different. If so, then her position would be no different in kind from that of Brennan and Jaworski. The "action" in the debate between such a theorist and Brennan and Jaworski would no longer focus on the claim that "[t]here are some things that people are normally allowed to own or possess in some way, but which should not be for sale," as Brennan and Jaworski originally claimed.[57] Instead, both sides would agree that questions that the moral appropriateness of certain market exchanges should be addressed by paying attention to the time, place, and manner of their occurrence.[58] The only disagreement would be over which markets would be permissible in which circumstances.

The debate between Brennan and Jaworski and a theorist who offers a contingent semiotic objection to markets would thus only be about where the contingent limits of markets should lie. And within this (very circumscribed) debate Brennan and Jaworski's criticisms of (possible) contingent semiotic objections to markets are sound. But this should provide only cold comfort to Brennan and Jaworski. For this victory has less to do with the power of their arguments than it has to do with the extraordinary weakness of the semiotic objections (whether essentialist or contingent) that they criticize.[59]

Recall again that Brennan and Jaworski hold that semiotic objections to markets are independent of other possible concerns about the effects of a market in the good or service in question. A semiotic objection (whether essentialist or contingent) holds that the market at issue would be wrong even if

> [it] would not lead to any exploitation, would not undermine distributive justice or result in morally bad distributions, would not cause inefficiencies, would not violate anyone's rights, would not cause self-destructive behavior, would not lead to others being harmed, and would not corrupt us.[60]

This market would be wrong *only* because it would "express or communicate something disrespectful, or would violate the meaning of some relationship."[61] Brennan and Jaworski also (correctly) note that what a person's acts express can be independent of her intentions.[62] And they take semiotic arguments to be deontic: That if a market in a certain good or service would communicate a wrongful attitude, then participation in that market would be wrongful independently of the consequences of this.[63]

Putting these claims together, then, for Brennan and Jaworski, someone who objects to an action (e.g., a certain good or service being exchanged for cash) on semiotic grounds (whether essentialist or contingent) would object to it even if (1) she recognized that it was not intended to communicate the (wrongful) attitude that observers would typically understand it to communicate in the cultural context in which it was made; and (2) she recognized that there was thus no reason to attribute that attitude in question to the actor; and (3) she recognized that the observers of the act understood that it was not intended to communicate that attitude, and so they recognized that there was thus no reason to attribute it to the actor; and (4) she recognized that this act would have no adverse consequences at all; and (5) she recognized that *not* performing this action would have serious adverse consequences. A person who objected to an action on semiotic grounds would thus be committed to holding that it was wrongful simply because persons within the cultural setting in which it was performed held it to be wrongful, where they held it to be wrongful for no other reason than they held it to be wrongful, and where any costs associated with maintaining that it was wrongful for no other reason than this were simply ignored.[64] When stated, this clearly makes even contingent semiotic objections to markets appear utterly implausible, holding as they do the wrong of certain transactions to be bare wrongs—wrong simply because they are wrong in themselves.[65] And, as Hume famously remarked in the context of his discussion of promissory obligation, it is mysterious how merely declaring something to be wrongful could make it so.[66]

But while Brennan and Jaworski are correct to reject semiotic objections to markets (whether these are essentialist or contingent), this does not advance the debate over the moral limits of markets as much as they (and others) believe.[67] Once the theoretical commitments of semiotic objections to markets are clarified, it becomes clear that they are utterly implausible. Indeed, so implausible are such objections that the principle of charity should dictate that they should not be attributed to persons who oppose markets in certain goods and services unless there is sufficient evidence to justify this.

Conclusion

There are two reasons to be suspicious of Brennan and Jaworski's specific attribution of essentialist semiotic objections to those they identify as anti-commodification theorists as they define this term. First, as I argued in Chapter 1, the theorists whose views they criticize do not endorse the Asymmetry Thesis. They are not anti-commodification theorists as Brennan and Jaworski define this position. Since Brennan and Jaworski have misunderstood the positions of those they criticize, we should be concerned that they have similarly misunderstood the arguments of those they identify as anti-commodification theorists. Second—and in a related vein—Brennan and Jaworski are correct to hold that essentialist semiotic arguments would (if sound) support the Asymmetry Thesis. But the theorists that Brennan and Jaworski criticize do not endorse this Thesis. There is reason to be suspicious of Brennan and Jaworski's claim that they advocate the essentialist semiotic arguments that would (if sound) support it.

There are also two reasons to be suspicious of Brennan and Jaworski's more general claim that essentialist semiotic arguments are the "*most common* class" of objections to markets.[68] First, such arguments are based on the view that the meanings of some signifiers are "logically essential."[69] This view is widely rejected by philosophers—and for good reason. To hold that essentialist semiotic objections are commonly advanced by those who oppose markets in certain goods and services is thus to hold that the critics of markets have widely adopted an implausible and heterodox view of meaning—and have done so without realizing this. Second, not only are essentialist semiotic objections implausible in themselves, they are supposed to support (according to Brennan and Jaworski) the (again, heterodox) equally implausible conclusion that certain acts are simply bare wrongs. Given this compound implausibility, the principle of charity requires that semiotic arguments not be attributed to persons unless there is good reason to do so.

Brennan and Jaworski might respond to these suspicions by asserting that they *have* provided sufficient evidence to justify the attribution of essentialist semiotic arguments to Sandel, Anderson, Satz, Walzer, and Archard. In Chapters 3, 4, and 5, I will argue that this is not the case. Not only have Brennan and Jaworski failed to provide evidence that these theorists have offered such arguments, but a proper understanding of their views will show that they have not offered any semiotic arguments at all.

Notes

1 See, too, Chapter 7.
2 That this critique is the "argumentative core" of their work has been recognized by Daniel Layman, "Review: *Markets Without Limits*," *Business Ethics Quarterly* 26, 4 (2016), 561. See also Luke Semrau, "Review: *Markets Without Limits*," *Economics and Philosophy* 33, 2 (2017), 328, and Jonathan Anomaly, "Review: *Markets Without Limits*," *Notre Dame Philosophical Reviews*, available at: https://ndpr.nd.edu/news/markets-without-limits-moral-virtues-and-commercial-interests/
3 That semiotic arguments—especially essentialist semiotic arguments—are rare (or, in the case of essentialist semiotic arguments, possibly even non-existent) in philosophy has not prevented people from being wrongly convinced by Brennan and Jaworski that they are widespread. See Chapter 6, note 2.

4 Jason Brennan and Peter M. Jaworski, "Markets Without Symbolic Limits," *Ethics* 125, 4 (2015), 1053.
5 Jason Brennan and Peter M. Jaworski, *Markets Without Limits* (New York: Routledge, 2016), 49. Italics in original.
6 Ibid., 49. Brennan holds that semiotic arguments are also widespread in democratic theory; see his *Good Work If You Can Get It: How to Succeed in Academia* (Baltimore, MD: Johns Hopkins University Press, 2020), 103, and *Against Democracy* (Princeton, NJ: Princeton University Press, 2016), Chapter 5. They are not. See James Stacey Taylor "The Myth of Semiotic Arguments in Democratic Theory and How This Exposes Problems with Peer Review" (*International Journal of Applied Philosophy*, forthcoming).
7 Ibid., 68.
8 See W.D. Ross, *The Right and the Good*, (Ed.) Philip Stratton-Lake (Oxford: Clarendon Press, [1930] 2002),. 37–39, 46–47.
9 Brennan and Jaworski attribute in passing a semiotic objection to prostitution to Carole Pateman (misspelling her name as "Carol") in *Markets Without Limits*, 63. In support of this, they cite not Pateman but Satz, observing in an endnote that Satz writes that Anderson and Pateman both advance an "essentialist thesis" that "reproductive labor is by its nature something that should not be bought or sold" (*Markets Without Limits*, 73, n. 3, citing Debra Satz, *Why Some Things Should Not Be for Sale* [Oxford: Oxford University Press, 2010], 117–119 as the source of these quotations.) These quotations from Satz do not support the attribution of a *semiotic* objection to Pateman. Moreover, in the passage that *Satz* cites from Pateman, Pateman makes it clear that she objects to prostitution as she believes that it is analogous to slavery: "when a prostitute contracts out use of her body she is thus selling *herself* in a very real sense" (ibid., 119; Satz quotes Pateman, *The Sexual Contract* [Stanford, CA: Stanford University Press, 1988], 207. Satz omits the italics that appear in the original.) This is not a semiotic objection. In Brennan and Jaworski's defense, one could argue that Pateman later holds that "what is wrong with prostitution" is that through prostitution "men gain public acknowledgement as women's sexual masters" and so the wrong of prostitution is grounded on the view of the relationship between men and women that it communicates (*The Sexual Contract*, 208). But this defense fails. It is not the *acknowledgment* of women's subordinate status to men that renders prostitution wrongful for Pateman, but that prostitution enables johns to attain actual mastery over prostitutes—women who "in a very real sense" sell themselves to men (i.e., to be mastered by men).
10 Brennan and Jaworski, *Markets Without Limits*, 47.
11 Ibid., 47.
12 Ibid., 49.
13 Ibid., 49.
14 Ibid., 49.
15 Ibid., 52.
16 Ibid., 52–53.
17 Ibid., 52–53. See also Chapter 3, note 43.
18 Ibid., 21, 54. Brennan and Jaworski respond at length to corruption objections in *Markets Without Limits*, Part III.
19 Ibid., 63.
20 Ibid., 63.
21 Ibid., 63. Brennan and Jaworski fail to cite any source for this story; see note 30, below.
22 Ibid., 63.
23 Ibid., 63. Note that while this claim about the Merina is correct, other claims that Brennan and Jaworski make about their practices are unsupported. See Chapter 9.

24 Ibid., 68.
25 Ibid., 68.
26 Ibid., 68.
27 Ibid., 69.
28 Ibid., 68–73. Brennan and Jaworski's argument that social codes should be revised has been persuasively criticized by David G. Dick, "Impure Semiotic Objections to Markets," *Public Affairs Quarterly* 32, 3 (2018), 234–235 and Ryan W. Davis, "Symbolic Values," *Journal of the American Philosophical Association* 5, 4 (2019), 457–460.
29 Brennan and Jaworski, *Markets Without Limits*, 63.
30 Herodotus, *The Histories*, trans. A.D. Godley (Cambridge, MA: Harvard University Press, 1920), Book III, Chapter 38, sections 2–4.
31 Ferdinand de Saussure, *Course in General Linguistics*, Eds. Charles Bally and Albert Sechehaye, trans. Roy Harris (La Salle, IL: Open Court. 1983).
32 Michel Foucault, *The Order of Things* (London: Tavistock, 1970); Michel Foucault, *The Archaeology of Knowledge* (London: Tavistock, 1974).
33 Ernst H. Gombrich, *The Image and the Eye: Further Studies in the Psychology of Pictorial Representation* (Ithaca, NY: Cornell University Press, 1982), 150–151.
34 At that time the V-sign (with the palm facing inwards, not outwards, which represented "V for Victory") was considered to be *very* rude!
35 On the history of the meaning of the term "queer," see Erin J. Rand, *Reclaiming Queer: Activist and Academic Rhetorics of Resistance* (Birmingham, AL: University of Alabama Press, 2014). The comedian Lenny Bruce attempted this with racial slurs; see David Emblidge, "The Sick/Healthy Humor of Lenny Bruce," *Revue française d'études américaines* 4 (1977), 104–105.
36 Margaret Jane Radin also explicitly rejects this claim; see (e.g.) *Contested Commodities* (Cambridge, MA: Harvard University Press, 1996), xi, 12, 14, 92, 103, 160–161.
37 J.L. Austin, *How to Do Things with Words* (New York: Oxford University Press, 1965), Lecture III.
38 Ludwig Wittgenstein, *Philosophical Investigations*, trans. G.E.M. Anscombe, 3rd edn (Harlow: Pearson, 1973).
39 H.P. Grice, "Meaning," *The Philosophical Review* 66, 3 (1957), esp. 377–378. I note the relevance of Grice's views for semiotic arguments in Chapter 6.
40 John Skorupski, *Symbol and Theory: A Philosophical Study of Theories of Religion in Social Anthropology* (Cambridge: Cambridge University Press, 1976), 120.
41 W.V.O. Quine, *Word and Object* (Cambridge, MA: MIT Press, 1960). In developing her feminist epistemology, Anderson draws on Quine's work on the underdetermination of scientific theory to argue that theories determine the significance of facts through how they organize them. Putting this in semiotic terms, Anderson's view is that facts (e.g., a particular action) have no significance (meaning) independent of the theory (of meaning) that is used to organize them and render them intelligible. (Elizabeth Anderson, "Feminist Epistemology: An Interpretation and a Defense," *Hypatia* 10, 3 [1995], 77; citing Quine, *Word and Object*, 22.) Recognizing such indeterminacy, Anderson notes, should lead one to reject the assumption "that the way the world appears to oneself is the way it appears to everyone" (Anderson, "Feminist Epistemology," 80). Thus, that one understands by a certain action that the actor has communicated disrespect should not lead one to think that such actions *necessarily* communicate disrespect. Rather than endorsing the semiotic essentialism that Brennan and Jaworski attribute to her, Anderson's Quineian approach to epistemology thus commits her to rejecting it. I discuss Anderson's views further in Chapter 4.
42 David Lewis, *Convention* (Cambridge, MA: Harvard University Press, 1969), esp. 147, 152–159.
43 Hilary Putnam, *Mind, Language, and Reality: Philosophical Papers*, vol. 2 (Cambridge: Cambridge University Press, 1975).

44 Michael Dummett, *The Seas of Language* (Oxford: Oxford University Press, 1993), 447–449, 451, 460.
45 Simon Blackburn, *Spreading the Word* (Oxford: Oxford University Press, 1984), 118–122.
46 G.P. Baker and P.M.S. Hacker, *Language, Sense, and Nonsense* (Oxford: Blackwell, 1984), esp. Chapter 10.
47 Donald Davidson, *Inquiries into Truth and Interpretation* (Oxford: Oxford University Press, 2001), esp. Chapter 18.
48 Torin Alter, "Symbolic Meaning and the Confederate Battle Flag," *Philosophy in the Contemporary World* 7, 2–3 (2000): 1–4.
49 David Archard, "'A Nod's as Good as a Wink': Consent, Convention, and Reasonable Belief," *Legal Theory* 3 (1997): 273–290. Archard's work on this issue shows (as I will note in Chapter 5) that Brennan and Jaworski are wrong to hold that he endorses an essentialist semiotics.
50 Alex Silk, "Theories of Vagueness and Theories of Law," *Legal Theory* 25, 2 (2019): 132–152.
51 Andreas L. Mogensen, "Meaning, Medicine, and Merit," *Utilitas* 32, 1 (2020), 97–100.
52 Anne Phillips, *Our Bodies, Whose Property?* (Princeton, NJ: Princeton University Press, 2013), 9.
53 The above list becomes even longer if we include not just recent work but that of all of the philosophers who, over the last two and a half millennia, have rejected essentialism about meaning in favor of some form of conventionalism. See, for example, Hermogenes' view in Plato's *Cratylus*, and Aristotle's view as expressed in *De Interpretatione*, 16a 3–8. (Plato, *Cratylus, Parmenides, Greater Hippias, Lesser Hippias*, trans. H.N. Fowler [Cambridge, MA: Harvard University Press, 1926], 1–192; Aristotle, *Aristotle Categories and De Interpretatione*, trans. J.L. Ackrill [Oxford: Oxford University Press, 1975].)
54 Although Georg Simmel does not draw on semiotic essentialism to object to transactions in certain goods and services, he does hold that the symbolism associated with money precludes it from being "an adequate mediator of personal relationships ... that are intended to be permanent and based on the sincerity of the binding forces" (Georg Simmel, *The Philosophy of Money*, 3rd edn, Ed. David Frisby, trans. Tom Bottomore and David Frisby [London: Routledge, 2004], 378). Simmel's discussion of this issue indicates that he holds this because he believes that the use of money naturally (in a sense that appears akin to Grice's) has a certain symbolic meaning. He is thus not necessarily committed to endorsing the type of semiotic essentialism that Brennan and Jaworski correctly reject. This observation about Simmel's views is compatible with his claim concerning the inadequacy of money as a mediator of personal relationships being wrong; see the discussion of the use of money as a gift in Alternative America in Chapter 3, and Chapter 9, note 49.
55 In Chapter 6 I discuss recent attempts—stimulated by Brennan and Jaworski's critique—to develop new sorts of essentialist semiotic objections to markets.
56 Brennan and Jaworski, "Markets Without Symbolic Limits," 1053.
57 Brennan and Jaworski, *Markets Without Limits*, 15.
58 Ibid., 62.
59 I will explain further why such objections are so weak in Chapter 6 when I consider the implications (no pun intended) that Grice's theory has for them.
60 Brennan and Jaworski, *Markets Without Limits*, 47.
61 Ibid., 48.
62 Ibid., 61.
63 Ibid., 68, 69, 70–72, 82.
64 This account of the semiotic wrongfulness of an action would be accurate whether the semiotic objection was essentialist or contingent; the former would simply hold that persons in all cultural settings would hold this action to be wrong.

65 Ross, *The Right and the Good*, 37–39, 46–47. David G. Dick also notes how implausible such objections are; "Impure Semiotic Objections to Markets," *Public Affairs Quarterly* 32, 3 (2018), 230.
66 David Hume, *Treatise on Human Nature* (Oxford: Oxford University Press, 1978), 524.
67 See, for example, Semrau, "Review: *Markets Without Limits*," 328 and Anomaly, "Review: *Markets Without Limits*." The belief that Brennan and Jaworski's rejection of essentialist semiotic arguments provides a significant contribution to the debate over the moral limits of markets is becoming widespread—see Chapter 6, note 2. But this belief is unfounded. Not only is there no reason to believe that anyone offers the semiotic objections that they criticize, there is good reason (for the reasons I discuss in this chapter, as well as in Chapter 6) to believe that no-one does. I address the question of how the false view that semiotic arguments are widespread could have become so entrenched in the literature on the morality of markets in Chapters 8 and 9.
68 Brennan and Jaworski, *Markets Without Limits*, 49.
69 Ibid., 65.

3
SANDEL, SEMIOTICS, AND MONEY-BASED EXCHANGE

Introduction

In *What Money Can't Buy*, Michael J. Sandel challenges us "to rethink the role and reach of markets in our social practices, human relationships, and everyday lives."[1] His work on this issue is one of the primary targets of Brennan and Jaworski's critique in *Markets Without Limits*. Yet although they address Sandel's work at length, they have fundamentally misunderstood his position and so much of their criticism misses its mark. I have already argued (in Chapter 1) that Brennan and Jaworski were wrong to attribute the Asymmetry Thesis to Sandel. In this chapter I will argue that they were also wrong to attribute to him essentialist semiotic arguments.

Sandel's Putative Semiotic Objections to Markets

Recall that Brennan and Jaworski hold that semiotic objections to markets take the form

> to allow a market in some good or service X is a form of communication that expresses the wrong attitude toward X or expresses an attitude that is incompatible with the intrinsic dignity of X, or would show disrespect or irreverence for some practice, custom, belief, or relationship with which X is associated.[2]

Recall, too, that with this general account of semiotic arguments in hand they develop a tripartite taxonomy of what they believe to be their various types. The first is "The Mere Commodity Objection": that "buying and selling certain goods or services shows that one regards them as having merely instrumental value."[3] The second is "The Wrong Signal Objection": "that buying and selling certain goods and services communicates, independently of one's attitudes, disrespect for the objects in question."[4] The third is "The Wrong Currency Objection": "that inserting markets and money into certain types of relationships communicates estrangement and distance, and is objectionably impersonal."[5]

Brennan and Jaworski claim that Sandel offers semiotic objections to adoption auctions, the use of money or gift certificates as gifts, and speculative markets concerning future acts of terrorism or the deaths of third parties.[6] They hold that he objects to "a market in children" as this "would express and promote the wrong way of valuing them" for "[c]hildren are not properly regarded as consumer goods but as beings worthy of love and care."[7] They hold that he objects to giving money or gift certificates as gifts as these do not convey the same "attentiveness" as "traditional gift-giving," and that he objects to persons gambling on death or using markets to generate information about possible acts of terrorism on the grounds that "[i]f death bets are objectionable, it must be ... in the dehumanizing attitudes such wagers express."[8]

Brennan and Jaworski offer little exegetical support for their claim that Sandel offers semiotic objections to these markets. (Indeed, they offer nothing more than the above quotations in support of this claim.[9]) This is unfortunate for not all of the worries that they quote him as expressing fit neatly into their tripartite taxonomy of semiotic objections. It is true that Sandel's concern with the use of cash and gift certificates as gifts could be construed as a version of the Wrong Currency Objection. This is because their use for this purpose could be understood to communicate a lack of attentiveness on the part of the giver and hence her "estrangement and distance" from the recipient.[10] (Although as I will argue below, Sandel's concern here should not be construed in this way.) But his use of the term "express" in his discussions of markets in children, betting on death, and information markets in terrorism renders his objections to these practices ambiguous between Mere Commodity Objections and Wrong Signal Objections. This should make us wary of Brennan and Jaworski's exegesis of his views. One might attribute to Sandel a Mere Commodity Objection to markets in children or financial speculation concerning death or future acts of terrorism on the grounds that he believes that to participate in such markets is to express an attitude that children or the persons whose lives one is betting on are of merely instrumental value.[11] Or one might attribute to Sandel a Wrong Signal Objection to these markets on the grounds that he holds that participation in them would express the "wrong way of valuing" children or the persons whose lives are being bet upon independently of whether the participants in these markets valued them in this way. It should be stressed that this difficulty in placing Sandel's concerns within Brennan and Jaworski's framework owing to this ambiguity is noted merely to raise suspicion of their exegesis of his view—nothing more. And this difficulty can be resolved once we recall that Brennan and Jaworski's argument against Mere Commodity objections will (as they recognize) lead their proponents to modify them so that they are no longer semiotic objections but corruption objections. Thus, if Sandel *is* to be understood as offering a semiotic objection to markets in children and information markets in terrorism and death, his objection must be taken to be a Wrong Signal objection.

Markets in Children and Information Markets in Terrorism and Death

As I noted in Chapter 2, the semiotic objections that Brennan and Jaworski outline are so implausible that the principle of charity requires that they not be ascribed to anyone unless there is good exegetical reason to do so. But not only do Brennan and Jaworski provide little exegetical justification for their ascription of semiotic objections to Sandel, there is good reason to believe that he does not offer them.

Sandel objects to "a market in children" on the grounds that it "would *express and promote* the wrong way of valuing them."[12] This objection is most naturally understood not as a semiotic objection but as an objection that this market would be wrong because it would promote the wrong way of valuing children. It would promote viewing children as "consumer goods" rather than as "beings worthy of love and care."[13] This shift in how children are viewed (both by some or all of those who participate in this market and by some or all of those who are aware of its existence) could lead to their mistreatment, either through active abuse or neglect. It could also lead the persons whose attitudes are thus adversely affected by the market to come to view other adults as similarly having primarily (or exclusively) instrumental value rather than being valuable in themselves. Rather than being understood as a semiotic objection, this is most naturally understood as a corruption objection: A market in children will "cause us to develop defective preferences or character traits."[14] Similarly, Sandel's objection to speculative markets concerning terrorism or death is most naturally read as a corruption objection rather than as a Wrong Signal objection. He objects to such markets on the grounds that they promote "a callous indifference or, worse, a ghoulish fascination with the death and misfortune of others."[15] Indeed, not only are Sandel's objections here most naturally read as corruption objections rather than semiotic objections, they *cannot* be semiotic objections as these are defined by Brennan and Jaworski. This is because such objections "are independent of worries about ... character corruption."[16] Thus, on Brennan and Jaworski's own terms, Sandel does not offer semiotic objections to markets in children or speculative markets concerning terrorism or death.[17]

Before I turn to show that Brennan and Jaworski are also mistaken to hold that Sandel offers semiotic arguments against the use of gift certificates or cash as gifts, I should note that Sandel does not believe that the possibility of character corruption that could arise from markets in children or speculative markets concerning terrorism or death establishes that such markets are necessarily wrongful, all things considered. He acknowledges that even if these markets are "morally corrosive," we might still decide to allow them "for the sake of the social good" they would provide.[18] In this respect, Sandel's view—like that of Satz, as I discussed in Chapter 1—is similar to the consequentialist approach advocated by Brennan and Jaworski.[19] Their view is thus not as different from that of some of the market critics they critique as they make it out to be.

Inappropriate Gifts? Gift Certificates and Cash

Brennan and Jaworski assert that Sandel offers a semiotic objection to "gifts of money or gift certificates."[20] Given that he is writing in contemporary America, Sandel's concern here cannot be with the *commodification* of cash and gift certificates. American cash is fiat money. It is simply a medium of exchange and not something (*qua* money) that can be commodified.[21] Similarly, gift certificates can be understood as a form of representative money with the owner having a claim on a certain range of commodities.[22] Rather than being commodifiable *qua* money, gift certificates are also simply mediums of exchange.

Sandel's concern thus cannot be with the moral question of whether cash and gift certificates should be commodified. (Indeed, he is not even offering an objection to these practices, let alone a semiotic objection. More on this below.) Instead, he is addressing the question of whether gift-giving in contemporary America should be governed by the norms of money-based market exchange. In discussing semiotic objections to markets, Brennan and Jaworski claim that those to whom they attribute such objections (including Sandel) hold the view that "certain markets *essentially* signal disrespect."[23] Given that they claim that Sandel "objects to gifts of money or gift certificates" on semiotic grounds, it would be reasonable to infer that they believe that his objection is based on the view that such gifts "essentially signal disrespect."[24] (Support for this inference can be found in the fact that they note that Sandel holds that "'traditional gift-giving' expresses 'attentiveness' while these gifts do not."[25]) But Sandel is not concerned with making essentialist claims such as this. As I noted in Chapter 1, his project is to address the question of whether in addition to being a market *economy* the contemporary United States should also be a market *society* (in which all human interactions are governed by the norms of money-based market exchange).[26] His concern with the increasing use of gift certificates and cash as gifts is thus to be understood as a concern about their increasing use within the contemporary United States. That Sandel's focus is parochial in this way (rather than being concerned with making universal, essentialist, claims) is supported by his discussion of Joel Waldfogel's work on the economic inefficiency of gift-giving as well as Stephen Dubner and Steven Levitt's popularization of Waldfogel's views.[27] He notes that Waldfogel observes that "cash is considered a 'tacky gift'" and that Dubner and Levitt note that the reluctance to give cash gifts is a "social taboo."[28]

Neither of these are essentialist claims. Instead, both merely note how the use of gift certificates and cash as gifts is viewed within contemporary American society.[29] Insofar as Sandel is concerned with the signals that are sent by the increasing use of gift certificates and cash as gifts, he is only concerned with those that would be sent by this way within the cultural milieu in which he is writing. He is not committed to making any essentialist semiotic claims concerning the use of gift certificates or cash as gifts (such as "the use of cash as a gift necessarily signals disrespect"). Brennan and Jaworski's objections to essentialist semiotic arguments thus fail to engage with Sandel's work given the (culturally situated) project that he is pursuing in *What Money Can't Buy*.

Money and the Norms of Friendship

That Sandel's concern with the symbolism of the increasing use of gift certificates or cash as gifts is a parochial one (and not essentialist, as Brennan and Jaworski claim) can also be seen by paying attention to the structure of his arguments. Sandel observes that differing conceptions of types of interpersonal relationships will lead to the adoption of different norms that are held to be appropriate to govern the interactions of persons in those relationships.[30] To illustrate this, consider how differing conceptions of friendship could lead to the adoption of differing norms governing how friends should interact with each other. One might, for example, conceive of friendship as being a type of relationship in which friends attempt to enable each other to satisfy their preferences more than they do for persons with whom they are not friends. The norms governing the actions of persons who conceived of friendship in this way would direct them to act to enable their friends to satisfy their preferences. However, if one conceived of friendship differently, then other norms might be appropriate to govern the interactions between friends. One might, for example, conceive of friendship as being a type of relationship in which friends express their appreciation of the non-instrumental value that they recognize in each other in virtue of each other's unique characteristics. On such a conception of friendship, the interactions between friends would be appropriately governed by norms that direct them to express thoughtfulness and concern for each other. These norms might direct persons to interact with their friends in a way that is different from the way that persons who conceived of friendship in terms of preference-satisfaction would be directed to act by the norms appropriate to their conception of friendship. It is possible, for example, that the norms that would be appropriate for a preference-satisfaction conception of friendship would direct persons to express their friendship for each other through gifts of money. This way of expressing these norms could arise from the belief that persons are most likely to be able to satisfy their preferences when they choose for themselves how to expend their available resources. Similarly, it is possible that the norms that would be appropriate for an appreciation-based conception of friendship would direct persons to avoid gifts of money to express their friendship for each other. These norms could direct persons to take time to learn about their friends' values and interests and then to make the effort to choose gifts that they believe that their friends would value, with their choices expressing their appreciation for their friends' individuality.

As noted above, Sandel observes that differing conceptions of what certain interpersonal relationships involve could lead to differing views of which norms should govern the interactions of persons in those relationships. He then notes that some ways of conceiving of certain types of relationship might be more conducive than others to enable these relationships to contribute to the flourishing of the persons within them. It is, for example, possible that friendships that are conceived of by the persons within them as essentially involving appreciating the non-instrumental value of their friends are more conducive to the flourishing of those within them than are friendships that are conceived of by the persons within them as being vehicles for enabling one's friends better to satisfy their preferences. If so, then this would give us reason to prefer the former conception of friendship to the latter. This, in turn, would give us reason to prefer friendships to be governed by the appreciation-based norms that are appropriate to this conception of friendship rather than the preference-orientated norms of its (inferior) rival.[31]

Sandel's argument is thus that interpersonal relationships (such as friendship) should be governed by the norms appropriate to the conception of the relationship that would be most conducive to the flourishing of the persons within it. He is thus concerned to establish that certain conceptions of interpersonal relationships are more conducive to human flourishing than others, and, from this, to identify the norms that would appropriately direct the interactions of the persons within those relationships as so conceived. He is *not* concerned with offering an essentialist argument that certain norms can only be expressed in certain (non-market) ways. He thus does not offer the essentialist semiotic argument against commodification that Brennan and Jaworski attribute to him and then proceed to criticize.[32]

To see this, let us turn back to the above account of two of the possible ways in which persons could conceive of friendship. It was noted that it was possible that the norms appropriate for a preference-satisfaction conception of friendship would direct persons to express their friendship for each other through gifts of money. It was also noted that the norms appropriate for an appreciation-based conception of friendship could direct persons to buy thoughtfully chosen gifts to express their friendship with others. These ways of expressing these differing norms as they arise from these competing conceptions of friendship are those of contemporary American society, as Sandel notes.[33] But these norms could be expressed differently in another cultural context. Consider, for example, the ways in which they could be expressed in Alternative America.[34] In Alternative America, persons who accept the preference-satisfaction conception of friendship do not give their friends gifts of money. Instead, believing that persons frequently suffer from false consciousness and hence frequently acquire things that do not satisfy their "true" preferences, they hire expert psychologists to draw up profiles of their friends to help them decide what gifts to purchase for them. The more elaborate the effort that a person makes to determine what her friends' "real" preferences are, the more the gift is valued by its recipient as reflecting her "true" desires. For persons in Alternative America who accept the preference-satisfaction conception of friendship, a gift of money would be insulting, indicating that the giver did not care much about satisfying the "real" preferences of her friend. Conversely, in Alternative America, persons who accept the appreciation-based conception of friendship give carefully chosen gifts to casual acquaintances, reserving gift certificates and gifts of money only for very close friends. This is because those in Alternative America who accept the appreciation-based conception of friendship believe that true friendship only *begins* with an appreciation of the peculiar traits of one's friend. (After all, if that was all that there was to it, one would have just as much reason to act in friendship toward strangers who shared the traits of your friends as you would toward your friends themselves![35]) Accordingly, in Alternative America, those who accept this conception of friendship consider it appropriate to give carefully chosen gifts reflecting knowledge of the recipients' traits only to acquaintances or new friends. To give such gifts to one's close friends would express that one's friendship with them was shallow, based solely on their publicly knowable traits. As one's friendship progresses, one indicates one's deeper appreciation for one's friends as unique individuals by avoiding gifts based on their known traits, first, by giving them gift certificates and, then, in the ultimate expression of intimacy, money, to express that their value as a friend can never be captured by any gift whose choice was based merely on their observable traits. It is thus common in Alternative America for people who conceive of friendship in appreciation-based terms to measure increasing intimacy in terms of fungibility, with increasingly fungible gifts expressing increasing intimacy.[36]

Given that Sandel believes that the appreciation-based conception of friendship is superior to its preference-satisfaction rival, he would not be alarmed were Alternative America to see an increase in the proportion of gifts welcomed by their recipients that were gift certificates or money. These gifts would be expressions of the norms that he believes should govern appropriate interactions between friends. His concern with the increase in the use of money or gift certificates as gifts in (Actual) America is thus not based on the view that "[i]nserting markets and money into certain kinds of relationships [necessarily] communicates estrangement and distance, is objectionably impersonal, and/or violates the meaning of that relationship," as Brennan and Jaworski believe.[37] Instead, it is based on the view that given how the norms governing gift-giving relationships between friends associated with the preference-satisfaction conception of friendship and its appreciation-based rival *are expressed in (Actual) America today*, the increasing use of money and gift certificates as gifts indicates that the conception of friendship that he believes is superior is losing ground to that which he believes to be its inferior rival.

Once Sandel's concerns with the increasing use of gift certificates and cash as gifts in contemporary America are properly understood, three things become apparent. First, Sandel is not offering an "objection" to this practice, as Brennan and Jaworski claim.[38] He is not objecting to the use of gift certificates and cash as gifts; he does not think that this practice is somehow morally wrong. Instead, his concern is that the expansion of this practice is indicative of the growing popularity of an understanding of friendship that he believes is inferior to an alternative that is losing ground. Since Sandel is not objecting to the use of gift certificates and cash as gifts, he is clearly not offering a semiotic *objection* to this practice, as Brennan and Jaworski claim. Second, even if Sandel was objecting to this practice (and he is not), his objection would not be a semiotic objection as Brennan and Jaworski define these. Brennan and Jaworski are clear that the hallmark of a semiotic argument is that its proponent is concerned solely with what a particular act expresses with this concern being *independent* of any other moral concerns that she might have.[39] But Sandel's concern with the increasing use of gift certificates and cash as gifts is not that the use of these items as gifts somehow expresses something wrongful and it is for this reason that their use for this purpose is wrongful. Instead, he draws on contemporary American norms that govern the giving of gifts to infer that the use of gift certificates and cash for this purpose indicates that those who use them in this way understand friendship in a way that he believes is suboptimal for the flourishing of those within this relationship. The moral concern that Sandel has is associated with the use of gift certificates and cash as gifts and focuses on how persons understand friendship. This concern, in turn, is motivated by a concern that certain ways of understanding friendship would compromise the ability of those who adopted them properly to flourish within friendships. His concern with the use of gift certificates and cash as gifts is thus not that this practice would in itself somehow express something wrongful. Instead, the normative claim that underlies his concern with certain forms of gift-giving has to do with human flourishing. Thus, even if he did object to the increasing use of gift certificates and cash as gifts (and he does not), this objection could not be a semiotic objection, as these are defined by Brennan and Jaworski. Finally, Sandel's concern with the increasing use of cash and gift certificates as gifts is based on his understanding of what their use for this purpose evinces within the cultural context of the contemporary United States. His concern is thus not based on an essentialist understanding of semiotics, as Brennan and Jaworski claim. Since his concern is dependent upon a certain contingent social understanding of what the use of money and gift certificates as gifts signifies concerning the gifter's conception of friendship, it is not only compatible with, but is supported by, Brennan and Jaworski's (orthodox) view that the symbolic meanings of both money and cash transactions are culturally dependent.

Intrinsic Value, Instrumental Value, and Yosemite

So far, I have addressed the putatively semiotic objections that Brennan and Jaworski attributed to Sandel. But, as I noted in Chapter 1, Sandel raises the question of whether there are any goods that should not be distributed in accord with market norms because to allocate them in this way would (given the prevailing understanding of the social symbolism of market distribution) be wrongful to treat them as having mere instrumental (rather than intrinsic) value. Sandel considers this issue in the context of the scalping of tickets to campsites in Yosemite National Park, and, at first sight, it appears that he is there endorsing a Mere Commodity Objection to such scalping.[40] It thus seems that at least in this case Brennan and Jaworski would be justified in attributing a semiotic argument to Sandel (even though they do not actually do so).

But there are three reasons why this conclusion should be resisted. First, Sandel does not expressly endorse the view that some things (such as campgrounds at Yosemite) should not be exchanged according to market norms as this would be "a kind of sacrilege."[41] Instead, he is merely reporting an objection that was raised (in *The Sacramento Bee*) against scalpers auctioning such items off to the highest bidder. Second, as noted above, Sandel is not committed to endorsing an essentialist semiotics. Indeed, he expressly rejects semiotic essentialism in the context of this very discussion when he notes that "norms change."[42] He thus recognizes the possibility that the current norms that govern the symbolic meaning of paying a high price for a Yosemite campground could shift. To illustrate this, let us accept, for the sake of argument, that in contemporary Actual America the auctioning of such a campground will signal that the value of this good is commensurable with that of money. It thus signals that it is not a "sacred" good but merely one that is profane. But the symbolic meaning of paying money for a good or service could change. It is thus possible that paying an exceptionally large amount of money for something such as a Yosemite campground could come to symbolize that one held it to be "sacred."[43] Thus, even if Sandel does endorse the view that auctioning certain goods or services to the highest bidder would (in contemporary Actual America) be "a kind of sacrilege," this does not commit him to opposing this way of distributing such goods or services in all situations. Finally, as Brennan and Jaworski recognize, when faced with Brennan and Jaworski's objections, the proponents of Mere Commodity objections would be wise to respond by holding that "when people buy and sell certain objects, this tends over time to *cause* them to view the objects as mere commodities."[44] Thus, *even if* Sandel endorses the Mere Commodity objection that he reports, then his response to Brennan and Jaworski's criticism of it should follow this trajectory. Rather than offering a Mere Commodity objection (and, note again, one that would rest on contingent rather than essentialist semiotics), Sandel would really be offering a *corruption* objection. Even on the reading of Sandel that is most favorable to Brennan and Jaworski, then, Sandel would not endorse an essentialist version of the Mere Commodity semiotic objection to auctioning campsites at Yosemite (or similar "sacred" goods or services).

Conclusion

Brennan and Jaworski misunderstand Sandel's views in four important ways. First—as I discussed in Chapter 1—they wrongly attribute to him the Asymmetry Thesis.[45] But Sandel's concern is not with establishing that certain goods and services should never be bought or sold but with the quite different question of when it would be morally inappropriate for the norms of the market to be used to direct human relationships.[46] Second, they wrongly believe that he holds that his objections to the use of markets (or, more accurately for Sandel, the use of market norms) in certain situations (e.g., the distribution of children, or to generate information about possible future terrorist activity) are definitive. But Sandel expressly disavows this, noting that his concerns about the adverse effects of the expansion of market norms in such ways could be outweighed if the social utility that they generated was sufficiently high.[47] Third, Sandel's concern with the increasing use of cash and giftcards as gifts is not that this expresses something wrongful. Instead, his concern is that their increasing use as gifts indicates that a conception of friendship that he believes is suboptimal is supplanting a conception of it that he believes is superior. His objection is thus not to the increasing use of cash and giftcards as gifts but to the changing conception of friendship that this evinces. His objection is thus dependent on non-semiotic concerns. Hence, he does not offer a "semiotic objection" to the use of cash and giftcards as gifts, as such objections are defined by Brennan and Jaworski. Finally, Sandel recognizes that the meaning of actions is dependent upon the social context in which they are performed. He thus does not endorse the essentialist semiotics that Brennan and Jaworski attribute to him.

Notes

1 Michael J. Sandel, *What Money Can't Buy* (New York: Farrar, Straus and Giroux, 2012), 15.
2 Jason Brennan and Peter M. Jaworski, *Markets Without Limits* (New York: Routledge, 2016), 47.
3 Ibid., 49.
4 Ibid., 49.
5 Ibid., 49.
6 Ibid., 48.
7 Ibid., 48; Brennan and Jaworski are here quoting Sandel, *What Money Can't Buy*, 10.
8 Brennan and Jaworski, *Markets Without Limits*, 48; quoting Sandel, *What Money Can't Buy*, 106 ("attentiveness" and "traditional gift-giving"—which appears without the hyphen in the original), and 146 (for the claim concerning death bets that has been rendered ungrammatical by Brennan and Jaworski's editing).
9 This is in line with the paucity of citations they offer to support their attributions of views to Satz and Anderson (as I note in Chapter 1). I offer a possible explanation for the sparseness of their citations in Chapter 8.

10 As I will argue below, construing Sandel's concern in this way is mistaken. His concern is not that the use of cash or gift certificates as gifts between friends communicates estrangement but that within the cultural context of the contemporary United States it signals that the friends who use these items in this way have a conception of friendship that is inferior to an alternative. Moreover, the signal that is sent by the use of these goods within this cultural context concerns the conception of their relationship that is held by the person who uses them in this way and not with either the goods themselves or the quality of the relationship. Since this is so, Sandel's concern about the use of cash or gift certificates as gifts between friends fails to be a semiotic concern as Brennan and Jaworski define this. They state that semiotic objections hold that:

> to allow a market in some good or service X is a form of communication that expresses the wrong attitude toward X or expresses an attitude that is incompatible with the intrinsic dignity of X, or would show disrespect or irreverence for some practice, custom, belief, or relationship with which X is associated.
>
> (*Markets Without Limits*, 47)

11 To understand Sandel's concern with information markets in terrorism and death in this way would require a modification to Brennan and Jaworski's account of the Mere Commodity Objection, for the participants in this market would thereby express their view that the objects of the objects of trade (i.e., the persons whose lives are being bet upon, not the bets themselves) were of only instrumental value.
12 Sandel, *What Money Can't Buy*, 10. Emphasis added.
13 Ibid., 10.
14 This account of a corruption objection is from Brennan and Jaworski, *Markets Without Limits*, 21.
15 Sandel, *What Money Can't Buy*, 153. Sandel's discussion of these issues are thus examples of his addressing the question of whether the use of markets or non-market forms of distribution would be most likely to maximize social utility. Brennan and Jaworski respond to Sandel's "corruption" arguments in *Markets Without Limits*, Chapter 13.
16 Brennan and Jaworski, *Markets Without Limits*, 47.
17 My earlier work on this issue was thus mistaken as I wrongly believed the woozle that Sandel had developed semiotic arguments (albeit *contingent* semiotic arguments) for his position. See James Stacey Taylor, "Sandel, Semiotics, and Money-Based Exchange: What We Can Learn from Brennan and Jaworski's Failed Critique," *Public Affairs Quarterly* 33, 2 (2019): 159–176. For a discussion of woozles, see Chapter 8.
18 Sandel, *What Money Can't Buy*, 162.
19 Brennan and Jaworski, *Markets Without Limits*, 73.
20 Ibid., 48.
21 According to John Maynard Keynes:

> *Fiat Money* is Representative (or token) Money (*i.e.* something the intrinsic value of the material substance of which is divorced from its monetary face value) – now generally made of paper except in the case of small denominations – which is created and issued by the State, but is not convertible by law into anything other than itself, and has no fixed value in terms of an objective standard.
>
> (*[1930]* 1965, 7)

22 See W. Stanley Jevons, *Money and the Mechanism of Exchange* (New York: D. Appleton & Co., 1896), 191–192.
23 Brennan and Jaworski, *Markets Without Limits*, 68. Emphasis added. They repeat this claim in the context of criticizing Sandel in "Klotzes and Glotzes, Semiotics and Embodying Normative Stances," *Business Ethics Journal Review* 4, 2 (2016), 11.
24 Brennan and Jaworski, *Markets Without Limits*, 48, 68.

25 Ibid., 48; citing Sandel, *What Money Can't Buy*, 106.
26 Sandel, *What Money Can't Buy*, 10–11.
27 Ibid., 103. Sandel cites Joel Waldfogel, *Scroogenomics: Why You Shouldn't Buy Presents for the Holidays* (Princeton, NJ: Princeton University Press, 2009), and Stephen Dubner and Steven Levitt, "The Gift Card Economy," *New York Times*, January 7, 2007. Sandel presents Dubner and Levitt's work as though it offered independent confirmation of Waldfogel's. This is disingenuous; Dubner and Levitt were simply reporting on Waldfogel's earlier work on the inefficiency of gifting in "The Deadweight Loss of Christmas," *American Economic Review* 83, 5 (1993): 1328–1336.
28 Sandel, *What Money Can't Buy*, 103; citing Waldfogel, *Scroogenomics*, 48, and Dubner and Levitt, "The Gift Card Economy."
29 Waldfogel notes that such gifts are only considered "tacky" "in some circumstances," such as from younger persons to older persons. It is socially acceptable for parents or grandparents to give their children cash. (*Scroogenomics*, 48–49). Since Waldfogel's claims here occur on the pages that Sandel cites, it is reasonable to infer that Sandel is aware of them. This lends further support to the view that Sandel does not believe that the use of cash (or gift certificates) as gifts inherently signals disrespect, as Brennan and Jaworski believe. Having noted this, it must be admitted that it is possible that Sandel did not read Waldfogel carefully. After all, Brennan and Jaworski claim that Michael Walzer endorses essentialist semiotics and support this claim by citing pages where he explicitly denies that this is his view. See Chapter 5, note 8.
30 Sandel, *What Money Can't Buy*, 102–104.
31 Ibid., 101–104.
32 Indeed, it is not clear what it would even mean to offer an argument against the "commodification" of money, gift certificates, or giftcards!
33 Sandel, *What Money Can't Buy*, 98, 101–107.
34 Brennan and Jaworski draw on a "Twin America" thought experiment to show that Sandel is mistaken to hold that it is necessarily wrong to buy wedding speeches (*Markets Without Limits*, 67–68). But as should be clear from this discussion, this is not Sandel's view.
35 Noted by Niko Kolodny, "Love as Valuing a Relationship," *The Philosophical Review* 112, 2 (2003), 135.
36 This example counters Simmel's claim that money is inadequate to serve as a mediator within close personal relationships. See Georg Simmel, *The Philosophy of Money*, 3rd edn (London: Routledge, 2004), 378. See too Chapter 2, note 54, and Chapter 9, note 49.
37 Jason Brennan and Peter M. Jaworski, "Markets Without Symbolic Limits," *Ethics*, 125, 4 (2015), 1057.
38 Brennan and Jaworski, *Markets Without Limits*, 48.
39 Ibid., 47–48.
40 Sandel, *What Money Can't Buy*, 35.
41 Ibid., 37.
42 Ibid., 40.
43 Since outlining this account of a possible way of understanding the relationship between money and the sacred, I have learned that this view of the symbolic relationship between money and "priceless" works of art has been suggested by Igor Kopytoff, "The Cultural Biography of Things: Commoditization as Process," in Arjun Appadurai (Ed.), *The Social Life of Things: Commodities in Cultural Perspective* (Cambridge: Cambridge University Press, 1986), 82–83. According to the set of norms that would govern how the meaning of such monetary transactions is to be understood, in the art world large payments are understood as "sacrifices" that are willingly made to secure access to something whose value lies beyond that of mere money. These norms could be viewed as an extension of the account of the relationship between value and

sacrifice developed by Simmel, *The Philosophy of Money*, 72–98; see also Olav Velthuis, *Talking Prices: Symbolic Meanings of Prices on the Market for Contemporary Art* (Princeton, NJ: Princeton University Press, 2005), 172–176.
44 Brennan and Jaworski, *Markets Without Limits*, 54.
45 Note that Sandel's opposition to markets in children does not commit him to oppose the exchange of children for money. It is possible, for example, that he could approve of a system in which adoption fees must be paid to acquire children, with these fees being set not by the market but at a level that covers the expenses of the adoption agency. In any case, Sandel explicitly notes that his opposition to markets in children, or information markets in terrorism or death, is not definitive.
46 And, as noted above, why Brennan and Jaworski believe that Sandel objects to the "commodification" of cash and giftcards is utterly mysterious.
47 Sandel, *What Money Can't Buy*, 162.

4

SEX, SURROGACY, SEMIOTICS, AND SPHERES

Anderson on Market Exchange

Introduction

In Chapter 1, I argued that Brennan and Jaworski were mistaken to attribute the Asymmetry Thesis to Anderson. I will now argue that they were also mistaken to attribute to her essentialist semiotic objections to markets in certain goods and services.

Brennan and Jaworski Attribute Essentialist Semiotic Objections to Anderson

As I noted in Chapter 1, Brennan and Jaworski assert that Anderson

> has no problem with you having casual sex or with you serving, for free, as a pregnancy surrogate for your infertile sister. But she doesn't want people to sell sex or surrogacy. For her, you can give it away, but you can't sell it—and others shouldn't buy it.[1]

They also claim that Anderson offers semiotic objections in support of the view that while it is morally permissible to provide certain goods or services "for free" (e.g., sex or surrogate pregnancy), it is impermissible to buy or sell them.

In support of their latter claim, Brennan and Jaworski first attribute to Anderson a version of the Mere Commodity objection. They begin by extensively quoting her account of what is involved in treating something as a commodity:

> A practice treats something as a commodity if its production, distribution, or enjoyment is governed by one or more norms distinctive to the market.

Market norms structure relations among the people who produce, distribute, and enjoy the thing in question. For example, in market transactions the will and desire of the parties determines the allocation between them of their freely alienable rights. Each party is expected to look after her own interests, neither party is expected to look after the interests of the other, or of third parties, except to the minimal extent required by law.[2]

They then write that if Anderson intends this to be the definition of a commodity, then to hold that something is a commodity in Anderson's sense "just is to regard it as having purely instrumental value, and in buying and selling that good, people are expected only to observe some minimal set of negative moral obligations."[3] Thus, they hold, "[i]f we decide to define 'commodity' this way, it becomes trivial that thinking of something as a commodity is incompatible with thinking of that thing (or some practice associated with it) as deserving respect or reverence."[4] Hence, they argue, by defining "commodity" in this way, Anderson presupposes that "buying and selling certain goods or services shows that one regards them as having merely instrumental value."[5] If this regard were mistaken—if one should instead regard the goods or services themselves as having more than instrumental value, or if one should regard the practices associated with them as having more than instrumental value—then the buying and selling of these goods or services would be wrongful. It would wrongly treat them (or the things associated with them in the appropriate ways) as being of merely instrumental value.

Brennan and Jaworski also outline a second way in which they believe that Anderson offers a Mere Commodity objection to the sale of sex.[6] They note that "Anderson complains that in prostitution, the buyer gives the prostitute cash, while the prostitute gives the buyer her body."[7] The buyer and seller thus "do not exchange the same *kind* of good."[8] From this, they infer that Anderson "seems to conclude" that "the buyer necessarily treats the prostitute as a mere object."[9] They accordingly believe that Anderson holds that a person who buys sex will wrongfully treat their trading partner as a Mere Commodity.

Finally, Brennan and Jaworski note that Anderson objects to the commodification of sex on the grounds that this would impose restrictions on some person's freedom. "In particular," they claim, Anderson believes that commodifying sex would reduce "some people's freedom to have sex have the meaning they want it to have."[10] They note that Anderson believes that "a moral culture that accepts prostitution"[11] makes it difficult to "establish insulated social spheres where [sex] can be exclusively and freely valued as a genuinely shared and personal good."[12] As Brennan and Jaworski construe this:

> The idea here is that Jane might not just want to give sexual pleasure to Kevin. She also wants sexual pleasure to be insulated from the market, such that the sex they enjoy together is something they both recognize as a

"genuinely shared and personal good". In a world where Kevin (or Jane) can buy sex, then the meaning of sex if different. So, Anderson concludes, allowing people to buy sex reduces the freedom of those who want sex to have a certain meaning.[13]

Brennan and Jaworski do not identify which type of semiotic argument they take Anderson to be making here. However, since they discuss it in the context of their objections to the Wrong Signal and Wrong Currency objections, it appears that they believe that it is a token of one of these types of objections.[14]

Anderson Rejects Semiotic Essentialism

I provided an overview of Anderson's project and her account of the important of sphere differentiation to preserve persons' freedom and autonomy in Chapter 1. As I argued there, Anderson explicitly rejects the Asymmetry Thesis with respect to sex and surrogate pregnancy that Brennan and Jaworski attribute to her.[15] Since she does not endorse the conclusion that essentialist semiotic objections are intended to establish, there is no reason to believe that she offers them. But the argumentative structure of Anderson's position is not the only reason to reject Brennan and Jaworski's attribution of essentialist semiotic arguments to her. In developing both her account of rational action and her pragmatic account of how persons can justify both their value judgments and the actions that flow from them, Anderson explicitly *rejects* semiotic essentialism. And—and more importantly—none of Anderson's arguments against commodified sex (i.e., its exchange for money in accord with market norms) or surrogacy contracts rely on semiotic concerns.

Anderson notes that a theory of value should provide an account of how value should guide persons' rational actions. To supplement her pluralistic theory of value based upon sphere differentiation (which I outlined in Chapter 1), she develops an expressive theory of rational action. For Anderson, a rational action is that which "adequately expresses our rational attitudes towards people and other intrinsically valuable things."[16] She notes that since "expression is a meaningful activity" "it requires a publicly intelligible vehicle to make its point."[17] This is provided by the social norms that govern the communicative import of particular expressions and actions so that these can be used by persons within the spheres in which they are operative "to communicate distinctive meanings to others."[18] Rather than endorsing the essentialist semiotics that Brennan and Jaworski attribute to her in outlining her expressive theory of rational action, Anderson explicitly states that the meaning of certain expressions and actions is socially contingent.

Anderson's rejection of semiotic essentialism is also explicit in her development of her pragmatic account of how persons can justify both their value judgments and the actions that flow from them.[19] She holds that to "justify an evaluative claim is to appeal to reasons that make sense of particular attitudes toward the evaluated subject."[20] As noted above, Anderson holds that the evaluative concepts through which persons express their reasons for evaluating things in a certain way and acting accordingly are diverse, applying to particular social domains and guiding particular feelings that are supported and recognized within those domains. Such evaluative concepts are "thick" concepts whose appropriate use and ability to guide the attitudes of those who use them are determined by reference both to certain facts that obtain and by the norms that exist within a particular social setting. The concept of a "music snob," for example, is a thick concept that would operate within a social space in which reverence toward certain types of music is viewed negatively.[21] The appropriate use of this term is not merely guided by facts that obtain (i.e., it applies to a person who is reverential in a particular way) but also by an understanding of its evaluative point (i.e., that the person in question should not have the attitudes that typically accompany the type of reverence in question). This use, in turn, guides the evaluations, and hence actions, of persons within the social group that uses this term in this way (i.e., that one should avoid being a person of this sort). In outlining this pragmatic approach to justification, Anderson is clear that the use of evaluative thick concepts is partially determined by the "culturally specific meanings" of the social practices to which they apply—an explicit rejection of semiotic essentialism.[22]

Anderson Supports Revising Costly Norms

Like Brennan and Jaworski, then, Anderson believes that the meanings of expressions and actions are socially contingent. She thus does not believe (as Brennan and Jaworski claim) that "monetary transactions" must *necessarily* be viewed as "impersonal, instrumental, and selfish": She agrees with them that they might not be.[23] But this is not the only way in which her views are similar to (and anticipate) those of Brennan and Jaworski. In addition to her explicit rejection of semiotic essentialism, Anderson also argued that persons could have reason to alter the meanings that they attach to their social practices—a view that Brennan and Jaworski also argued for (and which they and others appear to believe is original to them).[24]

Brennan and Jaworski observe that in light of the ways in which cultures "imbue certain actions, words, and objects with symbolic meaning ... some behaviors will signify morally bad meanings."[25] But, they note, avoiding these behaviors merely to avoid signifying the morally bad meanings that they communicate could be costly, either because such avoidance is harmful in itself or because it carries with it high opportunity costs. If this is so, they argue, this will provide reason to modify or abandon the meanings attached to certain behaviors.[26] In this, they agree with Anderson. She expressly notes that her theory of rational action is not a form of conventionalism whereby an appropriate action in a situation is that which would be required by the prevalent norms. Instead, she notes that a "social order can be criticized for failing to provide adequate normative vehicles for the expression of attitudes that have come to make sense to its members."[27] For example, the norms in Western Europe and North America for bodily contact between heterosexual romantic partners (e.g., that the man lead his partner on the dance floor) also express a status hierarchy. This precludes couples that reject this hierarchy in favor of a more egalitarian relationship from adequately expressing their relationship.[28] Such couples thus have reason not only to ignore these norms but also to develop their own that would enable them to communicate their feelings for each other to third parties. Similarly, Anderson notes that the correct use of thick evaluative concepts (e.g., "rude" and "polite") is not simply a matter of following a set of descriptive rules. Traditional rules of etiquette, for example, encourage men to give women personal compliments (this is evaluated as "polite"); they also encourage persons to avoid giving personal compliments in a business setting (this is evaluated as "rude").[29] But in certain situations (e.g., when men are working with women), these descriptive rules can conflict. To determine whether a man paying a female co-worker a personal compliment is "rude" or "polite," we have to attend to the underlying purpose of the social rules that govern the use of these concepts. We could come to understand that the rules that encouraged men to pay personal compliments to women arose at a time when male and female interactions typically took place in social rather than business settings where such compliments could ease the development and sustenance of personal relationships. Now that women and men (should) interact as equals in business settings, the norms that govern such settings (e.g., that facilitate a focus on business performance rather than on personal relationships) should govern the interactions between men and women. It would thus be "rude" for a man to pay female colleagues personal compliments. Anderson notes that when the applications of such concepts becomes contested (as was the case with "rude" and "polite" when women first entered the workforce in significant numbers), we should reflect on the evaluative point of the attitudes that justify their use. This, in turn, could motivate those who participate in the social practices in question to consider adopting alternative norms that might better serve their ends.[30] Thus, when women were starting to enter the workforce, an enlightened manager could have instructed his male subordinates that he considered paying female colleagues personal compliments to be "rude" even though at the time this was still typically considered to be "polite." This change in social norms would be justified not only by a concern for equality but also by the (defeasible) belief that a gender-equitable workplace would be more productive than one that was not. Brennan and Jaworski could thus follow Anderson in agreeing that the meaning of a man paying a personal compliment to a female co-worker should change from being a "polite" action to one that was "rude."

Anderson Does Not Offer Semiotic Arguments Against Commodified Sex or Surrogacy

Given that Anderson endorses neither the Asymmetry Thesis (with respect to sex or surrogacy) nor semiotic essentialism, it would be surprising if she offered an essentialist semiotic argument in support of that Thesis with respect to either sex or surrogacy.

And she does not.

As I noted above, Brennan and Jaworski attribute a Mere Commodity objection to Anderson after extensively quoting her account of what is involved in treating something as a commodity. They note that she appears to believe that "by definition" a commodity just is "a thing governed by norms distinctive of the market, and the market norms are fundamental [sic] *a*moral, as they are about seeking maximum satisfaction."[31] They then hold that this entails that by definition to "think of something as a commodity ... just is to regard it as having purely instrumental value ... ."[32] It would thus be "trivial that thinking of something as a commodity is incompatible with thinking of that thing ... as deserving respect or reverence."[33] But, argue Brennan and Jaworski, such a Mere Commodity objection "cannot form the basis to an objection to universal commodification."[34] This is because "it is always an open question whether a person who buys or sells an object actually views the object as a commodity in the above sense."[35] Thus, they conclude, Mere Commodity objections (such as that which they attribute to Anderson) fail because "the fact that people buy and sell things does not automatically show us that those people have the wrong attitudes towards those things."[36] They might both buy and sell certain things "while at the same time maintaining an attitude of respect or reverence" toward them.[37]

Brennan and Jaworski are obviously correct to hold that exchanging goods or services for money is compatible with the parties to the exchange "maintaining an attitude of respect or reverence" toward them (or toward the "practices and customs" associated with them).[38] But Anderson does not deny this possibility. Instead, she affirms it. Her discussion of professional sex therapy makes it clear that she believes that in certain situations a woman's sale of her sexual services for money is compatible both with her maintaining respect for her own sexuality and with this sale *enhancing* respect for it on the part of her client.[39] Where Anderson diverges from Brennan and Jaworski—and the source of their mistaken attribution to her of a Mere Commodity objection—is her use of the term "commodity" to apply *only* to those goods and services whose "production, distribution, or enjoyment" are "governed by one or more norms distinctive to the market."[40] For Anderson, the category of "commodity" is a sub-set of the category of "goods or services that are exchanged for money." By contrast, for Brennan and Jaworski, a commodity "is simply anything with a price tag."[41] By failing to recognize that their use of this term differs from, and is wider than, Anderson's, Brennan and Jaworski take her to hold that "anything with a price tag" will be regarded as having "purely instrumental value" and that "in buying and selling that good, people are expected only to observe some minimal set of negative moral obligations."[42] But this is not Anderson's view. Instead, she believes that if goods or services are bought or sold according to *non-market* norms (e.g., sales of sex governed by the professional norms that have been reflectively endorsed by sex therapists), they would *not* be treated as commodities as she defines this.[43] Brennan and Jaworski are thus simply wrong to attribute to her the view that there is a "necessary connection between buying and selling something on a market, and regarding that object as a commodity in the loaded with negative connotations sense discussed above."[44] Their initial attribution to Anderson of a Mere Commodity objection is mistaken.

Brennan and Jaworski subsequently reiterate their claim that Anderson offers a Mere Commodity objection to the sale of sex.[45] They do this in the context of discussing "The Essentialist Objection." This objection is that "anthropologists and sociologists are just wrong to claim that the meaning of money and markets is contingent" and that "[s]ome markets are essentially disrespectful."[46] They attribute this objection to those they identify as "anti-commodification theorists" (such as, they claim, Anderson) who (they claim) offer essentialist semiotic objections to markets in certain goods and services. They hold that Anderson objects to the sale of sex as the parties to it "do not exchange the same *kind* of good"; "the buyer gives the prostitute cash while the prostitute gives the buyer her body."[47] From this they claim that Anderson holds that "the buyer necessarily treats the prostitute as a mere object" and so concludes that prostitution is wrongful as it is "essentially degrading."[48]

There are four responses that should be made to Brennan and Jaworski's claims here. First, as noted above, Anderson does not endorse the semiotic essentialism that they attribute to her—indeed, she explicitly rejects it. Second, as was also noted above, Brennan and Jaworski conflate the sale of sex with prostitution. But, for Anderson, these are distinct. Sale of sex by prostitutes (i.e., sales of commodified sex, as Anderson understands this) is a sub-set of the possible sales of sex (which includes sales of non-commodified or partially commodified sex by e.g., sex therapists). Anderson only objects to the sale of *commodified* sex and not to the sale of sex *simpliciter*.[49] Third—and most importantly—Anderson's argument against prostitution is not a semiotic argument. This argument is not that the payment of cash for commodified sex *symbolically communicates* the degradation of the prostitute. Instead, it is that the payment of cash for commodified sex *actually* degrades the prostitute by compromising her autonomy. Anderson holds that while the cash payment that a customer pays to a person whose sale of sex is governed by market norms is "impersonal and fully alienable," the prostitute yields power over their person in exchange. The prostitute's autonomy is thus compromised and so they are degraded.[50] The wrong of prostitution is not, for Anderson, derived from any symbolic meaning that the payment of cash for commodified sex might have. It is derived from the way in which the buyer of commodified sex treats its seller.[51]

Finally, Brennan and Jaworski's putative counterexample to what they take to be Anderson's argument demonstrates that they have failed to engage with her views. Brennan and Jaworski focus on the claim (that they attribute to Anderson) that prostitution is immoral because those party to it "do not exchange the same *kind* of good."[52] They then note that there is no reason to believe that the exchange of different kinds of goods is immoral. They support this by noting that "Anderson directly exchanges philosophy lectures for cash."[53] Thus, they conclude, since cash and philosophy lectures are different kinds of goods and since Anderson (clearly) believes that exchanging one for the other is permissible, there is no reason to believe that the exchange of different kinds of goods (e.g., philosophy lectures, or sex, for cash) is wrongful.

This putative counterexample to (what they take to be) Anderson's argument is based on directly comparing the moral status of the sale of professional services with the moral status of the sale of commodified sex. But, as outlined above, Anderson is clear that insofar as the sale of professional services and the sale of commodified sex are governed by different types of norms, their moral status differs.[54] For Anderson, then, if the sale of her professional services as a lecturer is governed (at least in part) by the professional norms of teaching that she has reflectively adopted, while the sale of commodified sex is wholly governed by the norms of the market, these transactions will differ in kind. That she holds the former to be morally permissible does not commit her similarly to endorsing the latter. It is thus not that different *kinds* of goods are exchanged that matters morally to Anderson, as Brennan and Jaworski assert. Instead, what matters morally for Anderson are the *norms* that govern the exchanges in question.

In addition to their mistaken attribution of a Mere Commodity objection to Anderson, Brennan and Jaworski also attribute to her another type of (what they believe to be a) semiotic objection: That legalizing the commodification of sex will limit "some people's freedom to have sex have the meaning they want it to have."[55] As Brennan and Jaworski understand it, Anderson's objection here is that if sex could be bought and sold, then the "meaning" of the sex that is enjoyed between persons who exchange it "as an exclusive gift" will be different.[56] It will no longer be a "genuinely shared and personal good" that has no price but will, instead, be simply a commodity with a price that happens in this instance to be freely exchanged.[57]

Brennan and Jaworski do not explain why they believe that this argument is a semiotic objection. (Although it appears that they believe that this is a semiotic argument as it refers to the "meaning" that sex will have in a situation where it is legally commodified. More on this below.) This is unfortunate, for this argument does not fit their definition of a semiotic objection. As they construe this argument, it begins with the claim that commodifying sex will reduce the freedom of some people to enjoy sex when this has a certain meaning, i.e., that which it would have in a situation where it could not be (legitimately) bought and sold. With this claim in place, this argument then moves to claim that this reduction in these persons' freedom would be wrongful. The argument then concludes that the commodification of sex would be wrongful as it would reduce the freedom of those who would prefer to enjoy sex with the meaning that it would have in a situation when it could not (legitimately) be bought and sold. This argument is thus (as Brennan and Jaworski explicitly note) grounded on a moral concern about the possible reductions in freedom that could result (for some people) from the commodification of sex.[58] But a semiotic objection is one that holds that "to allow a market in some good or service X" would be wrongful if this market would "express the wrong attitude toward X or express an attitude that is incompatible with the intrinsic dignity of X, or would show disrespect or irreverence for some practice, custom, belief, or relationship with which X is associated."[59] The (putative) proponents of such objections hold that the wrong-making property of a market "in some good or service X" just is that this would "express or communicate something disrespectful, or would violate the meaning of some relationship."[60] This argument is thus not a semiotic argument as these are defined by Brennan and Jaworski, for such arguments operate independently of other moral concerns (such as reductions in freedom).

To be fair to Brennan and Jaworski, I should note that they do not list freedom as one of the moral concerns that semiotic arguments must be independent of; this includes only "worries about exploitation, misallocation, rights violations, self-destructive behavior, harm to others, or character corruption."[61] It might be that freedom could be covered by moral concerns with rights violations (i.e., one has a right to be free to enjoy sex in a certain way) or harm to others (one harms those who wish to enjoy sex in the absence of its commodification by restricting their freedom to do so). But attempting to locate freedom within Brennan and Jaworski's taxonomy is unnecessary, for this could simply be expanded to accommodate other moral concerns (i.e., that are independent of purely semiotic concerns) that are not already listed. And if Brennan and Jaworski refuse to expand this taxonomy in this way, it will become unclear as to what exactly makes a semiotic objection semiotic.

It is also not open for a defender of Brennan and Jaworski's attribution of semiotic arguments to Anderson to claim that this argument would count as semiotic as it includes a semiotic premise (i.e., that the commodification of sex will limit "some people's freedom to have sex *have the meaning* they want it to have").[62] This is for two reasons. First, to claim that an argument that includes a premise that refers to the meaning that an action or an utterance has is a semiotic argument would be to expand the definition of such an argument far beyond that which was originally provided by Brennan and Jaworski. On this expanded account of what would constitute a semiotic objection, objections that are clearly not semiotic as Brennan and Jaworski define this would be counted as being semiotic.[63] Consider the objection that it would be wrong to shout "Fire!" in a crowded theater when no fire existed on the grounds that this would be likely to cause panic and lead to persons being injured. On the expanded account of what constitutes a semiotic objection outlined here, this would be a semiotic objection for one of its premises made essential reference to the meaning of the wrongful action (i.e., shouting "Fire!" means in the situation at hand that there is a fire in the theater). But this cannot be right, for Brennan and Jaworski explicitly note that semiotic objections, as they define them, are supposed to be independent of "worries about ... harm to others."[64] That one of the premises in an argument makes reference to the meaning of an action or an utterance thus cannot suffice for it to be a semiotic argument on their terms.[65]

But even this (mistaken) response is not open to those who wish to defend Brennan and Jaworski's claim that Anderson's freedom-based argument is a semiotic argument. This is because Anderson's freedom-based argument against legalizing the commodification of sex makes no mention of the different "meanings" of sex in a situation where it is (legally) commodified versus one where it is not. This terminology was introduced into the discussion of this argument by Brennan and Jaworski who then drew upon it (i.e., the claims about "meaning" that they introduced) to construe Anderson's freedom-based argument as a semiotic argument.[66]

That Anderson's freedom-based argument is not a semiotic argument becomes clear when her text is examined closely (i.e., without introducing terminology into it that did not originally exist). As noted above, Anderson argues that commodified sex (i.e., the sale of sex according to market norms) involves the "(de)valuation of women as rightfully male sexual property" such that the man does not need to "respond to the woman's own personal needs."[67] She holds that this type of sex is inferior to "sexual acts exchanged as gifts" which are founded on "a mutual recognition of the partners as sexually attracted to each other."[68] But the inferiority of commodified sex to sex exchanged as a gift does not support imposing legal restrictions on the former. Indeed, Anderson notes that the legal co-existence of both commodified and gifted sex would appear to promote freedom by allowing "those who value sexuality as a higher good enjoy it in non-commodified personal relations, and those who value it as a commodity exchange it on the market."[69] But Anderson holds that this is too simple. She argues that rather than being sharply contrasted, the way in which women's sexuality is valued in the commodified sphere influences how it is valued in the personal sphere. She holds that prostitution (i.e., the provision of commodified sex) provides "techniques and models" for sexual gratification that are based on viewing women as male sexual property that men "import back into the sphere of personal relations and make normative for their partners there."[70] Hence, argues Anderson, if women's sexuality "is legally valued as a commodity," this will undermine the possibility that "it can be exclusively and fully valued as a genuinely shared and personal good."[71] Nowhere in this argument does Anderson make mention of differing "meanings" that sex might have in either the commodified or the personal sphere. Instead, she focuses on the need not to legalize commodified sex to ensure that people have the freedom to express themselves sexually in certain ways. Thus, not only is this freedom-based argument not a semiotic argument as Brennan and Jaworski define this, it makes no semiotic claims at all.[72]

Conclusion

Brennan and Jaworski attribute the Asymmetry Thesis to Anderson with respect to sex and surrogacy. They also hold that she supports this, deploying semiotic arguments that are designed to show that one can "give ... away" each of these services "but you can't sell it—and others shouldn't buy it."[73] Both of these claims are false. As I argued in Chapter 1, Anderson does not endorse the Asymmetry Thesis with respect to either sex or surrogacy. And, as I argued both there, and in this chapter, she does not support her views concerning the morality of the exchange of these services for money by appeal to any essentialist semiotic objections. Not only are none of the arguments that she develops in support of her views concerning how sexual and surrogacy services should be distributed semiotic, but she expressly rejects semiotic essentialism.

But the conclusions to be drawn from this discussion of Brennan and Jaworski's treatment of Anderson's work are not merely negative. Just as elaborating Sandel's views helped to clarify the nature of the debates that he was engaged in, so too does this elucidation of Anderson's views clarify the moral concerns that she sees arising with the expansion of market norms into new domains. And, as I will discuss in Chapter 7, these clarifications contribute to a better understanding of the contours of the current debates over the appropriate limits of markets.

Notes

1 Jason Brennan and Peter M. Jaworski, *Markets Without Limits* (New York: Routledge, 2016), 12. As I noted in Chapter 1, Brennan and Jaworski neither quote from Anderson nor cite her work to support this claim. This absence of textual support is not surprising, for (as I argued) Brennan and Jaworski misrepresent Anderson's views. I offer a possible explanation for their lack of exegetical support for their claims in Chapter 8.
2 Ibid., 52. Quoting Elizabeth Anderson, "Why Commercial Surrogate Motherhood Unethically Commodifies Women and Children," *Health Care Analysis* 8 (2000), 19–20.
3 Brennan and Jaworski, *Markets Without Limits*, 52.
4 Ibid., 52.
5 Ibid., 49, 52.
6 Brennan and Jaworski do not identify this as a Mere Commodity objection although it seems from their claim (ibid., 76) that the prostitute is necessarily treated "as a mere object" by the buyer that they believe that this objection is a token of that type. However, they also offer this objection as an example of a Wrong Currency objection (ibid., 61). The difficulty of identifying what type of semiotic objection this is supposed to be is perhaps because, as Brennan and Jaworski note, Anderson's semiotic objections are "less explicit" (ibid., 49) than those of another author that they (also wrongly) identify as an anti-commodification theorist. (The author in this case is

Michael Sandel. That Brennan and Jaworski hold that he offers more "explicit" essentialist semiotic objections to markets than does Anderson is mistaken for, as was argued in Chapter 3, he does not offer such arguments at all.) As I will discuss below, Anderson's arguments are "less explicit" as semiotic objections simply because they are not semiotic objections at all.

7 Brennan and Jaworski, *Markets Without Limits*, 76.
8 Ibid., 76. Emphasis in original.
9 Ibid., 76. Again, Brennan and Jaworski neither cite nor quote Anderson to support their exegetical claims.
10 Ibid., 76.
11 Ibid., 76–77.
12 Elizabeth Anderson, *Value in Ethics and Economics* (Cambridge, MA: Harvard University Press, 1993), 155, as quoted by Brennan and Jaworski, *Markets Without Limits*, 77. Two points are worth making here. First, Brennan and Jaworski misquote Anderson. The correct quotation (with ellipses) is "establish insulated social spheres where… [sex]… can be exclusively and fully valued as a genuinely shared and personal good." Second, they wrongly attribute this (mis)quotation to Anderson's "Why Commercial Surrogate Motherhood Unethically Commodifies Women and Children," even though the page number they cite (155) lies outside the scope of that paper. (They make this mistake twice in this chapter; see *Markets Without Limits*, 84, notes 4 and 8. They also make this mistake in citing Radin; see Chapter 7, note 53.) I, too, have made similar careless mistakes. See James Stacey Taylor, "Buying and Selling Friendship," *American Philosophical Quarterly* 56, 2 (2019), 200–201, notes 8, 9, 39, 40.
13 Brennan and Jaworski, *Markets Without Limits*, 77; see also 48–49. Note that in their earlier outline of this argument they construe it to be grounded on a concern "to preserve Kantian autonomy" while here they construe it as being grounded on a concern to preserve freedom. But as Anderson makes clear, autonomy and freedom are distinct concepts. See *Value in Ethics and Economics*, 141–143.
14 The difficulty in placing Anderson's putatively semiotic objections into Brennan and Jaworski's taxonomy stems from the fact that, as will be discussed below, none of them are semiotic objections.
15 There is also no reason to believe that she endorses this thesis with respect to any other good or service.
16 Anderson, *Value in Ethics and Economics*, 17.
17 Ibid., 18.
18 Ibid., 18.
19 It is also clear from the Quinean basis of her epistemology. See Chapter 2, note 41.
20 Anderson, *Value in Ethics and Economics*, 97.
21 Ibid., 98.
22 Ibid., 101.
23 Brennan and Jaworski, *Markets Without Limits*, 68.
24 Ibid., 68–73. See, for example, Jonathan Anomaly, "Review: *Markets Without Limits*," *Notre Dame Philosophical Reviews*, available at: https://ndpr.nd.edu/news/markets-without-limits-moral-virtues-and-commercial-interests/
25 Brennan and Jaworski, *Markets Without Limits*, 68.
26 Ibid., 69. Brennan and Jaworski claim that opposition to organ sales is "an example of symbolism with a high opportunity cost." Assuming that allowing markets in human organs will "make sick people healthier, make poor people richer, and prevent hundreds of thousands of deaths per year," prohibiting them because "in light of pre-existing Western interpretative practices, markets in organs would still count as 'commodifying life'" is extremely costly. This interpretative practice should thus be revised to allow organ markets (ibid., 70). Brennan and Jaworski do not cite anyone who offers this objection to organ markets.

27 Anderson, *Value in Ethics and Economics*, 18.
28 Ibid., 18–19.
29 Ibid., 99.
30 Ibid., 101–102.
31 Brennan and Jaworski, *Markets Without Limits*, 52.
32 Ibid., 52. It is unclear how Brennan and Jaworski derive the claim that Anderson believes that to "think of something as a commodity ... just is to regard it as having purely instrumental value ... " from the passage that they quote from her, for there she makes no mention of the attitudes that persons take toward commodities (in her sense of this term).
33 Ibid., 52.
34 Ibid., 52.
35 Ibid., 52.
36 Ibid., 54.
37 Ibid., 54. See also Chapter 3, note 43.
38 Ibid., 54.
39 Anderson, *Value in Ethics and Economics*, 156.
40 Anderson, "Why Commercial Surrogate Motherhood Unethically Commodifies Women and Children," 19.
41 Brennan and Jaworski, *Markets Without Limits*, 52.
42 Ibid., 52.
43 This is not a minor mistake. By failing to recognize that Anderson is arguing not against the exchange of certain goods and services for money but against the exchange of certain goods and services for money *being governed by market norms*, Brennan and Jaworski fundamentally misunderstand her project. (The point that the exchange of a good or service for money does not entail the commodification of that good or service is also made by Radin, who notes "[t]hat money travels from John to Jane, and a child travels from Jane to John, isn't evil in itself, outside of our conceptualization of the interaction" [Margaret Jane Radin, *Contested Commodities* (Cambridge, MA: Harvard University Press, 1996), 14].) Note, too, that the giving of gifts or money after a service has been performed or a good received does not entail that the service or the good has been *exchanged* for the gifted-good or the money given. The practice (of men in certain groups in Madagascar) of leaving gifts of money for their sexual partners should thus not be understood either as the sale of sex according to market norms nor the exchange of sex for money. For further discussion of this last point, see Chapter 9.
44 Brennan and Jaworski, *Markets Without Limits*, 52. In their defense, one could try to hold that Brennan and Jaworski are only claiming that Anderson holds that there is a "necessary connection between buying and selling something *on a market* [i.e., in accord with market norms], and regarding that object as a commodity in the loaded with negative connotations sense discussed above." But this cannot be their view as they make it clear that they believe that Anderson would not accept the buying and selling of certain goods or services at all.
45 Brennan and Jaworski do not make the crucial distinction between the sale of sex and the commodification of sex.
46 Brennan and Jaworski, *Markets Without Limits*, 75.
47 Ibid., 76.
48 Ibid., 76.
49 In Brennan and Jaworski's terms, legitimate sex therapy of the type that Anderson would allow to be bought and sold would be traded on a *schmarket* rather than a market; ibid., 65.
50 Anderson, *Value in Ethics and Economics*, 154.

51 Brennan and Jaworski recognize this when they write that Anderson holds that "the buyer necessarily treats the prostitute as a mere object" (*Markets Without Limits*, 76). But they do not realize that this is not a semiotic objection to prostitution.
52 Ibid., 76.
53 Ibid., 76.
54 Anderson, *Value in Ethics and Economics*, 145–150.
55 Brennan and Jaworski, *Markets Without Limits*, 76.
56 Ibid., 77.
57 Ibid., 77; see also 48–49.
58 Ibid., 77.
59 Ibid., 47.
60 Ibid., 48.
61 Ibid., 47.
62 Ibid., 76. Emphasis added.
63 I discuss this further in Chapter 6.
64 Brennan and Jaworski, *Markets Without Limits*, 47.
65 See the discussion of Archard's argument in Chapter 5.
66 It is possible that Brennan and Jaworski confused the form of Anderson's freedom-based argument with that offered by Archard, which will be discussed in Chapter 5. But this is not the only time that Brennan and Jaworski attribute terms to Anderson that do not appear in her texts. In discussing Anderson's views of surrogacy, they write that she worries that commercial surrogacy arrangements communicate the view that women are merely "incubation machines," citing her "Is Women's Labor a Commodity?," *Philosophy & Public Affairs* 19, 1 (1990), 71, in support (Brennan and Jaworski, *Markets Without Limits*, 48, 50, note 5). But Anderson makes no mention of women as "incubation machines" in that article. Similar carelessness accompanies their citation practices; see note 12, above.
67 Anderson, *Value in Ethics and Economics*, 154.
68 Ibid., 154.
69 Ibid., 155.
70 Ibid., 155.
71 Ibid., 155.
72 It is puzzling as to why Brennan and Jaworski offered this argument as an example of a semiotic argument, especially since (once again) they provide no quotations or citations in support of their reading.
73 Brennan and Jaworski, *Markets Without Limits*, 12.

5
WALZER, SATZ, ARCHARD, AND SEMIOTICS

Introduction

In Chapter 1, I argued that neither Walzer, nor Satz, nor Archard endorse the Asymmetry Thesis that Brennan and Jaworski attribute to them. Without further ado, I will now argue that none of them endorse the semiotic objections that Brennan and Jaworski burden them with, either.

Michael Walzer's Spheres of Justice

Brennan and Jaworski assert that Michael Walzer both endorses the Asymmetry Thesis and supports this endorsement with essentialist semiotic arguments. They write that Walzer "says that distributions of goods are unjust when these distributions violate the social meaning of those goods."[1] They hold that, in Walzer's view, different goods "are governed by different norms, and represent autonomous spheres that must be kept apart" and note that he "complains that money can 'intrude' into other spheres."[2] They quote him as noting that the "words *prostitution* and *bribery*, like *simony*, describe the sale and purchase of goods that, given certain understandings of their meaning, ought never to be sold or purchased."[3] From this they conclude that Walzer believes that "certain things cannot be for sale because that violates the *meaning* of those goods" and thus that he supports an essentialist semiotic argument.[4] On the basis of this, they then conclude that he believes that certain things (e.g., sexual services, and ecclesiastical privileges) can be given away but never bought or sold and hence that he endorses the Asymmetry Thesis.[5]

As I argued in Chapter 1, Walzer does not support the Asymmetry Thesis. Nor does he offer any essentialist semiotic arguments in support of his view—although

DOI: 10.4324/9781003251996-7

a cursory reading of his work might give the impression that he does. His claim that "*prostitution* and *bribery*, like *simony*, describe[s] the sale and purchase of goods that, *given certain understandings of their meaning*, ought never to be sold or purchased" could be construed as Mere Commodity objections to these practices.[6] One could take this claim as supporting an objection to prostitution and simony on the grounds that the sale of sex and ecclesiastical privilege would express the inappropriate attitude that the prostitute and the privilege are of mere instrumental value. One could also take it to be objecting to simony on the grounds that buying and selling ecclesiastical privilege would communicate disrespect for it—a form of Wrong Signal objection.

Brennan and Jaworski are correct that Walzer believes that the "meaning" of certain goods precludes their sale.[7] This makes it appear that he offers semiotic objections to the commodification of certain goods and services. But even from the passages that Brennan and Jaworski quote, it is clear that Walzer does not offer *essentialist* semiotic objections to markets. In writing that "given *certain* understandings" of the meaning of certain goods, they ought never to be bought and sold, Walzer acknowledges that on *other* understandings of the meanings of these goods, they *could* be bought and sold. And Walzer spends considerable time making it clear that he *rejects* the essentialist semiotic position that Brennan and Jaworski attribute to him.[8]

Walzer notes explicitly that "[g]oods in the world have shared meanings because conception and creation are social processes. For the same reason, *goods have different meanings in different societies*."[9] From this, he claims that:

> it is the meaning of goods that determines their movement. Distributive criteria and arrangements are intrinsic *not to the good-in-itself but to the social good* ... All distributions are just or unjust *relative to the social meanings of the goods at stake*.[10]

Walzer is also clear that he believes that "*Social meanings are historical in character*, and so distributions, and just and unjust distributions, *change over time*."[11]

Walzer thus clearly rejects the essentialist view that there is a "deep metaphysical fact" about the meaning of certain goods. This can be also seen in his discussion of healthcare. Walzer believes that the social meaning of healthcare in the modern West requires that it be provided communally rather than through market means.[12] However, he expressly notes that his "conventionalist" view requires that healthcare be distributed in this way *only* because it has a particular "place" "in the life of a particular group of people" (i.e., those in America at the time he was writing).[13] He does not believe that healthcare has any intrinsic meaning that precludes its commodification.

Walzer acknowledges that "certain key goods have what we might think of as characteristic normative structures, reiterated across the lines ... of time and space."[14] He notes that it has been believed in many different societies that offices (i.e., positions of responsibility) "should go to qualified candidates" and so other ways of distributing them (e.g., by markets) have frequently been thought unjust.[15] But he observes that even in these cases there is *no* universal agreement concerning the correct method of distributing the goods in question, and so their (widely-shared) social meaning does not support an essentialist semiotic objection opposing their commodification.[16]

As well as attributing to Walzer a position that he takes pains explicitly to reject, Brennan and Jaworski also fail to recognize that his use of the term "social meaning" differs from theirs. This is not merely an exegetical nicety. Once Walzer's use of this term is understood properly, it can be seen that not only does he not offer any essentialist semiotic arguments to commodification, he does not offer semiotic arguments against markets at all.

Brennan and Jaworski's focus is on the "social meaning" of market transactions where transactions have social meaning if they communicate an attitude either toward the goods or services that are being traded or toward one's trading partner. Walzer's concern, however, is not with the social meaning of market *transactions*, but with the social meaning *of goods and services themselves*.[17] He argues that certain social understandings of the nature of particular goods and services within a culture will restrict the ways in which they can (or should) be distributed within that culture. Thus, he argues, within the United States in the early 1980s, marriage was understood such that "[c]itizens are limited to one spouse and cannot purchase a license for polygamy" and that the communal nature of citizenship precluded the purchase of "exemptions from military service, from jury duty, and from any other form of communally imposed work."[18] He also noted that, in that social milieu, political offices, many sorts of prizes and honors, and love and friendship could not be bought, for the understanding of these goods required that they be distributed according to merit and not merely purchased.[19]

Walzer is not claiming that if one attempted to buy a license for polygamy, a Pulitzer Prize, or someone's friendship, one would thereby express disrespect for one's intended trading partner or for the good or service that one was attempting to buy. Instead, his claim is that an attempt to buy one of these goods or services would indicate that one did not comprehend how the nature of the good in question was understood within that society. To offer someone money in exchange for friendship would not evince a lack of respect for friendship or for one's would-be friend. It would simply show that one does not properly understand the nature of friendship in a society in which "true" friendship could not be bought and sold.[20] On this understanding of friendship, it can only be directly conferred on someone through appreciating qualities that she has; this is what it "means to be" a friend. Since this is so, the distribution of friendship is beyond the scope of the market.[21] Similarly, to offer money in exchange for a Pulitzer Prize would not evince a lack of respect for the Prize. It would simply evince a failure to understand that, given the social understanding of the nature of the

Prize, it could only be distributed according to merit and not by market means.[22] On this understanding a purchased Pulitzer would be no Prize at all.

For Walzer, then, the nature of certain goods within a society—what it *means to be a good of a certain sort within a particular society*—is partially constituted by the means by which they are properly allocated within that society. But it would be mistaken to infer from this that instead of offering essentialist semiotic objections to the commodification of certain goods and services, he offers *contingent* semiotic objections to the market distribution of certain goods and services. (Recall from Chapter 2 that a contingent semiotic objection is one that holds that certain goods and services should not be bought and sold for money within particular societies because such commodification would, within that society, be "wrong because of what market exchange communicates or because it violates the meaning of certain goods, services, and relationships").[23] This is because Walzer's objections to commodifying certain goods and services are not semiotic at all.

To understand why Walzer is not offering *any* semiotic objections to markets, his claims about the social meanings of certain goods and services must be understood in the context of his overall project. As I outlined in Chapter 1, Walzer holds that theories of distributive justice should recognize that "*People conceive and create goods, which they then distribute among themselves*" with how goods are conceived determining how they should be distributed.[24] In some (if not all) societies, certain goods will be understood such that they are to be distributed by different criteria that are used to distribute goods that are understood differently. (For example, as I noted in Chapter 1, it might be understood in one society that offices should go to the meritorious while luxury goods could be purchased by anyone with the means to do so.) Walzer then notes that the autonomy of these different spheres of distribution is often violated so that "one good or one set of goods is dominant and determinative of value in all the spheres of distribution."[25] Rather than attempting to correct this by redistributing the dominant good to achieve "simple" equality, Walzer suggests that theories of distributive justice should instead focus on securing "complex" equality by reducing dominance. To achieve this, goods should be distributed throughout a society according to different allocative mechanisms that are appropriate to the social understanding of the nature of that good in that society. Walzer's project is to argue that this approach to distributive justice would lead to a more just distribution of goods through precluding money from becoming the dominant allocative mechanism in any society.[26]

Once Walzer's claims concerning the "social meaning" of goods are understood in the way that he intends and placed in the context of his political theory, it is clear that he does not offer semiotic objections to commodification, as these are understood by Brennan and Jaworski. Walzer's concern with goods and services being distributed according to their "social meanings" within a society is motivated solely by his concern for distributive justice. His argument that certain goods and services should thus not be distributed by market means within certain societies is not a semiotic argument. This is because (as Brennan and Jaworski define them) such objections operate independently of other moral concerns—including concerns about the unjust misallocation of goods and services.[27]

Debra Satz and Stanford's Student Newspaper

Brennan and Jaworski are also wrong to hold that Debra Satz offers essentialist semiotic arguments in support of her views.

To support their claim that "nearly every anticommodification theorist at some point relies upon or advances a semiotic objection" to the money-based exchange of certain goods or services, Brennan and Jaworski cite Debra Satz's mention of a case in which students were paid by the university that they attended to keep their dorm rooms neat and to be out of them by noon to impress prospective students and their parents.[28] They attribute to Satz the view that such a transaction is wrongful because it is "at odds with the kind of relationship a university should have with its students."[29] They hold that she is here offering a version of a Wrong Currency semiotic objection that holds that a particular transaction is wrongful because it "violate[s] the meaning" of the relationship in question.[30]

Brennan and Jaworski are mistaken. First, note that they do not attribute this objection to Satz on the basis of directly citing her work. Instead, they attribute it to her on the basis of a third party's (Beverly Momoi) account of her views.[31] Moreover, the account of Satz's views that they drew on was not from an academic source. It was simply a report from Stanford's student newspaper on the Senior Class Day Speech that Satz gave to graduating seniors at Stanford University; it was not an account of her considered academic position. These concerns might be minor quibbles: Momoi *might* have represented Satz's expressed views accurately, and Satz *might* be expressing her considered academic views in this speech. But even if Momoi represented Satz's views in this speech accurately, Brennan and Jaworski failed accurately to represent Momoi's account of Satz's views. In the article that Brennan and Jaworski cite, Momoi does not report that Satz argues that a university paying students to keep their rooms tidy is wrongful. Nor does she report that Satz claims that this is at odds with the proper relationship between a university and its students. Instead, she reports that Satz mentions this case merely as an example in a list of several examples of unusual market transactions. She also does not report Satz as offering a semiotic objection to a university paying its students to perform this service for it—indeed, she does not report Satz taking any normative stance on this practice at all.

As well as misattributing a semiotic objection to Satz on the basis of a student newspaper's report of a speech that she gave to undergraduates rather than on the basis of her published academic work, Brennan and Jaworski also overlooked the fact that Momoi reported that Satz offered only two types of objections against market transactions. And neither of these are semiotic objections, as these are outlined by Brennan and Jaworski.[32] First, Momoi reports that Satz argued that "the intrinsic nature of certain goods" (such as "friendship, a person's good name, various prizes and honors") entails that their value is diminished when they are sold.[33] This is not a semiotic objection, as these are defined by Brennan and Jaworski. It is not based on claiming that "buying and selling certain goods and services is wrong because of what market exchange communicates or because it violates the meaning of certain goods, services, and relationships" but on the nature of the goods in question.[34] Second, Momoi reports that Satz argued that certain extrinsic considerations could render particular market transactions immoral. A transaction might be "noxious" if the parties had differing levels of information about the transaction, or if one of them was not fully aware of the consequences of her actions. A transaction could also be immoral, for Satz, if it caused extreme harm to either individuals or society.[35] None of these extrinsic objections to markets are semiotic objections. As Brennan and Jaworski define them, semiotic objections operate independently of such extrinsic considerations.

Satz and the Meaning of Friendship, Love, and Prizes

But the above criticism of Brennan and Jaworski's claim that Satz has developed a semiotic objection to a market transaction might have moved too quickly. When one attends to Satz's *published, scholarly* work on noxious markets, it seems that both of the concerns about market limits that Momoi attributed to Satz could be construed as having semiotic components.

The first objection to the expansion of markets that Momoi attributed to Satz is the claim that owing to the nature of certain goods ("friendship, a person's good name, various prizes and honors"), their value would be diminished when sold.[36] As noted above, this is not, as stated, a semiotic objection. But rather than consider this claim, as stated by Momoi's report on Satz's views, it would be more charitable to Brennan and Jaworski to consider the corresponding claim that Satz states in her scholarly work: that "some goods do have a meaning that resists commodification—think of friendship, love, and Nobel Prizes … ."[37] This seems to be the claim that "friendship, love, and Nobel Prizes" have an essential meaning (i.e., one that is not socially constructed) that necessarily precludes them from being legitimately bought and sold for money. As such, it appears to be a semiotic objection to their commodification.

But to understand Satz's view in this way is mistaken. Satz is not claiming that it would be wrong to buy or sell "friendship, love, and Nobel Prizes" because doing so "would express or communicate something disrespectful, or would violate the meaning of some relationship."[38] Instead, like Walzer's similar discussion of friendship, her references to meaning should be understood as grounding ontological rather than semiotic claims. In claiming that the "meaning" of "friendship, love, and Nobel Prizes" precludes their commodification, Satz is claiming that what it means *to be* a friend, a lover, or a Nobel Prize-winner ("in our culture") precludes these goods from being bought and sold.[39] The "friendly" actions of a purchased "friend," for example, would arise not in response to the personal qualities of the individual who had (attempted to) purchase her friendship but to the financial inducements offered to her to perform them. For Satz, the acts of a true friend would be motivated only by the former considerations and not the latter: A bought friend would be no friend at all. Similarly, for Satz, one cannot purchase love or Nobel Prizes. To be genuine, these goods can only be bestowed in recognition of certain qualities of the recipient. These goods are thus partially constituted by the means by which they are distributed. For the friendship, love, or Nobel Prize that one receives *to be* friendship, love, or a Nobel Prize, one must receive it because the person who is bestowing it upon one is responding to qualities that she believes one has or accomplishments that she believes one has achieved. Hence, for Satz, the (ontological, not semiotic) meaning of these goods—*what it means to be* a friend, a lover, or a Nobel Prize-winner—precludes their commodification.

Satz, Semiotics, Surrogacy, and Sex

Satz's discussion of why goods such as friendship, love, and Nobel Prizes cannot be bought and sold is simply descriptive.[40] It thus fails to fall within the scope of Brennan and Jaworski's criticisms of those who prescribe limiting markets. But some of her other arguments that concern the limits of markets are both prescriptive and based on expressivist claims.[41]

In arguing against markets in women's reproductive labor, Satz holds that such markets "reinforce gender hierarchies—unequal status between men and women—in a way that other, accepted labor practices do not."[42] They do this by supporting "a vision of women as baby machines or mere wombs," reinforcing "an old stereotype of women as merely the incubators of men's seeds."[43] Satz thus holds that buying and selling women's reproductive labor is wrong (at least in part) because the transactions within this market communicate a wrongful attitude toward women. Similarly, in arguing against prostitution, Satz writes that this practice "contributes to and embodies the perception of women as socially inferior to men,"[44] "represents women as sexual servants to men,"[45] and "represents women as objects for male use."[46] She also suggests that "prostitution depicts an image of gender inequality by constituting one class of women as inferior."[47] "Prostitution," she writes, "is a theater of inequality; it displays for us a practice in which women are seen as servants of men's desires."[48] Satz thus objects to prostitution on the grounds that transactions in this market communicate wrongful attitudes toward women.

Yet although Satz believes that transactions in women's reproductive and sexual labor communicate wrongful attitudes toward women, she does not claim that this would *necessarily* be the case. Instead, she only claims that these transactions would communicate these wrongful attitudes *within the social milieu in which she is writing*. She explicitly states that she argues that "the sale of women's reproductive labor is not ipso facto degrading. Rather it becomes problematic only in a particular political and social context"[49]—a point that she takes care to note applies also to prostitution.[50] Satz repeatedly stresses that her claims concerning the meanings of market transactions in women's reproductive labor apply only to "our society" and to this market in "its current form and context."[51] She acknowledges that "under very different background conditions" her objections to contract pregnancy might not apply.[52] She similarly notes that her objections to prostitution apply only to "the practice of contemporary prostitution" which "is a very different phenomenon from earlier forms of commercial sex."[53] She states that her claims concerning prostitution's representation of women as sexual servants to men are limited to "our society" and "our culture" and notes that these claims would not apply in a society which had "different assumptions about men's and women's gender identities."[54] She stresses that the attitudes toward women that are expressed in the contemporary practice of prostitution "will reflect social facts about our culture" rather than any essential meaning conveyed by the buying and selling of sex.[55] Indeed, in criticizing Radin's objections to prostitution, Satz expressly notes that the meaning of actions are mutable rather than essential and can change over time.[56]

Thus, while Satz's objections to markets in women's reproductive and sexual labor include claims about the meanings of transactions in these goods, she does not claim that these transactions necessarily communicate wrongful attitudes toward women but only that they convey such attitudes in the social milieu in which she is writing. Her arguments are thus not based on the claim that these markets "essentially signal disrespect" and so they are not subject to Brennan and Jaworski's criticisms which are aimed only at essentialist semiotic criticisms of markets.[57]

But there is a more fundamental reason why Satz's arguments against markets in women's reproductive and sexual labor are not subject to Brennan and Jaworski's criticisms of semiotic objections: They are *not* semiotic objections, as these are defined by Brennan and Jaworski. Recall that, for Brennan and Jaworski, a semiotic objection is one that operates independently of considerations concerning exploitation, the unjust allocation of resources, violations of rights, paternalistic considerations, harms to others, or the development of "defective preferences or character traits."[58] Satz's argument against markets in women's reproductive labor is that the wrongful attitudes toward women (e.g., "baby machines," "mere wombs," or "the incubators of men's seeds") that transactions within such a market would convey in our society would contribute to gender inequality.[59] This, in turn, would contribute to (e.g.) the wrongful allocation of resources, harm to women, and the violation of women's rights. Similarly, she argues that in our society the wrongful attitudes toward women that would be conveyed through commercial transactions in sex would be likely to harm women as a class by influencing how they are seen in ways that would have harmful effects.[60] Satz's objections to markets in women's reproductive and sexual labor are thus based on the claim that allowing such markets in our society would have harmful effects. They are thus not semiotic objections, as these are defined by Brennan and Jaworski.

David Archard's Dominoes

As I noted in Chapter 1, Archard defends Richard Titmuss' objections to the commodification of blood. As part of this defense, he outlines a "Contamination of Meaning" domino argument against allowing markets in certain goods and services.[61] He observes that domino arguments begin with the premise that "it is important for a non-market regime to exist or that such a regime is morally preferable to the market regime."[62] They then continue with the premise that "the market and non-market regimes cannot co-exist, the former driving out the latter."[63] Brennan and Jaworski take the "Contamination of Meaning" version of domino arguments to be an essentialist semiotic argument against the commodification of blood. They conclude that Archard's use of it is subject to their criticisms of such arguments. They are mistaken.

Recall the outline of "Contamination of Meaning" arguments that I offered in Chapter 1. Such arguments begin with the premise that "With respect to some good, *P*, one must think of *P* in either exclusively monetary terms ... or exclusively non-monetary terms ... ."[64] It is then claimed that "the effect of a market in *P* ... is that *P* comes to be thought of in dominantly if not exclusively monetary terms."[65] Thus, "the market in *P* comes to dominate in the sense that there is no opportunity for a pure 'gift' of *P*, the donation of *P* being equivalent to the transfer of its monetary value."[66] This appears to be a semiotic objection for it is based on the view that the "*meaning* of non-market exchanges would have been contaminated by the existence of the market exchanges."[67] Archard explains that on this view the monetary value associated with the sale of blood will also become associated with blood that is donated, changing the meaning of the donation from one that was previously "priceless" to one that was the equivalent of a monetary donation. The meaning of donations would thus become "contaminated" by the presence of the market.[68]

But this is not a semiotic argument, as Brennan and Jaworski define these. A semiotic objection to a market in a certain good or service holds that it would be wrong to have that market because it would "communicate or express bad motives or disrespectful attitudes."[69] But the "Contamination of Meaning" objection to the commodification of blood is *not* based on the claim that transactions within a market in blood would express bad motives or disrespectful attitudes. Instead, it is based on the claim that the introduction of a market for blood would preclude persons from donating blood in a situation where their donations could not be construed as the donation of a good with a specific cash value. The focus of this objection is thus on protecting a "space" in which persons can give "pure" gifts of blood.[70] But protecting this "space" for pure gifts of blood is not itself valuable. Rather, argues Archard, it is valuable both to sustain a sense of community between the persons who live in the society in which such "pure" gifts of blood could take place and for its consequent effect in fostering pro-social behavior within that society.[71] This argument is thus not concerned with the communicative nature of a market in blood but with the effects that it might have upon community solidarity and pro-social behavior. It is thus not a semiotic objection for such objections are independent of other moral concerns.

One might attempt to defend leveling Brennan and Jaworski's critique of essentialist semiotic arguments against Archard's (non-semiotic) argument by holding that Archard's argument is *based on* an essentialist semiotic premise: That if blood is commodified, then the provision of a certain amount of blood (whether paid or not) *will mean* the same as the transfer of an amount of money equivalent to its market value.[72] But, the proponent of using Brennan and Jaworski's critique against Archard in this way continues, actions have no necessary meaning. It thus cannot be the case that the commodification of blood will necessarily result in the act of providing blood necessarily meaning that a provider has performed an action equivalent to transferring the monetary equivalent of the market value of the blood. This premise should thus be rejected. There is thus no reason to believe that the commodification of blood would lead to the "contamination of meaning" in the way that Archard's argument requires.

But Brennan and Jaworski's critique does not apply to this premise in Archard's argument for it is not an essentialist semiotic claim. Archard's claim concerning the effects that the commodification of blood would have on the meaning of those acts involved in its non-market provision should be understood as a *contingent* claim that might (or might not) be borne out in practice. On this understanding of Archard's argument, its putatively essentialist semiotic premise ("the effect of a market in *P* ... is that *P* comes to be thought of in dominantly if not exclusively monetary terms") should be understood as a conditional empirical claim ("*If* the effect of a market in *P* ... is that *P* comes to be thought of in dominantly if not exclusively monetary terms") about the semiotics of donation after commodification. Thus, rather than holding that the introduction of payment for blood would *necessarily* change the meaning of the non-market provision of blood, Archard is only committed to holding that *if* it did,, then it will have restricted the freedom of some providers to donate blood in a situation where such donations held a particular meaning.[73]

Holding that Archard construes this premise as a conditional claim about the meaning of the provision of blood in a situation in which it has been commodified is not only required by the principle of charity. It is also required by the recognition that Archard explicitly rejects the essentialist semiotics that Brennan and Jaworski attribute to him. Archard holds that the meaning of identical expressions will depend on the context in which they are made. For example, in challenging the idea that "there are conventions whereby women express their consent to sex," Archard notes that a convention establishes a relationship between an action and what that action is taken to be mean that would not naturally exist. Recognizing that in linguistics the signifier and signified are held to be related arbitrarily, Archard denies that there are any actions that have a "culturally universal" meaning beyond those that are required by "logical entailment or physical necessitation."[74] Similarly, when writing on "Insults, Free Speech, and Offensiveness," he notes that the meaning of expressive acts depends on the context ("when, where, how, by and to whom") in which they are made.[75] He observes that "[a] particular historical context may ... give a sinister significance to some communicative acts that would otherwise be innocent or at least not particularly problematic."[76]

But one might still attempt to defend the applicability of Brennan and Jaworski's critique of semiotic objections to criticize Archard's argument on the grounds that it is not the semiotic *essentialism* of his premise that is problematic but the fact that it is (putatively) *semiotic*.[77] Brennan and Jaworski accept that in some cases buying and selling certain goods would, in certain societies, communicate disrespect "given that culture's contingent semiotics."[78] They also accept that if "refraining from participating in these markets bears no significant cost or opportunity cost, and causes no significant harm," then persons "should refrain from participating in those markets."[79] But, they argue, if conforming to a culture's contingent semiotics would impose significant costs, then there is no duty to do so.[80] They hold that it is not the case that any such duty would be outweighed—it would simply disappear.[81]

As I noted in Chapter 2, Brennan and Jaworski's arguments thus apply to *contingent*, as well as to essentialist, semiotic objections to markets.[82] To ensure that their criticism of contingent semiotic objections is parallel to their criticism of essentialist semiotic objections, they should hold that a contingent semiotic objection is one that functions independently of other moral concerns. They should also hold that to be truly semiotic (in their sense) a semiotic premise (whether contingent or essentialist) is one that functions independently of other moral concerns. But once this expansion of their critique to both contingent semiotic arguments and semiotic premises (whether contingent or essentialist) has been clarified in this way, it can be seen that Archard's "semiotic" premise is not a semiotic premise at all. It is not the mere fact that in a particular society the commodification of blood would change the meaning of its non-market provision that is the basis for moral concern. Rather, it is that in this society this change in meaning would result in the erosion of a sense of a community and a diminution in pro-social behavior. This contingent and putatively "semiotic" premise thus does not function independently of other moral concerns. It is thus not (on what should be Brennan and Jaworski's understanding of what a semiotic concern is) a semiotic premise.[83]

Moreover, not only does Archard not offer a semiotic argument (nor offer a non-semiotic argument with a semiotic premise), his account is compatible with that developed by Brennan and Jaworski. Imagine that it would be instrumentally better to have a market in blood rather than not (e.g., this would secure more blood than would be secured, absent a market, and that this increase was beneficial). Assume, too, that the cost of the absence of such a market in a situation where a market in blood would lead to donations "to be thought of in dominantly if not exclusively monetary terms" would be considerable. In such a situation, it would be preferable either to try to alter persons' perceptions so that, despite the market for blood, it is no longer primarily thought of in monetary terms (where this way of viewing blood undermines pro-social behavior) or to take steps to alter persons' attitudes so that even though blood is thought of in monetary terms, this does not erode the sense of community or undermine pro-social behavior. Since there is nothing in Archard's argument that would preclude this approach, his account is compatible with Brennan and Jaworski's suggestion that the costs of particular practices could justify their revision.

Conclusion

Brennan and Jaworski's main criticisms of those that they consider to be prominent critics of markets (Sandel, Anderson, Walzer, Satz, Archard) are seriously flawed. Brennan and Jaworski systematically misunderstand both the positions of those they criticize as well as the arguments that they offer in support of them. This might come as a surprise: How could such work have been published in some of the "top venues" in philosophy?[84] It might also come as a surprise to find that *Markets Without Limits* is rapidly becoming highly influential, shaping the course of the current debate over the moral limits of markets.[85]

In Chapter 8, I will argue that none of this is surprising. In the current academic environment not only is there little incentive to detect errors of scholarship, there is considerable disincentive to do this. Moreover, not only are such errors likely to pass undetected, there are incentives in place that encourage the (unknowing) propagation of certain types of error: Those that lead to bold, striking claims, for example, that the "*most common* class of objections against commodifying certain goods and services" are all wrong.[86] I will then argue (in Chapter 9) that these (perverse) incentives stem from the commodification of academic research—and that given the adverse results of this, the norms of the market should not intrude into the academy. I offer a solution to restrict the influence of such norms in academic research in Chapter 10. But before turning to these issues, I will, in Chapters 6 and 7, turn to getting the debates over the appropriate limits of markets back on track.

Notes

1 Jason Brennan and Peter M. Jaworski, *Markets Without Limits* (New York: Routledge 2016), 49.
2 Ibid., 49.

3 Ibid., 49; quoting Michael Walzer, *Spheres of Justice* (New York: Basic Books, 1983), 9.
4 Brennan and Jaworski, *Markets Without Limits*, 49.
5 Presumably Brennan and Jaworski believe that Walzer holds that the service for which the bribe is offered is that which should not be bought or sold, and not the object of value that constitutes the bribe. But it is possible that they gave no thought to this complication.
6 Walzer, *Spheres of Justice*, 9. The final set of italics are added.
7 A more accurate account of Walzer's view would be that the "meaning" of certain goods would preclude their distribution being made exclusively through market means. See the discussion below.
8 Walzer explicitly rejects the universalist essentialist position in *Spheres of Justice*, 7–10. Brennan and Jaworski should be aware of this as this is precisely the span of pages that they cite when they address his work; see "Markets Without Symbolic Limits," *Ethics*, 125, 4 (2015), 1056, note 14.
9 Walzer, *Spheres of Justice*, 7. Emphasis added.
10 Ibid., 8–9. Emphasis added.
11 Ibid., 9. Emphasis added.
12 Ibid., 87–88.
13 Ibid., 88, footnote. Walzer drives home his unalloyed conventionalism by noting that it is possible that there could be a society in which haircuts had the cultural significance that healthcare has in the modern West, such that in that society healthcare could legitimately be commodified while haircuts would be distributed communally.
14 Ibid., 9.
15 Ibid., 9. The medieval Christian understanding of ecclesiastical office, for example, required that such office be distributed to persons on the basis of "their knowledge and piety and not for their wealth" (ibid., 10).
16 Ibid., 9. Walzer notes that in cultures different from the Christian Middle Ages ecclesiastical offices could be for sale: "if the gods can be appeased by sacrifices, why can't they be bribed by glittering gold?" (ibid., 97). And in the nineteenth century, Jeremy Bentham thought some offices should be bought and sold; see *The Rationale of Reward* (London: Robert Heward, 1830), 181–188. Note that while Brennan and Jaworski hold that "prominent theorists" like Walzer offer only *a priori* musings on the social meanings of certain goods and services, Walzer explicitly calls for "empirical investigation" into whether or not there are any goods whose social meaning has been universally shared. See Brennan and Jaworski, "Markets Without Symbolic Limits," 1066; Walzer, *Spheres of Justice*, 9.
17 At times Brennan and Jaworski conflate these in their discussion without realizing that they are different. For example, see "Markets Without Symbolic Limits," 1053, 1057.
18 Walzer, *Spheres of Justice*, 101.
19 Ibid., 101–102.
20 See Chapter 7 for further discussion of this general point; see also the discussion of Satz's views, below.
21 Although see James Stacey Taylor, "Buying and Selling Friendship," *American Philosophical Quarterly*, 56, 2 (2019): 187–202.
22 Although it is possible that Prizes could be partially commodified; see James Stacey Taylor, "What Can't Money Buy?," *Public Affairs Quarterly* 32, 1 (2018): 45–66.
23 Brennan and Jaworski, "Markets Without Symbolic Limits," 1053.
24 Walzer, *Spheres of Justice*, 6.
25 Ibid., 10.
26 Ibid., 3–63.
27 Brennan and Jaworski, *Markets Without Limits*, 46.
28 Ibid., 49.
29 Ibid., 48.

30 Ibid., 48.
31 Beverly Momoi, "Satz to Graduates: Some Things Should Never Be for Sale," *Stanford Report*, June 12, 2010. Available at: https://news.stanford.edu/news/2010/june/class-day-lecture-061210.html
32 The first is not even an objection to market transactions in the goods Satz mentions—see note 36.
33 Momoi, "Satz to Graduates." This view has clear affinities with the views of Sandel, Anderson, and Walzer, as outlined earlier in this volume and above.
34 Brennan and Jaworski, "Markets Without Symbolic Limits," 1053.
35 Momoi, "Satz to Graduates"; these objections to markets are outlined in Debra Satz, *Why Some Things Should Not Be for Sale* (Oxford: Oxford University Press, 2010), 9.
36 Although Momoi attributes to Satz the view that certain goods should not be bought and sold since this would diminish their value, it appears that this claim is not her primary focus. Instead, Satz's primary focus in discussing the limits that are imposed on markets by the nature of certain goods is not prescriptive but descriptive. Rather than focusing on the claim that the nature of certain goods is such that they *should not* be bought and sold, Satz instead focuses on the claim that the nature of certain goods is such that they *cannot* be bought and sold. This will be discussed further below.
37 Satz, *Why Some Things Should Not Be for Sale*, 84.
38 Brennan and Jaworski, *Markets Without Limits*, 48.
39 Satz, *Why Some Things Should Not Be for Sale*, 80.
40 For further discussion of this point, see Chapter 7.
41 See Chapter 6 for an extended discussion of expressivist arguments that are distinct from semiotic arguments.
42 Satz, *Why Some Things Should Not Be for Sale*, 117.
43 Ibid., 121, 130, 131.
44 Ibid., 135.
45 Ibid., 144.
46 Ibid., 149.
47 Ibid., 147.
48 Ibid., 147.
49 Ibid., 116.
50 Ibid., 222, note 4.
51 Ibid., 128.
52 Ibid., 131.
53 Ibid., 135, 137.
54 Ibid., 146, 148.
55 Ibid., 148.
56 Ibid., 142. On Satz's criticism of Radin, see Chapter 7, note 53.
57 Brennan and Jaworski, *Markets Without Limits*, 68. Brennan and Jaworski recognize that Satz rejects the view "that some markets necessarily have a particular meaning regardless of what people in different cultures think" (*Markets Without Limits*, 76) and draw on her observations here to criticize what they take to be Radin's objections to prostitution. But while they do not criticize Satz's objections to markets in women's reproductive and sexual labor on semiotic grounds, they do attribute to her an essentialist semiotic position concerning universities paying students to keep their dorm rooms tidy and vacated after noon. Since they draw upon her work rejecting such essentialist semiotics, that they attribute such an essentialist view to her is careless. But this carelessness is not surprising (and not entirely the fault of Brennan and Jaworski) for reasons that I will offer in Chapters 8 and 9.
58 Brennan and Jaworski, *Markets Without Limits*, 46–47.
59 Satz, *Why Some Things Should Not Be for Sale*, 121, 131.
60 Ibid., 148.

61 Margaret Jane Radin, *Contested Commodities* (Cambridge, MA: Harvard University Press, 1996), 95–99.
62 David Archard, "Selling Yourself," *The Journal of Ethics* 6, 1 (2002), 93.
63 Ibid., 93.
64 Ibid., 93.
65 Ibid., 94.
66 Ibid., 94.
67 Ibid., 95. Emphasis added. The discussion that follows has some affinity to the discussion of Anderson's freedom-based argument against the legalization of prostitution that I discussed in Chapter 4.
68 Ibid., 95.
69 Brennan and Jaworski, "Markets Without Symbolic Limits," 1055.
70 Archard, "Selling Yourself," 94.
71 Ibid., 92–102. The argument that Archard develops is complex and he notes that it is not definitive but requires further support, both theoretical and empirical; ibid., 102–103.
72 This attempted defense of Brennan and Jawiorski's attribution of an essentialist semiotic arguments to Archard is similar to the attempted defense of their attribution of this view to Anderson. This defense fails for similar reasons. See the discussion in Chapter 4.
73 Construing Archard's argument in this way not only renders it immune to Brennan and Jaworski's critique of essentialist semiotic claims. It also shows that Archard is not defending the Asymmetry Thesis with respect to blood. See Chapter 1.
74 Archard, "'A Nod's as Good as a Wink'," *Legal Theory* 3 (1997), 278–279. He does not, however, hold that the conventional meaning of an action is necessarily entirely arbitrary, allowing for the possibility that some actions could be related to their meanings metonymically. This is consistent with his denial that certain actions necessarily convey a particular meaning beyond that which can be drawn from them taken strictly in themselves.
75 David Archard, "Insults, Free Speech, and Offensiveness," *Journal of Applied Philosophy* 31, 2 (2014), 128.
76 Ibid., 128.
77 This attempted defense of the applicability of Brennan and Jaworski's critique could also be used as an attempt to defend its applicability to the views of Walzer and Satz. It fails with respect to their work for the same reasons that it fails with respect to Archard's.
78 Brennan and Jaworski, *Markets Without Limits*, 82.
79 Ibid., 82.
80 Ibid., 72–73.
81 Ibid., 73.
82 As noted in Chapter 1.
83 Dick refers to arguments where a semiotic concern is combined with a non-semiotic moral concern as "impure" semiotic arguments. But it would be better to refer to arguments that make appeal only to semiotic concerns as "semiotic" arguments and to those that do not as "non-semiotic" arguments. "Impure Semiotic Objections to Markets," *Public Affairs Quarterly* 32, 3 (2018), 227–246.
84 The term "top venues" is owed to Brennan and Jaworski. They take care to note that their work on the morality of markets has appeared in such places. *Markets Without Limits*, 227, note 3.
85 See Chapter 1, note 2, and Chapter 6, notes 1 and 2.
86 Brennan and Jaworski, *Markets Without Limits*, 49.

PART II
Getting the Debates Back on Track

6
EXPRESSIVIST ARGUMENTS

Introduction

In the previous chapters I argued that *Markets Without Limits* is seriously flawed. But as I took care to note in the Introduction to this volume, the primary aim of my criticism is positive: To redirect the contemporary discussion of the morality of markets away from the mirages of the Asymmetry Thesis and semiotic objections and back to the actual arguments and concerns of market critics. I will continue this redirection in this chapter and Chapter 7. In this chapter, I will offer a clarificatory taxonomy of expressivist arguments; in Chapter 7, I will offer a clarificatory taxonomy of the current debates over where the limits of markets (and market norms) do, or should, lie. But, as I will argue in Chapters 8, 9, and 10, the positive effects of my criticisms are not limited to putting the current discussion of the morality of markets back on track. Addressing the related questions of how flaws in academic work might arise and how they might escape detection in the peer-review process will lead to two further positive results. It will contribute to the debate over the proper scope of markets and market norms through supporting the view of market critics that there are some spheres of life where the norms of the market should not be dominant. And this, in turn, will lead to suggestions as to how to improve the quality of academic research.

Not All Expressivist Arguments Are Semiotic Arguments

In Chapters 2–5, I argued that semiotic arguments are not widely deployed in the literature on the moral limits of markets. Moreover, given how weak such arguments are it is unlikely that they will be widely deployed elsewhere in the philosophical literature. (This is especially true for essentialist semiotic arguments—those that are

DOI: 10.4324/9781003251996-9

the focus of Brennan and Jaworski's critique—since these rest on an account of meaning that is widely rejected.) But while semiotic arguments are unlikely to be common, arguments that appeal to what certain acts or practices express occur frequently in the philosophical literature. When combined with the fact that Brennan and Jaworski's (misguided) discussion of semiotic arguments has had a great deal of influence on recent debate, this leads to the worry that Brennan and Jaworski's work will mislead people into taking arguments that appeal to what certain acts or practices express to be semiotic arguments when they are not.[1]

While all semiotic arguments appeal to claims about what certain acts or practices express, not all arguments that appeal to what certain acts or practices express are semiotic arguments. This is an important point—and one that, if it is not recognized, could result in people continuing to tilt at the windmills of semiotic arguments.[2] This chapter thus makes a start in getting the debates over the moral limits of markets back on track after their (temporary) derailment by *Markets Without Limits*.

To this end—and to establish that not all arguments that appeal to what certain acts or practices express are semiotic arguments—I will in this chapter outline the different types of *expressivist* arguments that occur in contemporary moral and political philosophy. (As I noted in the Introduction to this volume, an expressivist argument is one that appeals to the expressive functions of acts or practices, either to identify them as a particular type of act or practice, or to justify or condemn them, where the expressive function of an act or practice could either be what it is taken to express or its effects on what other acts or practices are taken to express.) While many expressivist arguments have been developed in the context of debates over the moral limits of markets, some have been developed in the context of other discussions. I address these both for the sake of providing as complete a taxonomy of expressivist arguments as I can and also to forestall the possible misapplication of Brennan and Jaworski's critique of semiotic objections to the arguments in those areas.

This taxonomic outline of extant expressivist arguments will make clear that an argument that justifies (or condemns) an act or a practice by appeal to what it is taken to express is not necessarily a semiotic argument, as these are defined by Brennan and Jaworski. This is important. If one fails to recognize that semiotic arguments are merely one type of expressivist argument, then one might erroneously treat all expressivist arguments as semiotic arguments. And since Brennan and Jaworski's critique of semiotic arguments is sound, the assimilation of expressivist arguments to semiotic arguments will lead to an unjustified rejection of expressivist arguments that are not semiotic arguments. This taxonomic outline of expressivist arguments will also establish that even if expressivist arguments are common in contemporary moral and political philosophy, it is still possible that semiotic arguments are rare. The presence of expressivist arguments in the philosophical literature should thus not be taken as evidence that Brennan and Jaworski's critique of semiotic arguments undermines any *actual* argument that has been developed.[3] Indeed, since none of the non-semiotic expressivist argument-types that are outlined here are committed to the claim that any acts or practices have an essential meaning, it is possible that *no* actual argument will succumb to Brennan and Jaworski's critique.

This last point leads to the recognition that those who wish to establish that certain acts or practices are *necessarily* wrongful owing to what they convey should attempt to develop expressivist arguments that differ considerably from those that currently exist in the literature. This has been implicitly acknowledged by some (Anthony Robert Booth and Jacob Sparks) who wish to argue in favor of moral limits on markets and who have (in response to Brennan and Jaworski's critiques) developed ingenious arguments that they *believe* to be semiotic. I address their arguments in the final section of this chapter where I argue that Booth's is not a semiotic argument, and that both his and Sparks' arguments fail.

Expressivist Arguments

As I noted above, an expressivist argument is one that is offered to justify or condemn acts or practices by appeal to their expressive functions. As Brennan and Jaworski define them, semiotic arguments are expressivist arguments. Recall, for Brennan and Jaworski, a semiotic objection to an act (e.g., an exchange of sex for money) or to a practice (e.g., the routine commodification of sex) is wrongful if it communicates something wrongful, such as disrespect or some other wrongful attitude. Recall, too, that Brennan and Jaworski hold that semiotic objections to the commodification of certain goods or services are offered in support of the view that the purchase or sale of those goods or services would always be wrongful as this would necessarily (essentially) express something wrongful. They hold that in order to be a *semiotic* objection, an objection must hold that an act or practice is wrongful independently of any other moral considerations, such as harm, rights violations, or exploitation. They also hold that the proponents of such objections fail to recognize that censuring certain acts or practices on the sole grounds that they express wrongful attitudes or evince disrespect could be costly. By contrast, Brennan and Jaworski argue that if the costs (both consequential and opportunity) of continuing to censure acts or practices based on their symbolism is too great, then we should either change the meanings that we attribute to them or else cease attributing to them any meaning at all.[4]

Expressivist arguments can be either descriptive or prescriptive. A *descriptive* expressivist argument will identify a performance as being of a particular type (of act, law, policy, and so on) by making essential reference to what it conveys, either to the performer or to a third party. A *prescriptive* expressivist argument will justify or condemn a particular performance (of an act, a law, a policy, and so on) by making essential reference to what it conveys, either to the performer or to a third party. As defined by Brennan and Jaworski, semiotic arguments (both essentialist and contingent) are prescriptive expressivist arguments. But—as I noted above and will demonstrate below—not every prescriptive expressivist argument is a semiotic argument. I will establish this by outlining in this chapter the two main varieties of prescriptive expressivist arguments that are not semiotic arguments: Consequentialist prescriptive expressivist arguments, and non-consequentialist prescriptive expressivist arguments

Descriptive Expressivism

Before turning to outline the various kinds of prescriptive expressivist arguments that are not semiotic arguments, I will first address descriptive expressivist arguments. The reason for this is simple. My primary aim in this chapter is to head off any possible confusion (whether in the debates over the moral limits of markets or elsewhere) that might arise from the false belief that all expressivist arguments are semiotic arguments. And since descriptive expressivist arguments lack the prescriptive nature of semiotic arguments—and so are clearly distinct from them—considering them is a good place to begin.

Joel Feinberg offers a descriptive expressivist argument to distinguish punishments from (mere) penalties. Feinberg's is a *descriptive* expressivist argument because he is referring to what a particular performance (i.e., the imposition of "hard treatment") will convey to identify whether it would count as (i.e., be correctly *described* as) a punishment.[5] Feinberg argues that punishments can be distinguished from (mere) penalties by the fact that punishments have a "symbolic significance" that penalties lack.[6] Punishments (but not penalties) are conventional devices "for the expression of attitudes of resentment and indignation, and of judgments of disapproval and reprobation, either on the part of the punishing authority himself or of those 'in whose name' the punishment is inflicted."[7] Feinberg argues that it is part of the definition of punishment that in addition to its imposition of "hard treatment" on the person punished that it symbolically condemns her criminal acts—he notes that in many cases the "hard treatment" expresses this condemnation.[8] Feinberg explicitly notes that the expression of condemnation that is conveyed by certain ways of treating people is the result of convention. He notes that there is no more necessary connection between certain forms of hard treatment expressing condemnation than there is between the drinking of champagne and the celebration of important events.[9]

Feinberg's expressive theory of punishment differs from semiotic arguments as these are understood by Brennan and Jaworski in two respects. First, he explicitly rejects essentialist semiotics. Second (as I noted above), his expressivist argument is descriptive; its aim is to identify what makes a punishment a punishment. By contrast, the semiotic arguments that Brennan and Jaworski are concerned with are normative: They hold that certain actions are wrongful as they necessarily communicate something wrongful.

Feinberg's descriptive expressivist theory of punishment could play a role in normative arguments. If there is a reason why a person should not be punished for performing a particular act, then it will follow from Feinberg's expressivist view that there will be a reason why certain expressive actions (i.e., the hard treatment of punishment) should not be performed. But there is an important difference between the claim that certain expressive actions should not be performed *in a particular situation* and the claim that certain expressive actions should not be performed *simpliciter*. Feinberg is only committed to the former claim. Brennan and Jaworski's arguments address the latter.

To illustrate, consider Feinberg's discussion of when the difference between a punishment and a penalty will have practical import. Feinberg notes that the United States Constitution does not forbid the passing of all retroactive laws but only those that provide for punishment.[10] Whether the sanctions imposed by a law that was passed retroactively are penalties or punishments thus matters to that law's constitutionality. If the "hard treatment" imposed by a law that was passed retroactively would express condemnation—and thus be a punishment—then the law would be unconstitutional. It thus should not have been passed and the "hard treatment" should not have been imposed. The "hard treatment" imposed by a retroactively passed law would be wrongful because of what it communicated. But this is *not* because the communication of condemnation is itself wrongful. It would be wrongful because the communication of condemnation would be wrongful (as unconstitutional) *in this situation*.[11]

Consequentialist Prescriptive Expressivist Arguments

Feinberg's expressivist theory had a descriptive purpose: To distinguish between penalties and punishments based on what they express. Other expressivist arguments have a prescriptive purpose: To justify or condemn certain performances (acts, laws, or policies) based on their (expected or anticipated) communicative effects. This type of argument is a *consequentialist prescriptive expressivist argument*.

An example of this type of argument is that developed by Barry Maguire and Brookes Brown as an objection to certain types of markets. Maguire and Brown write that they are interested in developing "a broadly consequentialist semiotic objection" to markets.[12] They also note that their argument rests on the existence of "semiotic norms": Norms that in a certain context associate "a piece of behavior in some situation with some signal or expressive significance."[13] Since their objection takes the form of a *consequentialist* argument that rests on the view that certain behaviors owe their expressive significance to its *conventional* ascription to them, it is not a semiotic objection, as these are defined by Brennan and Jaworski. (Such objections are independent of consequentialist considerations and rest on the claim that a certain act or practice is essentially—not conventionally— endowed with a particular meaning.) It is, however, an *expressivist* argument for it is based on an appeal to the expressive functions of certain markets. Maguire and Brown observe that a compelling way to signal that you care about someone is to serve them at some cost to yourself.[14] But, they note, if you "serve someone for adequate consideration" (i.e., that which would compensate both for the loss of the welfare value of the good or service provided together with the costs of the exchange), this signal is lost.[15] They make similar points concerning testimony and esteem. The sale of acknowledgments in an academic text, book blurbs, or marketing campaigns in which persons are paid to recommend products to friends would, if they became widely used, undermine the efficacy of acknowledgments, blurbs, and personal recommendations.[16] Maguire and Brown hold that the commodification of the signals associated with caring, testimony, and esteem will impose significant costs. The ability to express effectively that we care about others and to communicate our sincerely held views to them are important to us, both instrumentally and intrinsically. If to preserve this expressive ability requires the imposition of restrictions on the scope of markets, then we have reason to impose them.

Such consequentialist expressivism plays a significant role in legal theory. It is widely held that "beyond establishing and enforcing rules" the law has the ability "to express those rules as a social meaning that can reinforce or change the norms of a community."[17] A law, for example, might be supported or condemned on the basis that it makes a "statement" that is "designed to affect social norms and in that way ultimately to affect both judgments and behavior."[18] This could occur in one of two ways. The passing of a law could be intended to make a "statement" that was intended to *reinforce* social norms. The passing of a law that criminalized a certain type of behavior might be intended to reinforce the widely held view that that behavior was wrong and so should continue to be avoided.[19] Such statement-making laws might frequently be used to reinforce social norms concerning the proper scope of markets. Sunstein, for example, holds that the use of the law to attempt to "fortify norms regulating the use of money ... is an important domain for the expressive use of law."[20] There are, for example, laws prohibiting the exchange of votes, body parts, and sex for cash.[21] Sunstein also holds that persons who endorse legal proscriptions against surrogate motherhood "are thinking in expressive terms," possibly aiming "to fortify existing social norms that insulate reproduction from the sphere of exchange."[22]

Statement-making laws could also be used to try to *change*—rather than merely reinforce—social norms. A law that prohibits littering might not be strongly enforced through legal sanctions. But it might express that littering is considered an inappropriate behavior and, though this, lead to persons expecting to be blamed by others if they litter. This, in turn, might lead them to change their behavior.[23]

As well as their direct effects on behavior through changing social norms, laws could also have indirect expressive effects that could lead to their being praised or condemned on consequentialist grounds. Laws that do not alter social norms through the expression of normative views might still lead to their revision through changing the background conditions against which they operate by altering the meaning of certain actions. For example, Sunstein observed that "many restaurant owners and inn-keepers actually supported the Civil Rights Act of 1964, which would have prevented them from discriminating."[24] Prior to the passage of this Act it would have been beneficial for white restaurant owners and inn-keepers to integrate their businesses. Doing so would increase the labor pool available to them (thus decreasing wages) and increasing demand for their services (provided that "whites did not shift their custom").[25] But while integration was still voluntary "for a white to serve or hire blacks was for the white to mark him or herself as having either a special greed for money or a special affection for blacks."[26] These were both stigmatized behaviors. However, the passing of the Civil Rights Act ambiguated acts of integration. They could now be understood either as the stigmatized behavior or as the result of a (legitimate) desire to abide by the law. As Lawrence Lessig notes, the law thus functioned "to reduce the symbolic costs of hiring blacks."[27] Although it did not directly change the social norms that worked against racial integration, the law altered the background conditions against which they operated. In so doing, it changed the meaning of certain acts in a way that eased the path to integration. It was thus justified on consequentialist expressive grounds. Since the expressive justifications of such laws appeal to their expected consequences, they are not semiotic arguments although they are expressive ones.

Non-consequentialist Prescriptive Expressivist Arguments

The above discussion of expressive justifications for performance have focused on the value of the states of affairs that could thus be brought about. A second class of prescriptive expressivist arguments—*non-consequentialist prescriptive expressivist arguments*—aims to justify performances independently of their consequences. These arguments can be offered either to justify the performance of individual expressive acts or to justify (or condemn) particular laws or social policies.

Non-consequentialist Prescriptive Expressivist Justifications of Individual Action

Robert Merrihew Adams offers a non-consequentialist prescriptive expressivist argument to justify the view that it could be rational to be "willing to pay the price of martyrdom for no obvious good result."[28] He holds that "it is a major part of virtue to be for the good and against the bad."[29] He then notes that the performance of certain actions will, given the existence of conventions that fix their meaning in certain contexts, express "commitment or loyalty to a belief or cause."[30] Actions that symbolically express that one is "for the good and against the bad" are not, for Adams, merely ways of communicating one's commitments to others. If one suppresses all outward expressions of one's commitments (such as, in Adam's example, one's opposition to Nazism) out of fear of persecution, one might start to question whether one is *really* opposed to (e.g.) Nazism or merely wishes that one were so opposed.[31] Acts that outwardly express one's inner commitments could thus affirm them, and this could provide the actions with value.[32] Expressive considerations can thus justify action independently of either its communicative effects on third parties or consequentialist import.[33] In arguing for this view, Adams does not ignore the possible costs of symbolic action. He recognizes that its value "can be undermined if its expected consequences are too costly to the concerns it is supposed to attest."[34] He also recognizes that the value of performing a symbolic action to attest to being "for the good and against the bad" will depend on "what other possibilities of action are available in the situation."[35] If there are ways other than the performance of symbolic action to "be for the good and against the bad," then pursuing these would be preferable. But if such means are absent, then the performance of symbolic action—even costly symbolic action—could be rational.[36]

Adams' account of how expressive but costly actions could be rationally justified was dependent on the assumption that "moral goodness has a more than merely instrumental value."[37] But other non-consequentialist prescriptive expressivist arguments could be developed to justify action without this deontic moral grounding. It is, for example, possible that the performance of expressive but costly actions could be justified by the (nonmoral) value that they would have to the performing agent.[38] Consider the reasoning that Paul Pennyfeather engages in Evelyn Waugh's novel, *Decline and Fall*, when offered £20 by Digby Vane-Trumpington as a "sort of damages" for his role in having him sent down from Oxford:[39]

> "If I take that money," he said to himself, "I shall never know whether I have acted rightly or not. It would always be on my mind. If I refuse, I shall be sure of having done right. I shall look upon my self denial with exquisite self approval. By refusing I can convince myself that, in spite of the unbelievable things that have been happening to me during the last ten days, I am still the same Paul Pennyfeather I have respected so long. It is a test case of the durability of my ideals."[40]

Pennyfeather's decision to reject the money was an expressive action but not one whose value lay in its communicative effects on third parties. Its value to him lay in its expression of his (non-moral) conception of himself as a gentleman (someone who has a "self respecting scorn of irregular perquisites") and hence his affirmation to himself that he was "still the same Paul Pennyfeather" he had "respected so long."[41] His acceptance of the money would have been justified by both compensatory and consequentialist considerations. (Vane-Trumpington was partly responsible for Pennyfeather's loss of his income and the marginal utility of £20 to Vane-Trumpington was far lower than it was for Pennyfeather.) But his decision to decline expressed and reinforced his continued adherence to his ideals, and it is this that justified it.[42] The value of such actions lies in their expression and affirmation of the agent's understanding of who she is, of her own commitments and the "narrative continuity" of her life.[43]

Non-consequentialist Prescriptive Expressivist Justifications of Law and Policy

The above types of expressive justifications for actions performed by individuals have analogs in similar expressive justifications for certain laws or social policies. Sunstein notes that: "sometimes people support a law, not because of its effects on norms, but because they believe that it is intrinsically valuable for the relevant 'statement' to be made."[44] (This type of justification could also be offered for repealing a law as well as passing one.) This expressive justification for law is akin to the expressive justification for symbolic action developed by Adams. It is the view that a law should make a "statement" as a way of expressing (and thus affirming) that the persons on whose behalf the legislator is understood to speak are for the good and against the bad. Sunstein states that: "the most important testing cases arise" for the proponents of such a view when "(a) people support laws because of the statement made by such laws but (b) the effects of such laws seem bad or ambiguous, even by reference to the values held by their supporters."[45] A response to this concern can be drawn from Adams' observation that the expressive value of an act will be diminished if its consequences are too costly for the position that it espouses.[46] Thus, to the degree that (b) holds, the expressive value of (a) will be diminished.[47] This does not entail that there will be no costly legal statements made. The supporters of such expressive laws might misjudge the costs of their effects. Or they might simply reject the cost-benefit analysis of law that implicitly undergirds Sunstein's observation and hold that the value of the statement is incommensurable with the costs of its effects.[48] (Although even in this case they would not necessarily ignore the cost of the legal statement for the reasons outlined by Adams.)

This account of how statement-making laws could be justified appealed to their symbolic value as vehicles for expressing that the polity in whose name they were enacted was for the good and against the bad. But there is another non-consequentialist justification for them that does not appeal to their symbolic value alone. This is that they are required by (or their repeal is required by) an independently justified moral or political principle, and that this is the case even if their enactment (or repeal) would make no practical difference. Anderson, for example, argues that racial segregation is wrong because it "expresses" "principles of contempt or inferiority."[49] This claim comes in the context of a discussion of whether the value of equality is reducible to its effect on welfare. Anderson argues that it is not, noting that even if the "expression" of contempt toward African-Americans through a policy of segregation had no effect on their welfare, it would still be wrongful—not because of the expression itself but because this would violate the principle of equality. Ronald Dworkin makes a similar argument when he discusses the need for voting assignments to "carry a symbolic declaration of equal standing for all."[50] For Dworkin, the principle of equality *prima facie* requires that democratic political structures that take equality seriously ensure that vote assignments reflect the equality of citizens by ensuring that in casting their votes, they will have a "horizontal equality of impact."[51] If this is not done, then the wrong would lie in the violation of the underlying principle of equality.

Such arguments are sometimes stated in terms of the law "expressing" an instantiation (or violation) of the moral or political principle in question. But this need not imply that the primary justificatory basis for endorsing (or condemning) it is that it communicates a particular attitude. Instead, the justificatory basis of such arguments is that the law is required (or condemned) by the principle in question. It "expresses" the instantiation (or violation) of the principle in a way analogous to how a phenotype expresses a gene. (Although this analogy should be taken neither to imply that there is a causal connection between the principle and the law nor that the content of the law that expresses the principle is unmediated by convention.) This justification for statement-making laws is non-consequentialist for it operates independently of any positive effects that they might have. But it need not appeal to their symbolic value alone. It could appeal to the effects that such laws would have on persons' rights. It could, for example, appeal to the claim that the legal instantiation of a principle is required by respect for persons' rights (e.g., to equality) or that a law should be repealed as its existence violates their rights independently of its effects on welfare.[52]

None of these non-consequentialist prescriptive expressivist arguments are committed to the claim that certain performances are *essentially* required to express allegiance to particular ideals. Adams, for example, notes that "it is only by virtue of our systems of *conventional symbolism* that we are able to be 'for' or 'against' most goods and evils."[53] Dworkin similarly recognizes that the meanings of actions are contingent. This is why he believes that the need to express the principle of equality through ensuring that citizens will have a "horizontal equality of impact" in casting their votes is only *prima facie*.[54] He observes that the meaning of the distribution of votes among a population will depend on both the history of the society in question and the conventions that it accepts. It is thus possible that the requirement that citizens will have a "horizontal equality of impact" in casting their votes "would not necessarily hold in a community whose history showed that unequal voting did not itself display contempt or disregard."[55] The symbolic equality of citizens could co-exist with an *unequal* distribution of votes if (for example) people were to "gain votes as they grow older, or ... acquire more votes by pursuing a course of study genuinely open to everyone ... ."[56] To justify a law (or the repeal of a law) on the grounds that it makes a certain "statement" thus does not commit one to endorsing essentialist semiotics. One might hold that the law only makes the (desired or objectionable) statement in a particular cultural situation. Moreover, none of these non-consequentialist prescriptive expressivist arguments are committed to claiming that the expressive acts that they justify (or condemn) should be performed without consideration of the costs that would thus be incurred. For these reasons, they are not essentialist semiotic arguments.

New Expressivist Arguments in the Debate Over the Moral Limits of Markets

None of the above prescriptive expressivist arguments are intended to establish that certain acts or practices are *necessarily* wrongful (or required). They are merely intended to establish that, given the conventional meanings of the acts or practices that they are concerned with, these acts or practices should be condemned (or supported). But Brennan and Jaworski's critique of (possible if not actual) essentialist semiotic objections to markets in certain goods and services has been influential. As well as generating the widespread (but mistaken) view that such objections are common, it has also motivated some persons to develop what they believe to be essentialist semiotic objections to markets that are intended to avoid Brennan and Jaworski's objections.

Although I did not address the substance of the expressivist arguments outlined above (for my purpose was merely to provide a taxonomy of such arguments), I will address that of the two (putatively semiotic) arguments that I will outline below. Addressing these arguments will be useful in furthering the discussion of the role that semiotic arguments both do (and do not) play in the debate over the moral limits of markets.

Booth's Argument

In response to Brennan and Jaworski's critique of semiotic arguments Anthony Robert Booth has developed and defended what he takes to be a new semiotic criticism of markets—the "Argument from signaling value choice."[57] Booth's argument is both ingenious and complex, and so I will spend some time reconstructing it before explaining both why it is not a semiotic argument, and why it fails.

Booth begins his argument by noting that two values are commensurable if one of them "can be determined to be *all things considered* more valuable, or both values can be determined to be equally of all things considered value."[58] Booth then holds that goods could be "bought and sold without treating them as having commensurable value."[59] This is because goods could be comparable (i.e., one could make a rational choice when choosing between them) even if their values are incommensurable. Such comparable but incommensurable goods would be "on a par."[60] To illustrate this, Booth offers the example of a choice between a career in banking and a career in philosophy. The values of these two careers are incommensurable; one option is not better than the other, all things considered. But a rational choice could still be made between them; they are *comparable* options. The values of these two careers are thus *on a par*. They are incommensurable, but it is *possible* for them to be compared. However, to compare goods with comparable but incommensurable values, one must *decide* which criteria are appropriate for this. These criteria are not provided for one as would be the case were the values of the goods to be commensurable. It is the choice of these criteria that renders the incommensurable goods comparable. In Booth's terms, this choice moves the values of the goods from being *on a par* (i.e., they are incommensurable but it is possible for them to be compared according to some as-yet-unspecified criteria) to being *proto-on-a-par* (i.e., the criteria to compare them has been chosen).[61]

Now to markets. If a good can be bought and sold, then this signals that its value is either commensurable with that of another good (e.g., money) or else it is proto-on-a-par (i.e., its value is comparable and incommensurable and the criteria to compare it to other values have been chosen).[62] The value of some goods (e.g., candy bars) will be commensurable with that of other goods (e.g., money). But the value of other goods (in Booth's example, a 10-minute friendship) will be incommensurable with that of certain other goods (for Booth, £10).[63] If goods whose values are incommensurable with those of other goods are bought and sold, this will signal that they have been assigned proto-on-a-par value. That is, their commodification signals that a mechanism has been created by which their value can be compared to that of other goods even though the values of the goods that can thus be compared are incommensurable. The presence of a good on the market signals that a value-choice has been made: That it has been decided that this is the sort of good that can be compared with other goods according to the norms of the market.[64]

Booth then notes that just as a person can "choose to make a value choice between two goods that are on a par," they "can also *choose not* to make such a value choice."[65] They can "reflect who they have decided to be by *not* making a choice, and thus by not turning a good that is on a par, into a good that is *proto-on-a-par*."[66] A person who chooses whether or not to "choose to make a value choice between two goods that are on a par" will thereby signal "who they have decided to be."[67] If they decide *not* to choose criteria to compare goods with comparable but incommensurable value—and so choose not to turn a good whose value is on a par with that of others into a good whose value is proto-on-a-par with that of those others—but signal that they *have* chosen a criterion of comparison, this would, argues Booth, be wrongful. They would be sending a false signal about who they have decided to be. This would, Booth holds, be either hypocritical or dishonest.[68]

Just as a person could act wrongly in this way by signaling that she has decided to be a certain sort of person when she has not, so too, argues Booth, could a community. A community would signal what type of community it has decided to be ("at a macro level") through its decision as to whether or not it will treat two goods whose values are on a par as having values that are proto-on-a-par.[69]

If the commodification of a good or service would signal that the society had decided that its value should be proto-on-a-par with that of other goods when the society had not in fact decided this, then its commodification would be wrongful as it would be a form of dishonest communication. For example, if a society decides that (e.g.) sex can be commodified, then by making sex proto-on-a-par with money, it will signal that it has evaluated the exchange of sex for money to be permissible. If, however, the society has chosen not to be the sort of society in which sex can be exchanged for money, then the commodification of sex in that society would be wrong. This would not be because the commodification of sex leads to bad consequences or violates rights. It would be because the commodification of sex would wrongly signal that the society had decided that it would be the sort of society where sex was proto-on-a-par relative to money when it had not.[70]

This is an ingenious argument. But while it is an expressivist argument, it is not a semiotic argument, as these are defined by Brennan and Jaworski. Recall that, on their view, semiotic objections to markets are intended to demonstrate that certain goods or services should *never* be bought or sold: "According to the semiotic objection, the act of commodifying certain objects is *essentially* disrespectful and degrading of those objects (or of something associated with those objects) because of a meaning that attaches to market activities."[71] But Booth's argument does not support the conclusion that markets in certain goods or services (e.g., sex) are *essentially* (i.e., always) wrong. Instead, it supports the weaker conclusion that in *some* circumstances it would be wrongful to have markets in certain goods and services (i.e., those where their commodification would falsely signal that the society in which they were commodified endorsed being the sort of society in which they were bought and sold).[72] Booth's argument does connect the wrongfulness of certain markets to a "meaning that attaches to market activities" (i.e., that the value of the good commodified is proto-on-a-par with that of other goods). But the signal sent by the commodification of (e.g.) sex will not, on Booth's view, be wrongful because it is "disrespectful or degrading" of sex or of "something associated with sex."[73] Instead, on the occasions when this signal would be wrongful (and hence when the market that sent it would be wrongful), this would be because it would misrepresent the market in question as occurring in a society that endorsed it when this was not the case. The wrong of the market would be grounded in the hypocrisy or dishonesty of the signal that it sent. It is this hypocrisy or dishonesty, not the signal, that is wrongful. Thus, while Booth's is an expressivist objection to the commodification of certain goods and services in certain societies, it is not a semiotic one.

I will argue below that Booth's argument fails. But before doing so I will outline another recent attempt to provide a semiotic objection to commodification that has been developed in response to Brennan and Jaworski's critique: Jacob Sparks' preference-based argument.

Sparks' Argument

Sparks writes:

> My main aim ... [is] ... to provide a recipe for generating semiotic objections that are immune to Brennan and Jaworski's point about the contingency of the meaning of market exchanges. You look for a market good (like sex) and think about what attitude is being expressed towards a related non-market good (like loving sex) when people engage in that market. In some cases, engaging in the market (on the part of an individual) or allowing the market (on the part of society) involves a failure to value the non-market good appropriately. In such cases, there's a semiotic critique that does not depend on the way we impute meaning to money or markets.[74]

Sparks' argument begins with the observation that there are some goods whose nature precludes their commodification.[75] The good of loving sex, for example, can only be received from someone who shares it without being paid to do so, for the nature of the good is partially constituted by the reasons for which it is distributed. Similarly, if one pays to be acknowledged in an academic work, the good that one will receive will be different in kind from an acknowledgment that was given in thanks.[76] But although these goods cannot be bought and sold, goods that are similar to them can be. It is possible to purchase sex from someone who will pretend to be providing it lovingly and it is possible to purchase acknowledgments in academic texts.[77]

Sparks then notes that market transactions express preferences. If a person consistently pursues the market version of the good rather than its commodification-resistant alternative, this would provide evidence that she prefers the former to the latter. The evidence for this view of her preferences would become stronger if the latter version of the good was available to her and the costs to her of obtaining it were not prohibitive.[78] Sparks holds that a person's actions could reveal that she has a preference for paid sex over loving sex. This, he asserts, would give observers reason to believe that she had "the wrong attitude toward love."[79] Sparks acknowledges that a person might occasionally exhibit a preference for the market version of a good over its commodification-resistant alternative without thereby revealing that she has the wrong attitude toward the latter good. But he holds that if a market in the commodified version of the good is allowed, we would then "*collectively* express the wrong attitude" to its commodification-resistant alternative.[80] Sparks supports this claim by appeal to the possibility that markets in certain goods could make it more difficult for persons successfully to provide those goods to others through non-market means. For example, a market in expressions of approval on social media could make it more difficult for persons successfully to signal genuine approval on social media. Sparks' argument is not the consequentialist point about the possible adverse effects that certain markets could have on persons' ability to express themselves that was made by Maguire and Brown.[81] Rather, his concern is that if we recognize that allowing a market in certain goods will make it more difficult to distribute their commodification-resistant versions, we are showing that we have the wrong attitude toward the latter versions of those goods. As he writes: "[A]llowing an expansion of the market for admiration-like-goods can show that we collectively have the wrong attitude towards admiration, even if that particular expansion doesn't exclude the giving and receiving of real admiration."[82]

Unlike Booth's argument, Sparks' argument is a semiotic argument. He holds that markets in certain goods would be wrongful because their commodification would express disrespect for the commodification-resistant goods that are associated with them, and that this disrespect would be expressed "because of a meaning that attaches to market activities."[83] But both Booth's and Sparks' arguments fail as objections to markets. And they fail for similar reasons.

Responses to Booth's and Sparks' Arguments

Both Booth's and Sparks' arguments rest on the claim that a society's commodification of a good will necessarily communicate that it endorses a normative propositional claim. For Booth, this is the claim that the value of a good (e.g., sex) is rightly considered to be proto-on-a-par with the value of (at least) one other good (e.g., money). For Sparks, it is the claim that the commodification-resistant version of a certain good has a particular value relative to its commodified version (where this relative value is too low, and hence its attribution evinces a wrong attitude toward the version of the good that resists commodification).

These arguments fail because it is not true that a society's allowing the commodification of a particular good or service will necessarily communicate either of these claims. I will address Booth's argument first. It is possible that a society might permit the commodification of sex as it believes that the value of sex is proto-on-a-par with that of money. But it is also possible that a society might believe that the value of sex is neither commensurable with money nor proto-on-a-par with it but permits the commodification of sex as it does not consider the adjudication of such issues to be within its purview.[84] It might even express its *opposition* to commodified sex by refusing legally to enforce contracts for sexual services while permitting them to be made and enforced by others. The existence of a market in (e.g.) commodified sex within a society thus tells us nothing about that society's views concerning the legitimacy of treating sex as though its value is proto-on-a-par with that of money.

The same point can also be made at the individual level. A person might believe that the value of a good should not be proto-on-a-par with money and yet still voluntarily exchange that good for money. Imagine a society with very few wealthy people and a lot of poor people. This society allows votes to be traded for money. A self-interested and prudentially rational poor person would be willing to sell her vote to the Wealthy Persons' Party (even though its policies are against her interests) as she realizes that this trade would be of no consequence to the electoral outcome. The other poor voters would reason similarly. Since the Wealthy Persons' Party only needs >50 percent of the votes to win, the poor voters would rush to sell their votes at just above transaction costs. In this situation a poor voter might believe that it is wrong for the value of votes to be proto-on-a-par with that of money. But, given her situation, she would still participate in the market.[85]

It is also possible that a society could commodify a good and have a thriving market in it when *no-one* endorses the view that its value should be proto-on-a-par with money. Consider again a market in votes. The poor are motivated to participate as sellers for the reasons outlined above. The wealthy are all civic-minded egalitarians who deplore vote markets. But they are all *timid* civic-minded egalitarians, and they all believe that the *other* wealthy people in their society are self-interested plutocrats who oppose egalitarianism. To avoid antagonizing their fellow wealthy citizens, each wealthy person thus behaves as they believe that they are expected to behave—as self-interested plutocrats who oppose egalitarianism.[86] They thus buy up votes and cast them for anti-egalitarian legislation while secretly opposing the policies that they outwardly support.

It is thus possible that a society could commodify a good without endorsing the view that its value is proto-on-a-par with that of other goods. Since this is so, the commodification of a good would not necessarily communicate that the society in which it is commodified believes that it should be treated as though its value was proto-on-a-par with other goods. Booth's claim that the commodification of a good would necessarily communicate this view is thus mistaken.

Similar points can be made with respect to Sparks' argument. Sparks holds that allowing markets in goods or services that are variants of goods or services that resist commodification will *necessarily* communicate a wrong attitude toward the commodification-resistant version of the goods or services in question. But this is not the case. Consider Sparks' argument against markets in votes. Sparks holds that gifted votes are superior to bought votes as he believes that the "connection between votes and a certain kind of political approval ... [is] important and worth maintaining."[87] Gifted votes maintain this connection while purchased votes do not. If we were to allow a market in votes, we would "therefore express the wrong attitude towards this important kind of political approval."[88]

This might be case in our society. But it is not necessarily the case. Consider again Alternative America. The population of Alternative America agrees with Sparks that the "connection between votes and a certain kind of political approval ... [is] important and worth maintaining."[89] But to express this, they facilitate a market in votes.[90] They require those who purchase votes publicly to identify which political party they will cast them for. They do this because they believe that the more purchased votes a party receives, the less its supporters are interested in securing the proper political approval of the electorate. Allowing a market in votes, they believe, where information about who purchases votes is publicized thus provides more information about parties than could be secured were such a market to be prohibited. Information about vote purchases is provided in real time throughout an election so voters can judge which parties are genuinely concerned with securing their approval and which merely claim to be. On learning that Actual America prohibits vote markets, the citizens of Alternative America are scandalized. Isn't it important to you, they ask, which parties really care about representing you and which only care about winning elections? And if this is important, then why do you prohibit the public vote markets that will help you determine whether a party cares about representation or merely winning?

A similar story could be told about markets in sex. In Alternative America, commodified sex is freely available. But this is not because its citizens have the wrong attitude toward loving sex. Instead, they value it highly—and use the ready availability of commodified sex to express this. In Alternative America, the purchase of sex conveys that the purchaser is not worthy of loving sex. Casual sex partners pay each other for sex (either in money or in gifts that are explicitly exchanged for sex) to express their lack of commitment. A person who has angered their partner and who wishes to atone for this might inform them that they will only have sex with prostitutes for the next week to express that they are currently unworthy of loving sex. The citizens of Alternative America are puzzled when faced with the sexual mores of Actual America. When they are told that committed couples sometimes express temporary estrangement by not having sex, they note that this method of signaling is ineffective. It does not identify who the wronged party is as neither partner has sex. It is thus unclear who is worthy of loving sex and who is not. Moreover, they note that since couples might not have sex for a period of time for many reasons, refraining from sex would not effectively communicate estrangement. Far better, claim the citizens of Alternative America, for the party in the wrong to signal that they are unworthy of loving sex by buying sex in its place. Rather than the widespread commodification of sex expressing that the citizens of Alternative America have the wrong attitude toward loving sex, it is instead used to express just how much they value it.

Booth's and Sparks' arguments fail because a society's allowing a market in a good or service does not necessarily express anything about the content of the preferences held by that society.[91] Note that in both cases the point of the objections to their arguments is not that the society did not intend to communicate a wrongful message by allowing a market to exist. It is possible that a wrongful message could be communicated without any intent to communicate it. Instead, the point of the responses to Booth and Sparks is that a society's allowing a market in a certain good or service could communicate many different things depending on context. It is thus not the case that a society's commodification of certain goods or services would necessarily communicate the normative propositions that Booth and Sparks attribute to it. All that the commodification of a good or service would necessarily communicate is the claim that those who treat it as a commodity believe that the market enables them to identify how much monetary value it has at a particular time and in a particular place.[92] This is merely a descriptive claim. It will thus not conflict with any normative views concerning "the society that one wants to be" as Booth's argument requires.[93] Nor will it express a normatively wrongful attitude in the way that Sparks' argument requires. Booth and Sparks are thus mistaken to hold that the commodification of certain goods and services would thus communicate something wrongful, whether this be about the decisions that the society had made concerning what sort of society it wanted to be or about the way in which the society valued the goods or services in question.[94]

Implications of These Responses

But while Booth's and Sparks' attempts to develop cogent semiotic objections to commodification fail, they fail in an interesting way—and one that helps clarify the role that expressivist arguments can play in the debate over the moral limits of markets. Booth's and Sparks' arguments fail because the only propositional content that will necessarily be communicated by a person's participation in a market transaction—or a society's allowing a particular market to exist—will be descriptive. This is because the only propositional content that could necessarily be communicated by an act or a state of affairs is that which would be instantiated by a causal relationship between the act or state of affairs and the meaning it conveyed. For example, the appearance of certain spots on a person's skin (a state of affairs) "means" that she has measles (i.e., this conveys that she has measles) in the sense that these spots show that she has measles.[95] Similarly, a certain muscle spasm that causes one to raise one's eyebrows "means" that one has a nervous tic. The meanings that are necessarily conveyed in this way are limited to descriptive claims. To introduce a normative element into them will require that a further meaning be ascribed to them by appeal to convention. Thus, for example, the raising of one's eyebrows might "mean" that one is expressing disapproval as this is the conventional meaning of raising one's eyebrows.[96] These spots on a person's skin are "bad" as they "mean" that she has measles and having measles is considered (in this society) to be a bad situation to be in. Since the normative meaning of an act or a state of affairs ("disapproval," "bad") will be dependent on a conventional system of symbolic meaning, it is always (in principle) subject to revision. Since this is so, neither acts nor states of affairs can necessarily communicate particular normative content. Essentialist semiotic objections to commodification—and essentialist semiotic arguments more generally—are based on the denial of this claim. Attempts to develop such objections are thus doomed to fail.

Conclusion

The conclusion that essentialist semiotic objections to markets are doomed to fail might appear to vindicate Brennan and Jaworski's critique of them. And it does—although there is still no reason to believe that such objections are widespread.[97] Although noting that essentialist semiotic arguments are doomed to fail might appear to be merely a negative observation, this note should have a positive effect on the debate over the moral limits of markets. It should redirect effort away from an unproductive focus on such arguments and toward more promising lines of inquiry—including (but not limited to) non-semiotic expressivist arguments of the sort outlined above. Like semiotic arguments, these will condemn (or justify) performances (such as individual actions, or the passing or repeal of laws or policies) by appeal to their symbolic value. But they differ from essentialist semiotic arguments in two important respects. None of them are committed to essentialist semiotics. And their proponents recognize that the costs of their symbolically valued performances are relevant to whether they can be expressively justified.[98]

Encouraging participants in the debates over the moral limits of markets to redirect their efforts away from tilting at the windmills of semiotic arguments will (with luck!) contribute to getting these debates back on track. Chapter 7 will continue in this endeavor by showing that rather than being "where the action is," the Asymmetry Thesis plays little role in the current debates over the limits of markets and market thinking.[99]

Notes

1 This conflation of semiotic arguments with expressivist arguments has already begun. See Dustin Crummett, "Expression and Indication in Ethics and Political Philosophy," *Res Publica* 25, 3 (2019), 387–388. See also note 2, below.
2 Brennan and Jaworski's unwarranted claim that semiotic arguments are common in the literature on the moral limits of markets is (worryingly) becoming widely accepted. (I explain why this might be so in Chapter 8.) See, for example, Matthew Caulfield, "The Expressive Functions of Pay," *Business Ethics Journal Review* 6, 1 (2016), 5, citing Brennan and Jaworski as evidence that semiotic objections "abound in academic literature"; Leef, "What's Really Disgusting?," *Regulation* (Spring 2016), 63, following Brennan and Jaworski in holding that semiotic arguments are among those "most frequently" offered against certain markets; Daniel Layman, "Expressive Objections to Markets: Normative, Not Symbolic," *Business Ethics Journal Review* 4, 1 (2016), 2, accepting Brennan and Jaworski's attribution of semiotic objections to Sandel; James Stacey Taylor, "Book Note: Jason Brennan and Peter M. Jaworski, *Markets Without Limits: Moral virtues and commercial interests*," *Choice Reviews* 54, 1 (2016), accepting that semiotic arguments are "common" (available at: www.choicereviews.org/review/10.5860/CHOICE.198180; yes, I, too, made this error); John Danaher, "The Symbolic-Consequences Argument in the Sex Robot Debate," in J. Danaher and N. McArthur, (Eds.), *Robot Sex: Social and Ethical Implications* (Cambridge, MA: MIT Press, 2017), 116, following Brennan and Jaworski in holding that "many moral philosophers" endorse semiotic objections to markets; Anthony Robert Booth, "The Real Symbolic Limits of Markets," *Analysis* 78, 2 (2018), 199, following Brennan and Jaworski in attributing semiotic objections to Anderson, Sandel, and Walzer; Jacob Sparks, "You

Give Love a Bad Name," *Business Ethics Journal Review* 7, 2 (2019), 7–8, following Brennan and Jaworski in holding that "[a] common complaint in the anti-commodification literature depends on what it means to buy or sell something"; Ryan W. Davis, "Symbolic Values," *Journal of the American Philosophical Association* 5, 4 (2019), 456, following Brennan and Jaworski in holding that objections to kidney markets are founded on persons being "symbolically opposed to the idea of paying money for human body parts"; Robert Sparling, "Blocked Exchanges and the Constitution: Montesquieu on the Moral and Constitutional Limits of Markets," *Polity* 51, 3 (2019), 535, accepting that Brennan and Jaworski are correct to impute essentialist semiotic objections to Walzer and Sandel; and Crummett, "Expression and Indication in Ethics and Political Philosophy," 387–388, who holds that if Brennan and Jaworski "are correct that what our actions communicate is solely a matter of social convention, their argument would undermine many currently existing arguments … ." (Crummett then follows Brennan and Jaworski in attributing essentialist semiotic objections to markets to Satz, Sandel, and Anderson; ibid., 389–391). See also Barry Maguire and Brookes Brown, "Markets, Interpersonal Practices, and Signal Distortion," *Philosophers' Imprint* 19 (2019), 1, who accept that Brennan and Jaworski are correct to attribute semiotic objections to markets to Walzer, Anderson, Satz, Sandel, and Archard.

3 The only argument that I am aware of that meets Brennan and Jaworski's conditions of being a semiotic argument is that developed by Jacob Sparks. See his "Can't Buy Me Love: A Reply to Brennan and Jaworski," *Journal of Philosophical Research* 42 (2017): 341–352, and his "You Give Love a Bad Name," *Business Ethics Journal Review* 7, 2 (2019): 7–13. Sparks' argument was developed in response to Brennan and Jaworski's criticisms of semiotic arguments and so successfully avoids their criticisms because it is compatible with the orthodox view concerning the conventional nature of meaning. (Although—as I discuss below—it fails for other reasons.) It is thus a different type of semiotic argument than that which Brennan and Jaworski criticize.

4 See Jason Brennan and Peter M. Jaworski, *Markets Without Limits* (New York: Routledge, 2016), Part II.

5 Joel Feinberg, "The Expressive Function of Punishment," *The Monist* 49, 3 (1965), 397.

6 Ibid., 400.

7 Ibid., 400.

8 Ibid., 400, 402. Feinberg characterizes this condemnation as the "fusing of resentment and reprobation," where "resentment" contains the vengeful attitudes persons have toward the person being punished and "reprobation" consists of "the stern judgment of disapproval" (ibid., 403). Feinberg identifies four further (and derivative) expressive functions of punishment: (1) authoritative disavowal of acts that might otherwise have been taken to be condoned by the government; (2) the public denunciation of certain actions; (3) the vindication of the law; and (4) the absolution of persons who might otherwise have been partially blamed for the transgressions of the person punished (ibid., 404–408).

9 Ibid., 402.

10 Ibid., 411

11 Feinberg similarly holds that the symbolic condemnation of persons subject to certain forms of "hard treatment" will preclude it from being legitimately imposed on persons convicted of strict liability offenses for which no fault or culpability is needed. This, he holds, is because the symbolism of those forms of hard treatment identifies them as punishments rather than mere penalties—and "there is something very odd and offensive in punishing people for admittedly faultless conduct" (ibid., 416). Again, the claim that it is wrong to impose "hard treatment" on persons in such cases is not justified by the claim that communicating condemnation is necessarily wrongful. It is

justified by the claim that communicating condemnation *in this situation* is wrongful and that this is so for reasons independent of the communication itself.
12 Maguire and Brown, "Markets, Interpersonal Practices, and Signal Distortion," 3.
13 Ibid., 4.
14 Ibid., 7.
15 Ibid., 8.
16 Ibid., 8–9. A similar point is recognized by Jacob Sparks, although this consequentialist objection is not the focus of his concern. "Can't Buy Me Love," 344.
17 Thomas A.K. McGinn, "The Expressive Function of Law and the *Lex Imperfecta*," *Roman Legal Tradition* 11 (2015), 2.
18 Cass R. Sunstein, "On the Expressive Function of Law," *University of Pennsylvania Law Review* 144, 5 (1996), 2025.
19 Conversely, a law that decriminalized or enabled certain behavior (e.g., marijuana use or gay marriage) might be intended to reinforce a growing consensus that such behavior was acceptable.
20 Sunstein, "On the Expressive Function of Law," 2039.
21 Ibid., 2039.
22 Ibid., 2039.
23 Ibid., 2032.
24 Ibid., 2043. Sunstein cites Lawrence Lessig, "The Regulation of Social Meaning," *University of Chicago Law Review* 62, 3 (1995), 965–967.
25 Lessig, "The Regulation of Social Meaning," 966.
26 Ibid., 966.
27 Ibid., 966.
28 Robert Merrihew Adams, *Finite and Infinite Goods: A Framework for Ethics* (New York: Oxford University Press, 1999), 215. Adams notes that martyrdom could be secular as well as religious. Someone might, for example, accept martyrdom for a political cause.
29 Ibid., 217.
30 Ibid., 218. A similar point is made by Robert Nozick, *The Nature of Rationality* (Princeton, NJ: Princeton University Press, 1993), 29. Both Adams and Nozick expressly note that symbolic meaning is conventional. See Adams, *Finite and Infinite Goods*, 217–218; Nozick, *The Nature of Rationality*, 29. Note, though, that Nozick believes that some actions will "presumably" always represent certain attitudes, "so that an action of handwashing always symbolizes removing guilt or whatever" (ibid., 28). Since Nozick is discussing the utility of symbolic action in the context of Freudian theory, it appears that he is here attributing to Freudians the view that certain actions "show" (in Grice's sense) that the performing agent has an underlying psychological issue.
31 Adams, *Finite and Infinite Goods*, 218.
32 Adams also holds that the performance of symbolic actions to affirm to ourselves that we are "for the good and against the bad" can have value—and thus be rational—even if they do not internally affirm one's commitments in this way. The performance of such actions, he holds, will be "important to the moral quality of our lives" (ibid., 219). This is not an expressive justification.
33 Sunstein notes that considerations such as these could also justify certain legal rulings. In this case, the value of the rulings is derived from their affirmation of a legal system's endorsement of certain underlying principles, such as opposition to racial segregation or affirming the value of free speech. As with personal expressive actions such as Pennyfeather's decision to reject "irregular perquisites" (discussed below), the value of such legal expressive actions is not (necessarily or solely) derived from their communicative effects on third parties but from their affirmation on behalf of those ruled by the legal system that *we* are a body that is committed to *these* values. Sunstein notes that he does not claim that in the legal context such expressive considerations could not be

overridden by consequentialist concerns. Sunstein, "On the Expressive Function of Law," 2027–2028.
34 Adams, *Finite and Infinite Goods*, 220.
35 Ibid., 220.
36 Ibid., 220.
37 Ibid., 218, note 5.
38 Bernard R. Boxhill draws on this sort of consideration to argue that persons should protest the wrongs done to them. "Self-Respect and Protest," *Philosophy & Public Affairs* 6, 1 (1976): 58–69.
39 Evelyn Waugh, *Decline and Fall* (London: Chapman & Hall, 1955), 51.
40 Ibid., 52. Pennyfeather's conception of a gentleman is not a *moral* ideal, but a *cultural* one—just as someone who adhered to the ideal of "coolness" would be adhering to a cultural rather than a moral ideal.
41 Ibid., 53, 52.
42 Fortunately for Pennyfeather his unscrupulous and utterly self-interested friend Captain Grimes pre-empted his decision to decline by accepting the money on his behalf.
43 Sunstein, "On the Expressive Function of Law," 2027. This was also recognized by Nozick, *The Nature of Rationality*, 28.
44 Sunstein, "On the Expressive Function of Law," 2026, 2024. To support the possibility of such endorsement, Sunstein cites Tom R. Tyler and Renee Weber, "Support for the Death Penalty: Instrumental Response to Crime, or Symbolic Attitude?," *Law and Society Review* 17, 1 (1982): 21–46. (Cited by Sunstein, "On the Expressive Function of Law," 2026, note 19.) But Tyler and Weber do not address the question of whether some persons support a law "because they believe that it is intrinsically valuable for the relevant 'statement' to be made" (Sunstein, "On the Expressive Function of Law," 2026). Instead, they ask whether variations in support for the death penalty "result from differences in concern about the problem of crime" or if "they are a function of differences in basic political and social values" (Tyler and Weber, "Support for the Death Penalty," 21). It is in the context of addressing the latter differences that they refer to the "symbolic perspective" on the death penalty. (See, for example, ibid., 26.) But by this they do not mean that some persons support (or oppose) the death penalty because they believe that it symbolically communicates a statement that they intrinsically value (or disvalue). Instead, they hold that support for (or opposition to) the death penalty arises from the "symbolic perspective" if it originates in social attitudes (e.g., "authoritarianism, dogmatism, and/or conservatism") instead of "utilitarian concerns about crime" (ibid., 26).
45 Sunstein, "On the Expressive Function of Law," 2045. Sunstein holds that "at least for purposes of law, any support for 'statements' should be rooted not simply in the intrinsic value of the statement, but also in plausible judgments about its effect on social norms and hence in 'on balance' judgments about its consequences."
46 Adams, *Finite and Infinite Goods*, 220.
47 A similar point is made by Nozick, *The Nature of Rationality*, 27.
48 Or—as Nozick suggests—the (apparently) costly statement-making law will symbolically stand for certain positive results. If this is so, then its supporters will impute a symbolic utility to it, derived from the utility that they would impute to the effects that it is (putatively) intended to achieve. (The value of this utility might be incommensurable with the costs that the legal statement imposes.) This symbolic utility is valuable to the supporters of such laws independently of the value of the effects that the law is (putatively) intended to achieve. Their efforts to retain them can explain why they might "refuse to look at or countenance … evidence [that the laws do not have their desired consequences] or other evidence about harmful consequences of the … policy" (*The Nature of Rationality*, 27). The law would still be costly, but for its supporters these costs would be outweighed by the symbolic value that it has for them.

But while this might be the correct way of understanding the motivations of some persons who support costly expressive legal statements, this approach assimilates their justification to a consequentialist framework, albeit possibly one that acknowledges pluralism of value. (See also Robert Nozick, *The Examined Life: Philosophical Meditations* [New York: Simon & Schuster, 1989], Chapter 25.) And it is likely that for some supporters of such statements, such consequentialist considerations play no role.

49 Elizabeth Anderson, "Reply," *Brown Electronic Article Review Service*; available at: www.brown.edu/Departments/Philosophy/bears/9912ande.html. Although he misleadingly terms it as a "semiotic" objection, Mogensen's egalitarian objection to rationing healthcare on the basis of persons' perceived contribution to society is of this type. "Meaning, Medicine, and Merit," *Utilitas* 32, 1 (2020), 100–106. This type of argument has also been drawn upon by Joseph Raz to explain the wrong of interpersonal deception and manipulation. (Raz explicitly notes that the symbolic meaning of deception and manipulation as expressing "disregard or even contempt" is conventional, and he accepts that the expressive wrong of such acts could in certain circumstances be outweighed by their positive consequences.) See *The Morality of Freedom* (Oxford: Oxford University Press, 1986), 378.
50 Ronald Dworkin, *Sovereign Virtue: The Theory and Practice of Equality* (Cambridge, MA: Harvard University Press, 2000), 200.
51 Ibid., 200.
52 In Nicholas Wolterstorff's phrase (offered in another context), the wrongful law would "count as" a violation of rights. "Would You Stomp on a Picture of Your Mother? Would You Kiss an Icon?," *Faith and Philosophy* 32, 1 (2015), 21. Wolterstorff is clear that he believes that the meaning (and, hence, in some cases, the nature) of actions are conventional.
53 Adams, *Finite and Infinite Goods*, 218. Emphasis added.
54 Dworkin, *Sovereign Virtue*, 200.
55 Ibid., 200, 201.
56 Ibid., 201.
57 Booth, "The Real Symbolic Limit of Markets," 200.
58 Ibid., 201.
59 Ibid., 202.
60 Ibid., 202. Booth draws here on Ruth Chang's work on incommensurability and comparability; see "The Possibility of Parity," *Ethics* 112, 4 (2002): 659–688.
61 Booth, "The Real Symbolic Limit of Markets," 202–203.
62 Ibid., 202.
63 Ibid., 202.
64 Ibid., 205.
65 Ibid., 205.
66 Ibid., 205.
67 Ibid., 205.
68 Ibid., 205.
69 Ibid., 203, 205.
70 Ibid., 205.
71 Brennan and Jaworski, *Markets Without Limits*, 47. Emphasis added.
72 Booth does not support the Asymmetry Thesis in support of which Brennan and Jaworski believe semiotic objections to markets have been developed.
73 Brennan and Jaworski, *Markets Without Limits*, 47.
74 Sparks, "You Give Love a Bad Name," 10.
75 Sparks, "Can't Buy Me Love," 343–344. See also the discussions of this point in Chapters 5 and 7.

76 Just as "paid" and "loving" sex do not exhaust the different types of sex that it is possible to receive (one could be the recipient of vengeful sex, pity sex, lustful sex, and so on), so too are there more types of acknowledgements than merely those provided for pay or in gratitude. See Eyal Ben-Ari, "On Acknowledgements in Ethnographies," *Journal of Anthropological Research* 43, 1 (1987): 63–84.
77 Brennan and Jaworski, *Markets Without Limits*, 226–227.
78 Sparks, "Can't Buy Me Love," 345.
79 Ibid., 344.
80 Ibid., 347. Sparks' move from claims about the expressive import of individual's preferences to that of "collective" preferences is similar to Booth's move from claims about what an individual signals by choosing or refraining to choose to treat values as proto-on-a-par to claims about what a society would similarly signal by its decisions to treat values in certain ways.
81 Ibid., 347. Maguire and Brown, "Markets, Interpersonal Practices, and Signal Distortion," 7–10.
82 Sparks, "Can't Buy Me Love," 348.
83 Brennan and Jaworski, *Markets Without Limits*, 47.
84 Consider a society whose citizens all believe that the value of money and the value of sex are neither commensurable nor proto-on-a-par. None participate in sex markets. But their polity has a thriving market in commodified sex sold and purchased by tourists. They permit this as they consider moral issues to lie outside their legal jurisdiction.
85 I offer a similar version of this example to make a different point in James Stacey Taylor, "Autonomy, Vote-Buying, and Constraining Options," *Journal of Applied Philosophy* 34, 5 (2017), 711–723.
86 This example is not as fictitious as it might appear. See Cristina Bicchieri on how many persons support norms they oppose as they mistakenly believe that support for them is widespread. *Norms in the Wild* (New York: Oxford University Press, 2017), 42–47.
87 Sparks, "Can't Buy Me Love," 349. It is not clear that casting a vote for a candidate is the same as "gifting" it to her, but let this pass.
88 Ibid., 349.
89 Ibid., 349.
90 For an argument that a market in votes would need to be facilitated rather than merely allowed, see James Stacey Taylor, "Markets in Votes, Voter Liberty, and the Burden of Justification," *Journal of Philosophical Research* 42 (2017): 325–340.
91 I assume for the sake of argument that it is possible for a society to have preferences in the way Booth and Sparks believe.
92 A similar point is made by Julian Jonker, "The Meaning of a Market and the Meaning of 'Meaning'," *Journal of Ethics and Social Philosophy* 15, 2 (2019), 188.
93 Booth, "The Real Symbolic Limits of Markets," 203.
94 Booth's and Sparks' arguments have another feature in common: They are both incomplete. To be sound, Booth must provide an argument for the view that a dishonest communication is necessarily wrongful. And Sparks must provide an argument for the view that the commodification-resistant versions of goods are objectively superior to their commodified counterparts that would ground the claim that a preference for the latter (or even an evaluation of the latter that is not sufficiently lower than that accorded to the former) would be wrongful.
95 This example is from Wayne A. Davis, "Grice's Meaning Project," *Teorema: Revista Internacional de Filosofía* 26, 2 (2007), 42. Davis uses it to illustrate Grice's views on meaning.
96 Note again that one might communicate an attitude without intending to do so.
97 Indeed, it seems that only Sparks has developed one.

98 Satz, for example, observes that there is a reason for people to wait in line as this "is a convention that has come to symbolize our quality" (Debra Satz, *Why Some Things Should Not Be for Sale* [Oxford: Oxford University Press, 2010], 107). However, she also recognizes that the costs of particular distributive policies (such as queuing) are morally relevant (ibid., 9).
99 Brennan and Jaworski, *Markets Without Limits*, 15.

7
WHAT WE TALK ABOUT WHEN WE TALK ABOUT THE LIMITS OF MARKETS

Introduction

In Chapter 6, I distinguished semiotic arguments from other types of expressivist arguments. I then offered a clarificatory taxonomy of the latter with the aim of precluding further derailing of the debates over the appropriate limits of markets. In this chapter, I will continue to rerail these debates by providing a taxonomy of the current debates over the appropriate limits of market and market thinking.[1] This chapter is thus a continuation of the arguments that I offered in Chapter 1, where I argued that none of the prominent theorists to whom Brennan and Jaworski attributed the Asymmetry Thesis (Sandel, Satz, Anderson, Walzer, and Archard) endorsed it. That discussion showed that "the action" in the current debates over the moral limits of markets is not to be found in discussions of whether there are certain goods and services that it would be permissible to distribute "for free" but never for money. It also showed that rather than there being only one debate over the morally appropriate scope of the market and of market norms, there are several. The debates over the moral limits of markets are more varied than that which is dreamt of in Brennan and Jaworski's philosophy.

By providing a map to the argumentative terrain, the taxonomy that I will develop in this chapter will facilitate discussion of where the appropriate limits of markets and market thinking lie. It could achieve this in three ways. First, use of this conceptual map could reduce the number of times that participants in these debates talk past each other. It could achieve this by reducing the number of times that they fail to understand that, while their positions appear to oppose each other, they might not, as they are engaged in different debates.[2] Second, through clearly delineating the nature of each debate over the appropriate limits of markets and so possibly reducing the number of misplaced criticisms, this conceptual

DOI: 10.4324/9781003251996-10

map could also help to increase the number of sound criticisms within these debates. It is, after all, easier to hit one's target once one knows precisely what it is. Finally, delineating the nature and scope of the current debates will enable connections between them to be identified that have been hitherto overlooked. This could increase understanding of the issues at hand and so further propel discussion forward.

Inherent Moral Limits on Markets

Brennan and Jaworski claim that arguments for the view that there are inherent moral limits to markets are "where the action is."[3] As I noted in previous chapters, they understand the view that there are inherent moral limits on markets to be the view that there are certain goods or services that persons could legitimately own and distribute freely but which they should not exchange for money. This anti-commodification position has a long history. Many religions have historically forbidden the charging of interest: The service of lending money can be performed freely but cannot be sold.[4] In medieval Europe, both Thomas Aquinas and Francisco Suárez argued that certain spiritual goods should only be distributed freely and never be bought and sold, even though they recognized that they could be.[5]

The view that there are some goods or services that could be owned and freely distributed but not exchanged for money is not the only way in which the claim that there are inherent moral limits to markets could be understood. As Brennan and Jaworski recognize, it is widely accepted that there are certain goods (such as child pornography) or services (such as those of an assassin) that should never be bought or sold because they should never be possessed.[6] This view captures an alternative account of the view that markets have inherent moral limits.

But there is also a third way in which markets are claimed to have inherent limits—one that was overlooked by Brennan and Jaworski.[7] (This is not a criticism of Brennan and Jaworski. They focused on what they took to be objections to markets that held that market exchanges transformed what would otherwise be permissible acts of transferring goods or services into impermissible acts of transfer. Objections to markets that do not accord them this transformative power are thus outside the scope of their project.) This is the view that there are certain goods (or actions) that can be legitimately possessed (or performed) but which should not be distributed to (or performed for) another, whether this is done freely or for payment. I noted in Chapter 1 that this is Anderson's position concerning surrogate pregnancy. Pregnancy is not immoral. However, Anderson holds that to carry a surrogate pregnancy for another would be immoral independently of one's motives for doing so. Kant also endorses this type of inherent limits on markets. To support his claim that persons are not entitled to exchange their body parts for money, he writes:

a man is not entitled to sell his limbs for money ... for otherwise all the man's limbs might be sold off. One may dispose of things that have no freedom, but not of a being that itself has free choice. If a man does that, he turns himself into a thing, and then anyone may treat him as they please, because he has thrown his person away ...[8]

A plausible understanding of this "Argument from Worth" would treat it as reflecting Kant's views of the value of personhood.[9] For Kant, persons are to be distinguished from mere things insofar as the former possess dignity rather than being valued by price; persons, unlike things, cannot be replaced by something of equivalent value.[10] But in selling part of one's body one is, for Kant, improperly making oneself into a thing, "an instrument of animal gratification."[11] For Kant, then, the sale of body parts is inherently wrong. But since it is wrong to sell a body part as this would be to treat it as something that could be exchanged for something of equivalent value (e.g., a certain amount of money), it would, for Kant, also be wrong to give away a body part for transplant into another. This, too, would be to treat the body part as though it could be exchanged for something of equivalent value (i.e., the body part that it replaced).[12] For Kant, then, there are certain goods that can be legitimately possessed but which should not be distributed to another, independently of the motives for such distribution.[13] If Kant is right, then this will impose inherent moral limits upon markets.

Ontological Limits of Markets

The participants in the above debates over whether there are any inherent moral limits to markets (and, if so, where these lie) accept that the goods or services that they discuss *could* be bought and sold and so focus on the question of whether they *should* be bought and sold. But participants in other debates over the limits of markets question whether it is *possible* for all goods or services to be bought and sold.

Goods and Services that Cannot Be Bought and Sold

It is widely held that some goods or services simply cannot be bought or sold. Love, for example, is believed to be beyond the scope of the market, as is friendship. It is partially constitutive of love and friendship that they are conferred only upon persons that one is attracted to in the relevant way *and* that they are conferred upon them *because* one finds them attractive in the relevant way. If Abdul were to attempt to have Beth's friendship by paying her to be his friend, then he would fail to secure the good that he wanted to have. At best, he would secure merely the simulacrum of friendship with Beth treating him as she would treat a friend. But because Beth would not be treating him in this way because she valued his personal qualities but only because he was paying her to do so, her acts would not be acts of friendship. Abdul could (possibly) have Beth's friendship but he cannot buy it. Similarly, while Beth could give away her friendship to Abdul (i.e., she could bestow it upon him freely), it is widely believed that she cannot sell it to him.[14] She can only confer her friendship upon people that she is attracted to in the relevant way. Since this is not under her volitional control, she cannot bestow her friendship upon someone simply because he has paid her to do so; she could only treat him *as if* he were a friend.

The good of friendship is thus held to be market-inalienable because its nature is such that it cannot be distributed by market means. It can only be distributed to persons who are believed to merit it by their potential friends, and this distribution is outside their direct volitional control. Other goods are similarly held to be constituted such that they can only be distributed to persons who merit them. Sandel, for example, observes that one cannot buy a Nobel Prize as it is constitutive of the nature of this good that it cannot be bought and sold.[15] Prizes such as the Nobel Prize are the goods that they are because they cannot be bought and sold but only distributed on the basis of perceived merit. Prizes that are distributed independently of merit—such as those that Alice awarded to all of the participants in the caucus-race in *Alice's Adventures in Wonderland*, or those that are won by lot—are different kinds of goods than those that are awarded only to persons who are believed to merit them. Owing to its means of distribution, the Nobel Prize confers status whereas the confits that Alice distributed as prizes did not. Prizes such as the Nobel Prize can thus be had but cannot be bought; they can be given away, but they cannot be sold.

But while friendship and (certain) prizes are held to be market-inalienable as their nature precludes their distribution to anyone apart from those who merit them, the nature of other goods is held to preclude their commodification, as they can only be distributed to persons who stand in certain relationships to the distributor. The good of feuding might be one such good. In the O. Henry story "A Blackjack Bargainer," a backwoodsman, Garvey, who came into money desired to solidify his social status by buying into a feud. ("Quality people everywhar ... has feuds."[16]) The transaction took place, with Garvey paying to take over the Goree family's role in a feud. But Garvey failed to purchase participation in the feud. His (purchased) opponents (the Coltranes) had none of the animosity toward him that is partially constitutive of feuding. They felt this only for members of the Goree clan. Moreover, the animosity that the Coltranes felt toward the Gorees was based not on the personal characteristics of any of the members of the Goree clan but only because they were members of the Goree clan.[17] The good of feuding with the Coltranes could thus only be had by a Goree.

But it is not only merit-based and relationship-based goods whose nature precludes their commodification. Many goods that are components of games are subject to ontological limits on their distribution. For example, a chess player can acquire (e.g.) his opponent's rook by capturing it in accordance with the rules of chess. But he cannot acquire it *qua* chess piece (i.e., as a component of the game rather than as the item that *represents* the component of the game) by buying it. If he does offer to buy the rook and his opponent agrees, he would not have acquired the rook *qua* chess piece. Such an acquisition can only be achieved in accordance with the rules of chess, and these do not allow players to purchase pieces in this way. Similarly, a chess player could give away his rook to his opponent—he could sacrifice it in accord with the rules of chess to secure what he believes to be some strategic end. But he cannot sell it to her for money. (Although he could offer an exchange, allowing his rook to be captured in return for his being able to capture [e.g.] his opponent's knight.) Similar remarks could also be made about goods that are components of other games, such as the hotels and other real estate of *Monopoly*.[18] And, more generally, these remarks can also be made about other goods whose existence is partially (or wholly) constituted by the rules that govern their distribution. The good of membership in certain clubs can only be acquired by non-market means. The good of being a member of The Second Preceding Sentence Club, for example, can only be held by persons who have read the sentence that precedes this one. That act is both a necessary and a sufficient condition for membership.[19]

Market Transformation

The above discussions of the ontological limits of markets are not *moral* debates. But they do have implications for debates over the moral limits of markets. In the examples above, the good or service whose nature precluded its sale or purchase simply could not be bought or sold. (A purchased Nobel Prize would be no prize at all.) Attempted purchase of these market-inalienable goods would secure the buyer only a simulacrum of what she desired. But other market-inalienable goods and services are such that some versions of them could be purchased even if the market-inalienable original could not. As with goods such as friendship and Nobel Prizes, payment would extinguish the market-inalienable originals. But the buyer could receive in their place goods or services that are similar (but not identical) to the market-inalienable original. Anderson, for example, holds that commodified sex would be different from non-commodified sex. The buyer of commodified sex would still receive sex and not merely receive the simulacrum of sex, as the attempted buyer of friendship would only (allegedly) receive the simulacrum of friendship. But the sex that he would receive in exchange for payment would necessarily be a different kind of sex from that which he would have experienced had he received it as a shared good.[20] The purchase and sale of certain market-inalienable goods and services would thus not merely extinguish them but transform them into modified versions of the (market-inalienable) originals.[21]

This transformative power that market payments can exert over certain goods and services raises moral questions. These arise from the combination of a descriptive claim (that commodification will change certain market-inalienable goods and services into similar but distinct goods) and an evaluative claim (that the version of the goods and services that will result from this transformation of the market-inalienable originals would be inferior to them). If the descriptive claim is true—if it is impossible to exchange money for a particular good without this changing it to another, similar, good—then this will impose an ontological limit on markets with the original (market-inalienable) good being beyond their scope.[22] Since the original good cannot be exchanged for money, any moral argument that might be offered in favor of limiting attempts to exchange it for money will focus on restricting markets in the inferior good into which it metamorphoses. Such arguments could not consist only of the combination of the above descriptive and evaluative claims. (After all, as Anderson observes, "Why shouldn't people have the freedom to enjoy inferior goods?"[23]) They must consist of these two claims combined with two more: That a market in the inferior good will crowd out the superior (market-inalienable) version and that this should (morally) be prevented.

Holding that a market in a certain good or service should be limited because it will lead to the crowding out of its superior alternative does not commit the proponents of this type of argument to claim that there is *necessarily* a moral limit on the market in the inferior good. They might believe that whether the inferior version of the good will crowd out the superior alternative is an empirical matter. If so, then their argument against the market in the inferior good will be contingent on whether this crowding out occurs. Other proponents of this type of argument might believe that there is a conceptually necessary connection between the generation of the inferior good through market exchange and the crowding out of its superior alternative. If they believe that this should (morally) be prevented, then they are poised to endorse the view that there is an inherent moral limit to limits, such that the inferior version of the good in question should not be exchanged for money.

Since such a crowding-out argument for holding that there are moral limits on markets is based on the ontological claim that the nature of certain goods will change once they are commodified, it does not commit its proponents to the position that Brennan and Jaworski believe is the hallmark of "anti-commodification critics." Recall, Brennan and Jaworski assert that such critics hold that some goods that "people are normally allowed to own or possess in some way" "should not be for sale." On this view, the goods that people are allowed "to own or possess" are the same as those that "should not be for sale."[24] But this is precisely what the proponents of the crowding-out arguments against the commodification of certain goods and services deny. On their view, the superior good is partially constituted by its non-commodification. Its distribution by norms other than those of market partially makes it the type of good that it is. Similarly, the inferior good that this superior good would metamorphose into, were an attempt made to commodify it, is partially constituted by its commodification. Its distribution by market norms partially makes it the type of good that it is. The proponents of these crowding-out arguments intend to establish the immorality of markets in the inferior version of the good with the aim of thereby protecting its superior alternative. But given that this (inferior) good is partly constituted by its commodification, it cannot be owned or possessed without being commodified. The proponents of these arguments thus do not intend to establish that there are some goods that can be owned or possessed but which should not be for sale. Instead, they intend to establish something more radical: That some goods that are partly constituted by their commodification should not be commodified. Their arguments are thus intended to establish that some goods (such as commodified sex) should not exist at all.

The Importance of Ontological Clarity

Debates over the inherent limits of markets are not always about the inherent *moral* limits of markets. A systematic examination of those goods and services that are widely held to be market-inalienable owing to their nature could also be fruitful. Such an examination would begin by identifying those goods and services whose nature is held to preclude their market alienability and then determining what (if anything) they have in common that could explain this. This would serve two purposes. First, it might transpire that the conditions that must be met for a good or service to be market-inalienable are not met by goods or services that are pretheoretically taken to be market-inalienable. The scope of goods and services that it is possible to buy and sell for money would thus be wider than is usually thought.[25] Second, any normative debate over which goods and services should not be bought and sold would presuppose that the goods and services in question *could* be bought and sold. Determining which goods are market-inalienable should thus be prior to, and fix the scope of, the debate over which goods should be exchanged for money.

Contingent Objections to Markets

Brennan and Jaworski (usually) hold that the anti-commodification view is that there are some goods that could be held and distributed freely but which should not be exchanged for money. But they also characterize the aim of anti-commodification theorists as being to "find limits to the market in which the market itself is the thing that introduces wrongness when there wasn't any to begin with."[26] This is a very vague characterization. It applies to the debate over whether there are any goods that could be possessed and given away freely but should not be exchanged for money. It also applies to the debate over whether there are any goods that should not be exchanged for money as such payment would both transform them into an inferior alternative and crowd out the superior version of them. And it applies to *another* debate over the moral limits of markets: The question of whether the introduction of markets in certain goods and services where no such market previously existed would be wrongful.[27]

This debate differs in two ways from the debates over the morality of commodification that were outlined above. First, those debates addressed the issue of whether it was morally permissible to exchange certain goods and services for money. In addressing this question, they were working with the assumption that there was nothing in the nature of the goods or services at issue (in the latter of those debates, the inferior, market-alienable goods or services) that would pose a barrier to their commodification. By contrast, the question of whether it would be morally permissible to *introduce* a market in certain goods and services rests on a particular presupposition: That the goods and services in question are such that their commodification must be facilitated in some way. The goods and services that are in question in this debate thus differ from those that can be readily traded without such facilitation (e.g., commodified sex or line-standing services). Second, this debate is not over whether it is inherently immoral to exchange the goods and services in question for money.[28] It is a debate over whether it would be morally permissible to *facilitate* a market in them in a particular situation. The answer to this question thus depends not on the goods or services in question but on the situation into which the market would be introduced.

Consider the debate over whether or not there should be a market in political votes. Unlike, e.g., sex and line-standing services, votes are socially constructed goods. Who receives a vote and the ways in which they can use it are determined by legal rules. The legal rules that govern the use of votes can either impede or facilitate their market exchange. The legal requirements that votes be cast in a secret ballot by the person to whom they were originally distributed would impede their market exchange. Even if markets in vote-casting services were legal (e.g., one could legally pay another to cast a vote at her behest), the requirement that they be cast in a secret ballot would result in there being few if any exchanges of such services for money. Unlike markets in goods whose effective use can be independent of legal rules (e.g., sex), an active market in votes requires institutional support. The relevant question for a market in votes is thus not whether it should be *allowed* (i.e., not prohibited) but whether it should be *introduced* (i.e., provided with the institutional support that would be necessary to facilitate it).[29] If the answer to this is negative, then if this market were to be facilitated, then this would introduce wrongness into a situation where it did not previously exist. Whether a market in votes should be introduced will depend on the social circumstances in which it would function. Introducing such a market could be wrongful if there was a marked disparity in wealth and income between rich and poor voters and a market for votes would enable the former politically to dominate the latter. In this situation, the introduction of a market in votes would introduce wrongness (the political domination of the poor by the rich) where none existed before. (See the discussion of vote markets in Chapter 6.) But the moral opposition to the introduction of a market in votes on these grounds might not hold in the absence of such economic inequality. In such a situation it might be morally permissible to introduce a market in votes. It is thus not true that persons who believe that the introduction of a market in X would introduce wrongness where none previously existed must believe that the commodification of X is inherently wrongful.[30] They could merely hold that whether X should (morally) be exchanged for money is contingent upon the social and economic conditions of the society in which X would be exchanged.

The debate over whether a market in a certain good or service should be introduced addresses the question of whether the good or service in question should be exchanged for money in a particular society at a particular time. This is a debate over the *contingent* moral limits of markets: Those that should (morally) be in place to restrict the exchange of certain goods or services at certain times, or places, or between certain types of people.[31] Most debates over whether certain goods or services should be exchanged for money are of this sort. Debra Satz, for example, argues that there are four criteria that should be used to assess whether a particular market is wrongful: vulnerability, weak agency, extremely harmful outcomes for individuals, and extremely harmful outcomes for society.[32] She does not argue (as I noted in Chapter 1) that there are "things that are normally permissible for adults to possess, own, have, occupy, provide, or use, but which are not permissible for those adults to trade, sell, and/or buy."[33] She does not object to particular markets on the grounds that their participants are trading in goods or services that it is inherently wrong to exchange for money. Instead, she argues that certain markets are wrongful because *given the particular social and economic circumstances in which they take place*, they "produce harmful outcomes, manifest weak agency, exploit underlying vulnerabilities, or support extremely harmful and inegalitarian social relationships ... ."[34] Satz *does* argue that certain markets are "*much more likely*" to be wrongful than others.[35] But holding that a market is *likely* to be wrongful is not the same as holding that it is *necessarily* wrongful.

This point can be generalized. Arguments that hold that certain goods or services should not be exchanged for money because one of the parties to the transaction would either be exploited or economically coerced into participating hold only against a particular social and economic background. For example, arguments that a market in kidneys is wrongful as this would exploit the poor or allow them to be economically coerced into selling their organs are intended to support only a *contingent* moral limit on the market that holds only under conditions of economic inequality.[36] A similar point can be made concerning arguments that hold that owing to the social and economic conditions in which a particular market would occur, one of the parties to transactions within it would typically be unable to consent to it in a way that would morally authorize her participation. Such arguments only support limiting the market in question under those conditions. And objections to markets in certain goods and services that are based on the view the market would misallocate them are not intended to establish that they should never be allocated by market means. Instead, they are intended only to establish that, given the contingent distribution of wealth in the society in which the goods or services in question would be allocated by the market, this would lead to their misallocation. Indeed, this latter type of objection is not even leveled against the commodification of the goods and services in question. It is compatible with this argument that, even given the nonideal distribution of wealth in a society, the goods and services in question (e.g., healthcare) should be procured for money (by, e.g., a non-profit agency) and then distributed in accord with non-market criteria (e.g., medical need).

The majority of the arguments in the current literature on the morality of markets focus (variously) on the claims that markets in certain goods and services would be exploitative, coercive, involve compromised consent, or would result in the misallocation of the goods and services whose market distribution is in question. The discussion of where the moral limits of markets lie in a particular society, at a particular time, is thus where the current "action" is in the commodification literature. Brennan and Jaworski are thus correct to hold that the focus of contemporary discussion of the moral limits of markets should be on *how* goods and services should be sold, not *which* goods and services should be sold.[37] But, as Dustin Crummett noted in another context, rather than being an iconoclastic position in the debate over the moral limits of markets, this is, in fact, the dominant one.[38]

Market Economy vs. Market Society

The debates outlined above address both the question of which goods and services *could not* be exchanged for money and the question of which goods and services *should not* be exchanged for money. But in addition to questions about the proper scope of the market *economy*, questions have also been raised about the proper scope of the market *society*. These questions do not address the issue of which goods and services should be bought and sold and which should not. Instead, they address the more fundamental question of how persons should understand the relationships that they have with each other. There are two approaches to addressing this question. The first asks whether the norms that govern the persons' actions should be those of the market or others, such as those appropriate to relationships between fellow citizens or between a professional and her clients. The second takes the expansion of market norms to be a *symptom* of a moral issue rather than a moral issue itself. This latter approach does not question whether the norms of the market should govern persons' relationships with each other. Instead, it asks how persons should conceive of the types of relationships (e.g., friendship) that they are in. How persons conceive of their relationships will be expressed by their actions toward each other. These actions will be governed by the norms that are, in their society, taken to be appropriate to govern the interactions of persons, given *both* the relationship that they have with each other *and* how they understand the nature of that type of relationship. The expansion of market norms governing the actions of persons who were in a particular type of relationship to each other would (holding the norms of the society constant) thus support the inference that how people conceived of this relationship was changing. The issue here would not be the question of whether this expansion of market norms was good or bad. The issue would be whether the changing understanding of the type of relationship in question that led to this expanded adoption of market norms was one that was to be applauded or decried.

Pluralistic Value and the Adoption of Norms

The first approach to addressing the question of whether we should be a market society as well as a market economy is exemplified in the work of Anderson. As I outlined in Chapters 1 and 4, Anderson offers an account of the social conditions that are needed for persons to have both freedom and autonomy. Anderson believes that for a person to be free, she must have a wide range of options to express her different evaluative positions. Certain evaluative positions can only be developed and expressed if there is a normative framework in place to support them. Hence, argues Anderson, for a person to be free, she must have access to a variety of different social spheres that are governed by different sets of norms and so support different modes of evaluation. This supports her view that the norms of the market should not replace alternative normative systems, such as those of (e.g.) the family or professions. But in addition to this general approach—which is similar to Walzer's descriptive account of how complex equality can be secured through the separation of different normative spheres—Anderson also provides accounts of when the norms of the market would be inappropriate to govern the distribution of certain goods and services.[39] For example, she argues that sex should not be commodified (i.e., distributed according to market norms), not only to preserve pluralistic freedom but also to enhance the dignity of women.[40] As I discussed in Chapter 1, Anderson is clear that this is not the claim that sex should not be bought and sold. It is the distinct claim that the buying and selling of sex should not be governed by market norms. Anderson's interest in where the proper limits of the market lie is with the proper scope of market norms, not with the question of which goods and services should not be bought and sold.

Understanding Relationships

The second approach to addressing the question of whether we should be a market society as well as a market economy is exemplified in the work of Sandel. Sandel addresses the question of how certain types of relationships between persons (e.g., that of friendship, of marriage, or of citizen and political representative) should, morally, be understood. (Which understanding would be the most "morally appropriate" is taken by Sandel to be decided by which would be the most conducive to the flourishing of the persons involved in the relationships in question, but it need not be understood in this way.[41]) Relationships can be understood in different ways. Friendship, for example, could be understood as a relationship in which the persons involved in it should especially seek to satisfy the desires of their friends. Or it could be understood as a relationship in which the friends should value each other for their own sake. Similarly, the relationship between a political representative and her constituents could be understood as (e.g.) one in which the former should paternalistically seek to fulfill the interests of the latter. Or it could be understood as a more reciprocal relationship in which political representatives should satisfy the desires of their constituents in exchange for direct or indirect payments. Recognizing that relationships could be understood in different ways raises the question of which understanding of a particular type of relationship would be the most morally appropriate to adopt. Some ways of understanding a particular relationship could (given the norms of the society in which they are in) lead those who accept them to adopt a more market-orientated attitude to those with whom they share them than others. A person who (in Actual America) understands friendship in terms of desire satisfaction is likely to adopt an attitude toward her friends that is similar to that adopted by an entrepreneur toward her potential customers. She would aim both to satisfy their desires and would expect that they would reciprocate by aiming to satisfy hers. By contrast, the attitude that a person who understands friendship in terms of mutual appreciation would adopt would focus less on satisfying her friends' desires and more on making them feel valued by her. She would value her friends in this way independently of any benefit that she could gain from this.

On this approach, the question of whether we should live in a more or less market society will turn on the question of whether it would be better (morally) for us to understand our relationships in terms that would lead them (in our society) to be governed by market norms. Note that this question is distinct from the question of the extent to which we should have a market economy. The question of whether a society is or is not a market society is a question that concerns how the persons within it understand their relationships with others. This is independent of the question of whether a society should or should not have a primarily market economy. The latter question asks nothing about how the persons within the society in question understand their relationships with each other. It only addresses the way in which goods and services are distributed within that society. Moreover, as I explained in Chapter 3, there is no necessary connection between adopting a market-orientated understanding of a relationship and endorsing market norms to express that understanding. Depending on their culture, persons might express a market-orientated understanding of a particular relationship according to non-market norms.

Norms and Assessing Competing Conceptions of Relationships

The discussion of which norms should govern the distribution of which goods and services within society and the discussion of how, morally, it would be best to conceive of different types of relationships could be conducted separately from each other. But it could also be beneficial to combine them.

Margaret Jane Radin, for example, has argued that how we understand both ourselves and our relationships with others will guide our understanding of which norms it would be appropriate to adopt to govern the distribution of certain goods and services, given the situation in which we find ourselves. These understandings will be guided by the worldview that we adopt.[42] We could, for example, have a view of the world in which "all things desired or valued ... are commodities."[43] On this worldview (that of universal commodification), persons are conceived of as commodity traders and it is believed that all values can be expressed in terms of price—and so all values are commensurable with each other.[44] Alternatively, we could have a view of the world in which not all values are commensurable.[45] On this alternative worldview, the value of some items could be incommensurable with that of money. If this were so, then not everything would necessarily be market-alienable.[46]

Radin notes that differing worldviews would support or preclude differing conceptions of personhood and interpersonal relations. The worldview of universal commodification, for example, "cannot support the traditional Kantian ideal of personhood" for "conceiving of persons or of essential attributes of personhood as fungible commodities tends to make us think of ourselves and others as means, not ends."[47] This worldview would also lead us to view personal relationships as having tradeable value. The act of a person who takes a job in a distant city that pays $100,000 more than her current job even though this would require that she forgo the company of her spouse would, on this worldview, be interpreted as revealing that she values the company of her spouse at less than $100,000. By contrast, on an alternative worldview (e.g., that endorsed by Radin, on which not all values are considered to be commensurable), one might hold that this person's acceptance of this job reveals nothing at all about the value that she places on the company of her spouse.[48] On this alternative worldview the financial value of the job is not commensurable with the value of the company of the job-seeker's spouse. She thus did not trade off the company of her spouse for an increased income.[49]

Like Sandel, Radin holds that certain conceptions of ourselves and our relationships will be more conducive to human flourishing than others.[50] If it is true that in a certain society the unbridled market provision of certain goods or services would foster a worldview (e.g., that of universal commodification) that would lead persons to a suboptimal conception of either themselves or their relationships, this would provide a reason to rein in (e.g., through regulation) or prohibit the market provision of those goods or services.[51] This debate is thus not merely about whether certain goods or services should or should not be market-alienable in a particular society. It also concerns the question of which goods or services should be *incompletely* commodified in that society through their provision and distribution being subject to regulation.[52]

However, Radin notes, considerations of the effects that the degree to which certain goods or services are commodified would have on persons' worldviews (and hence on their conceptions of themselves and their relationships) should not themselves determine whether certain goods or services should or should not be commodified. These considerations must be balanced against the effects that restricting the market will have on those who would participate in it. We might, for example, hold that the optimal conception of personhood (e.g., a Kantian one) requires that persons be prohibited from selling their organs on the grounds that such sales would injure them as persons. But it is possible that a would-be desperate seller's personhood would be injured more by forcing her to continue in her dire straits than by allowing her to sell an organ to escape them.[53] If so, then a concern for personhood should lead one to support, rather than oppose, organ markets.

The need to consider the effects that certain markets would have on those that would participate in them shows that the discussion of which norms should govern the distribution of which goods and services within a society should not be divorced from considerations of the social and economic conditions of the society in question.[54] Similarly, in assessing how best to conceive of certain relationships, one must recognize that this answer cannot be given merely by considering the likely advantages and disadvantages of adopting each conception independently of how it would be expressed within the social milieu in which it would be instantiated. One could not, for example, hold that a preference-satisfaction conception of friendship would be superior to one that focused on the value of one's friends for their own sake without determining how each of these conceptions would be expressed, given the prevailing norms in the society in which they would occur. It is *possible* that adopting a preference-satisfaction conception of friendship would be more conducive to the flourishing of friends than its alternatives independently of how the adoption of this understanding of friendship was expressed. But it is also possible that acting on the prevailing norms that govern how this understanding of friendship is expressed within a particular society would be harmful. And if this harm outweighed the benefits that would accrue to the friends from adopting this conception of friendship, this would provide a *prima facie* reason for preferring an alternative conception of friendship that would be suboptimal for those in the friendship relationship.

To illustrate this, consider the conception of political representation as being aimed at satisfying the preferences of the electorate. Assume that it has been determined that this conception is that which is most conducive to the flourishing of both the political representatives and those whom they represent. It is thus *prima facie* good that this conception of political representation is widely accepted within a particular society. The norms within this society direct holders of elected office who endorse this conception of political representation to guide their actions in accord with market norms. It is believed that this would maximize the satisfaction of their constituents' preferences. (The link between this conception of political representation and the endorsement of market norms is merely contingent; see the discussion in Chapter 3.) Markets in votes are both legalized and facilitated, and access to the legislature is only obtainable for payment. However, there is widespread economic inequality in this society with the poor greatly outnumbering the rich. Under these conditions it is unlikely that any political party would seek to represent the interests of the poor and so they would be *de facto* disenfranchised.[55] This, in turn, would be likely to lead to policies being adopted that would work to their detriment. Thus, even though the preference-satisfaction conception of political representation is (*ex hypothesi*) the optimal conception of the relationship between political representatives and those they represent, under certain conditions the norms that would be used to express it could result in its acceptance leading to more harm than good. It should thus be replaced (if possible) by a different conception of this relationship even though this alternative would in the abstract be less optimal than that which it replaces.

To emphasize that it is a contingent matter as to whether a particular conception of a relationship combined with a set of norms governing its expression would lead to more harm than good, consider a different example where the same conception of political representation as before is accepted and this is governed by the same market norms.

To facilitate the satisfaction of the preferences of both the representatives and their constituents, each constituent is annually provided with a sum of fiat money that she can use to buy political influence; she will be able to retain a quarter of any that is unused after a five-year period. (The ability to retain the allotted money makes it clear that this is fiat, and not merely token, money, while the ability to retain only a quarter of that which was unused is intended to alleviate concerns about this approach leading to the disenfranchisement of the poor who might not use their allotted money for political purposes so as to boost their income every five years.) It is believed by the proponents of this monetarized system of political expression that it would enable constituents better to express the strengths of their preferences for different political policies than they could achieve through voting. It is also believed that this would enable the representatives better to satisfy their constituents' preferences. In this situation the exchange of political influence for money would be considered to be morally appropriate as it would evince the correct relationship between representatives and constituents. Moreover, in this situation, the *unpaid* exercise of political influence would be morally condemned on the grounds that the beneficiary would thereby receive more than her "fair share" of political consideration. The participants in this monetarized political system would thus have accepted not only that the relationship between representatives and their constituents should be understood in market terms but that the norms that govern their interactions should be those (and only those!) of the market. And given the (politically induced) background conditions against which these interactions took place, there would be no concern that this approach was harmful to the poor.

Moving Forward to Improve Society

The question of which conceptions of particular relationships should be supported is thus not one that can be answered in isolation from the knowledge both of the norms that will govern their expression in a society and of the background conditions against which this expression will take place. As I noted above, it might be that the conception of a particular relationship that would be optimal under ideal conditions could be suboptimal in certain situations. But this raises questions that are relevant to the projects of those who are concerned with the issue of whether we should have a market society as well as a market economy. We should question how we would assess the relative merits of different ways of conceiving of a particular relationship under ideal conditions. We should also question how we should identify what these ideal conditions are. We should also question whether it would suffice to identify the optimal combination of the conception of a particular relationship and the norms that would govern its expression, given the background conditions that exist in the society in which this combination would be instantiated or whether it would be better were one of these variables to be altered. This latter non-ideal approach to the question of when endorsing market norms would be appropriate in a particular society could be drawn upon to encourage morally valuable change in that society. It could, for example, be used to determine if it would be morally valuable to work to change either the conception of the relationship that is adopted, the norms by which this is expressed, or the background conditions of the society in question. These questions must be answered before we can hold that a shift toward the use of market norms to govern the interactions of persons within a particular relationship is symptomatic of a shift to a conception of that relationship that is worse than that which preceded it.

Conclusion

It might be natural to think that discussion of the appropriate limits of markets focuses on the question of whether there are certain goods or services that could be legitimately possessed and given away freely but which should not be bought and sold. And there is some discussion of this issue—although this is a niche concern and one that was more popular in ecclesiastical circles in the thirteenth and sixteenth centuries than it is today.[56] But viewing the debates over the limits of markets in the binary way that this approach to the discussion encourages—with those in favor of expanding markets on one side and those who oppose this on the other—overlooks the multifaceted nature of the current debates over the limits both of markets and of market norms. This binary approach overlooks the question of how to identify those goods and services that it would be immoral to buy and sell because it would be immoral either to possess them, or to exchange them freely. It overlooks the question of which goods or services are beyond the scope of the market because their nature precludes their distribution by market means. It overlooks the question of which goods and services would be transformed into similar but distinct goods or services through being commodified. It overlooks the related moral question of whether these transformed goods or services should be produced (and distributed) through the attempted commodification of their originals. It overlooks the set of questions that concern whether certain goods or services should be procured and distributed by market means in certain contingent situations. And it overlooks entirely all of the questions that arise from considering whether in addition to being a market economy, we should also be a market society.

None of these questions are trivial—although some might find them boring.[57] As I noted at the start of this chapter, the above taxonomy of the contemporary debates over the morality of markets and of market norms serve three purposes. It will help persons engaged in different debates talking past each other as a result of failing to understand that they are addressing different issues. It will help persons develop sound criticisms of the views that they disagree with by enabling them properly to identify their targets. And it will foster discussion by facilitating awareness of the connections that might exist between discussions that have hitherto had little interaction. It is important to know what we talk about when we talk about the limits of markets.

With this outline of the various subjects that we might be addressing when we talk about the limits of markets in place, I will now turn to contribute substantively to one of these debates: The question of whether market or other norms should guide action in a particular sphere of activity.

Notes

1 The purpose of this chapter is thus similar to Judith Andre's aim in "Blocked Exchanges: A Taxonomy," *Ethics* 103, 1 (1992): 29–47. For the sake of concision, from now on, I will mainly refer to these debates as debates over the appropriate limits of markets; this should be read as the conjunctive claim where appropriate.
2 Brennan and Jaworski, for example, believed that critics of markets endorsed the Asymmetry Thesis. This mistake led them to criticize the views of those they considered to be critics of markets in ways that failed to engage with their positions.
3 Jason Brennan and Peter M. Jaworski, *Markets Without Limits* (New York: Routledge, 2016), 15.
4 Martin Lewison, "Conflicts of Interest? The Ethics of Usury," *Journal of Business Ethics* 22, 4 (1999), 330–334.
5 See Chapter 1, note 128.
6 Brennan and Jaworski, *Markets Without Limits*, 11.
7 I mistakenly conflated the first and third of these ways in which markets could have inherent limits in my brief "Book Note" (James Stacey Taylor, "Book Note: Jason Brennan and Peter M. Jaworski, *Markets Without Limits: Moral virtues and commercial interests*," *Choice Reviews* 54, 1 [2016]. Available at: www.choicereviews.org/review/10.5860/CHOICE.198180.) I was also mistaken to hold that these conflated accounts represented the current consensus view. As this chapter makes clear, they do not.

8 Immanuel Kant, *Lectures on Ethics*, Eds. Peter Heath and J.B. Schneewind, trans. Peter Heath (Cambridge: Cambridge University Press, 2001), 127.
9 For a discussion of why the argument is to be understood in this way, see James Stacey Taylor, *Stakes and Kidneys: Why Markets in Human Body Parts Are Morally Imperative* (Aldershot: Ashgate, 2005), 148–151.
10 Immanuel Kant, *Groundwork of the Metaphysics of Morals*, Eds. and trans. Mary Gregor and Jens Timmerman (Cambridge: Cambridge University Press, 2012), 46.
11 Kant, *Lectures on Ethics*, 70.
12 It would also presumably be wrong to accept a body part to replace one that had failed.
13 A similar point can be made with respect to Kant's second argument for the view that it is inherently wrong to commodify human body parts, the "Argument from Contradiction." For an outline and discussion of this Argument, see Taylor, *Stakes and Kidneys*, 151–153.
14 Although see James Stacey Taylor, "Buying and Selling Friendship," *American Philosophical Quarterly* 56, 2 (2019): 187–202.
15 Michael J. Sandel, *What Money Can't Buy* (New York: Farrar, Straus and Giroux, 2012), 94.
16 O. Henry, "A Blackjack Bargainer," in O. Henry, *O. Henry Stories* (New York: Platt & Munk, 1962), 167–188.
17 Note that the distributive conditions for feuding are not simply the opposite of those for friendship for feuding does not require that one's animosity toward one's opponents be motivated by any dislike of their individual characteristics but only of the relevant type of person that they are (e.g., "a Goree" or "a Coltrane").
18 For an earlier discussion of these points, see James Stacey Taylor, "What Can't Money Buy?," *Public Affairs Quarterly*, 32, 1 (2018): 45–66.
19 You dear reader, are now (presumably) a member of this Club! Membership in the (original) Preceding Sentence Club can only be acquired by reading a different sentence; see ibid., 49.
20 Elizabeth Anderson, *Value in Ethics and Economics* (Cambridge, MA: Harvard University Press, 1993), 154. See also Margaret Jane Radin, *Contested Commodities* (Cambridge, MA: Harvard University Press, 1996), 94.
21 Anderson, *Value in Ethics and Economics*, 154.
22 For a discussion of this point, see David G. Dick, "Transformable Goods and the Limits of What Money Can Buy," *Moral Philosophy and Politics* 4, 1 (2017): 121–140.
23 Anderson, *Values in Ethics and Economics*, 154.
24 Brennan and Jaworski, *Markets Without Limits*, 15.
25 This is the conclusion of Taylor, "What Can't Money Buy?."
26 Brennan and Jaworski, *Markets Without Limits*, 19.
27 See James Stacey Taylor, "What Limits Should Markets Be Without?," *Business Ethics Journal Review* 4, 7 (2016): 41–46, for a discussion of what their target is likely to be.
28 Brennan and Jaworski are thus mistaken to believe that a situation in which "the market itself is the thing that introduces wrongness when there wasn't any to begin with" (*Markets Without Limits*, 19) would entail that it is inherently morally wrong to exchange the goods and services in question for money.
29 See James Stacey Taylor, "Markets in Votes, Voter Liberty, and the Burden of Justification," *Journal of Philosophical Research* 42 (2017): 325–340.
30 Brennan and Jaworski appear to believe that these views are the same; *Markets Without Limits*, Chapter 3.
31 Brennan and Jaworski describe these debates as "boring" and "trivial";ibid., 15.
32 Debra Satz, *Why Some Things Should Not Be for Sale* (Oxford: Oxford University Press, 2010), 9.
33 This is how Brennan and Jaworski mistakenly characterize Satz's position; *Markets Without Limits*, 12.

34 Satz, *Why Some Things Should Not Be for Sale*, 9–10.
35 Ibid., 9.
36 See, for example, Paul Hughes, "Exploitation, Autonomy, and the Case for Organ Sales," *International Journal of Applied Philosophy* 12, 1 (1998): 89–95.
37 Brennan and Jaworski, *Markets Without Limits*, Chapter 4.
38 Dustin Crummett, "Expression and Indication in Ethics and Political Philosophy," *Res Publica* 25, 3 (2019), 392.
39 Anderson notes that her work resembles Walzer's; *Value in Ethics and Economics*, 143.
40 Ibid., 155.
41 Sandel, *What Money Can't Buy*, 103–104.
42 Radin, *Contested Commodities*, 6–15; see too E. Richard Gold, *Body Parts: Property Rights and the Ownership of Human Biological Materials* (Washington, DC: Georgetown University Press, 2007), 171–177.
43 Radin, *Contested Commodities*, 2.
44 Ibid., 5, 9.
45 For a discussion of commensurability in the context of the debate over property in the body, see Gold, *Body Parts*, Chapter 8.
46 Even if one considers the value of certain goods or services to be incommensurable with that of money, they could still be commodified if they are comparable and proto-on-a-par. See the discussion of Booth's argument in Chapter 6.
47 Radin, *Contested Commodities*, 84.
48 Ibid., 12.
49 Ibid., 11. See also Chapter 9, note 55.
50 Ibid., 88–94, 122, 144–148, 162. See also Anne Phillips, *Our Bodies, Whose Property?* (Princeton, NJ: Princeton University Press, 2013), Chapter 2.
51 Radin, *Contested Commodities*, 113, 144–148.
52 Ibid., xiii.
53 Ibid., 50–51; 124–126. In recognizing this, Radin explicitly rejects the view (attributed to her by Brennan and Jaworski, *Markets Without Limits*, 76) that certain goods or services should necessarily not be commodified. (See too *Contested Commodities*, xiii, 162.) Brennan and Jaworski are also wrong to attribute to her the view that prostitution is essentially wrongful and should be market-inalienable (*Markets Without Limits*, 76); indeed, she is explicit that her view is that "we should now decriminalize the sale of sexual services" (*Contested Commodities*, 135). Brennan and Jaworski are also in error when they write that "Margaret Jane Radin says that prostitution detaches intimacy from sex, and that widespread use of prostitutes might cause us not to see sex as intimate at all" (*Markets Without Limits*, 76). In support of this claim, they cite (in ibid., 76, 84, note 1) Radin's "Market-Inalienability," *Harvard Law Review* 100, 8 (1987), 1884. (Brennan and Jaworski miscite this as being published in 1997. They earlier miscite this view as being from "Radin, *Contested Commodities*, 1884"; Jason Brennan and Peter M. Jaworksi, "Markets Without Symbolic Limits," *Ethics* 125, 4 [2015], 1072, note 44. Surprisingly—or perhaps not, given my discussion in Chapter 8—neither Brennan, Jaworski, nor those who evaluated their work for publication noticed that these citations were erroneous—and that the latter citation implied that Radin's book is almost 2,000 pages long!) But Radin writes nothing about prostitution on that page (she is discussing how the worldview of universal commodification is an impoverished one to use to address the wrong of rape) and at no point in that article does she argue that prostitution is wrong as it detaches intimacy from sex; indeed, she never mentions intimacy in it at all. It seems that Brennan and Jaworski attribute this view to Radin not as a result of reading Radin, but as a result of reading Satz's criticism of Radin's objection to prostitution. (Their approach to scholarship is thus rather odd: They read Satz to discover Radin's views and read student newspapers to discover Satz's.) Brennan and Jaworski paraphrase Satz's response to Radin as "casual sex also detaches

intimacy from sex, and widespread casual sex could cause a cultural shift in which sex loses its intimate meaning" (*Markets Without Limits*, 76, citing Satz, *Why Some Things Should Not Be for Sale*, 142). Their paraphrase of Satz's view is accurate. But Brennan and Jaworski failed to recognize that it was *Satz*, not Radin, who introduced the worry that prostitution will detach intimacy from sex. She did so to illustrate her understanding of Radin's view of the problematic nature of prostitution (Satz, *Why Some Things Should Not Be for Sale*, 142). And, unfortunately for Brennan and Jaworski, Satz's exegesis is inaccurate. First, the quotation that she offers from Radin concerning the process by which we should decide which conception of human flourishing we should adopt did not occur in the context of Radin's discussion of prostitution, but in the context of discussing why we should reject market rhetoric to form our view of the world (ibid., 142; quoting Radin, "Market-Inalienability," 1884). Second, Radin, after recognizing that women's sexuality is currently incompletely commodified ("Market-Inalienability," 1923), argues that, in our nonideal world, prostitution should be decriminalized (to protect poor women from having illegally to sell sex) and structured so that its presence does not close off the possibility of our achieving a world in which men and women have more equal power (e.g., by banning advertising recruiting women into it [ibid., 1924–1925]). She makes no mention of prostitution leading to "the signs of affection and intimacy" becoming "detached from their usual meaning" with this (somehow) leading to a concern that "prostitution might undermine our ability to apply the criteria for coercion and information failure," as Satz holds (*Why Some Things Should Not Be for Sale*, 142). In (apparently) drawing on Satz without checking the accuracy of her exegesis, Brennan and Jaworski have been misled into misrepresenting Radin's views.

54 Radin, *Contested Commodities*, 162.
55 See Satz, *Why Some Things Should Not Be for Sale*, 103; Anderson, *Value in Ethics and Economics*, 158–163.
56 See notes 4 and 5.
57 Brennan and Jaworski, *Markets Without Limits*, 15.

PART III
From Market Norms to Academic Norms

8

WHY GOOD ACADEMICS PRODUCE BAD RESEARCH

Academic Incentives, Woozles, and Hoaxes

Introduction

In Chapters 6 and 7, I attempted to rerail the debates over the appropriate limits of markets and of market thinking. In this chapter and Chapter 9, I aim to contribute substantively to the debate over the proper scope of market thinking by offering support for the view that there are some spheres of life that should not be dominated by the norms of the market. I then will then move in Chapter 10 to offer suggestions as to how to encourage the production of academic research in accord with the norms of the academy rather than those of the market.

I will begin my contribution to the debate over the proper scope of market norms by offering a possible answer to a question that has no doubt been raised by my arguments and observations in Chapters 1–5: How is it that seriously flawed work can be published, and published in "top venues"? I will argue in this chapter that, given the external incentives that academics currently face, it is not surprising that seriously inaccurate work is published. I will also argue that responding to these incentives will motivate academics to conduct their research in accord with the norms of the market rather than the norms of the academy. (Ambitious and established academics do not publish to avoid perishing. They often publish to get paid.) I will continue my discussion of this latter issue in Chapters 9 and 10.

Why Good Academics Produce Bad Research: The Perversity of Current Academic Incentives

It is a truism in both economics and law that people respond to incentives.[1] When trying to determine how a surprising result arose from human action, it

DOI: 10.4324/9781003251996-12

would often be instructive to consider the incentives that might have led the actors in question to behave as they did. Thus, when asking both how flawed academic work might arise and then be published without its deficiencies being detected, we should attend to the incentives that are faced by academic researchers and referees to see if they would motivate action that could explain this.

Receipt of the external rewards that can accompany perceived academic success is strongly correlated with securing publications in "top venues."[2] As Jason Brennan and Phillip Magness put it: "[i]n general, the more and better you publish, the more you make."[3] The more publications an academic has in top venues, the more likely it is that she will be able to secure a tenured or tenure-track position in an academic department at a prestigious research institution. Such positions are valued in part because they have low teaching loads, freeing up time to do more research. As an academic's research profile rises, she could expect to receive lucrative job offers from institutions that compete with her own. Even if she does not accept such offers, she could use them as leverage to increase her remuneration from her current employer. A record of continuous and active publication in top venues will also make it more likely that she will receive invitations to give paid talks at other institutions, as well as grants, Fellowships, and other benefits that constitute "the spice of academic life."[4] And—as David Lodge has observed—the receipt of such benefits is often partially conditional on one having received similar benefits in the past.[5]

These professional incentives to publish in top venues are sometimes compounded by direct financial incentives. The McDonough School of Business at Georgetown University, for example, "pays faculty who publish in top venues ... a large summer research bonus."[6] Since at Georgetown "publications help raises, and raises build upon past raises, a good article or book now can easily be worth $300,000 over the course of a career."[7] Carlos III University of Madrid similarly offers financial rewards to academics for publication.[8] In some Danish universities academics are paid bonuses for each article that they publish; these range from 5000 DKK (approximately $800) to (in one case) 50,000 DKK (approximately $8000) an article.[9] Other examples abound.[10]

Faced with this set of incentives, a prudentially rational, ambitious, academic who desires to secure such professional rewards would strive to publish in top venues as often as possible.[11] She would avoid engaging in any professional activity whose time costs would not be repaid with an increased rate of publication.[12] She would accordingly avoid spending time on committee work or on teaching.[13] Instead, she would focus on producing publishable work. To this end, she would conduct her research in ways that she would expect would secure her the greatest number of publications for the time that she spends working.[14] And just as there are elements of her professional life (e.g., committee work, teaching) that would not repay the time spent on them with an increased number of publications, so too are there aspects of research that are less likely to repay the time spent on them with publications than are others. A prudentially rational researcher would thus orientate the time that she spends on research toward those activities that she expects would most likely repay her efforts with an increased rate of publication. She would spend as little time as possible on research activities that would be expected to provide a poor rate of publishable return for her efforts. She would accordingly avoid spending much time on those elements of academic research that would be both time-consuming and unlikely to increase her productivity.

A prudentially rational, ambitious, academic is thus unlikely to spend much (if any) time checking the references that are provided in the published works of others. Checking references is time-consuming and unlikely to lead to additional publications. It is *especially* time-consuming if the references in question refer to secondary rather than primary sources. Verifying them would require that the references in the cited sources also be checked. This could lead to the need to work through a chain of references before identifying the original source. But while time-consuming, checking references for accuracy is unlikely to increase one's rate of publication. (Very few top venues will publish research that focuses on identifying exegetical errors in previously published work.[15]) A prudentially rational academic who desires to publish as frequently as possible in top venues is thus unlikely to check others' references, instead trusting them to be accurate.[16] Indeed, that academics are unlikely to check their references is such an open secret in academia that it was mocked in a paper published by Orin S. Kerr. Kerr's paper (with the "impressive but generic title" of "A Theory of Law") was written and published solely to provide others with a source to append to claims they make that are either "so obvious or obscure" that they have not appeared before in the literature or that are "made up or false, making them more difficult to support using references to the existing literature."[17]

An ambitious academic would similarly have little external incentive to make sure that she accurately represents the views of those whose work she addresses. Consider, for example, someone who is drawing on the work of another to provide an example of a view that she is addressing (whether critically or otherwise). She might judge it sufficient for her purposes to cite a passage from the author whose work she addresses which, when read in isolation from his other work, appears to offer the view that she is addressing. It is possible that when read in the context of the rest of the author's work, the passage in question does not support this attribution of that view to him.[18] But an academic focused on publishing as much and as good as possible will have little incentive to verify that her use of this passage is legitimate by doing the extensive (and time-consuming) reading that this would require. She would, instead, be content with a plausible construal of the passage she cites (i.e., one that would pass muster with referees) even if this construal would transpire to be mistaken once the passage was placed in context.

An ambitious academic motivated by the desire for external reward would also be unlikely to spend much time ensuring that her citations to others' work was accurate. She would believe—with some justification—that if her arguments were interesting, referees would not reject her paper on the technical grounds that her citations were inaccurate. Instead, they might only require that she revise them prior to publication. Rather than spending time making sure that her references are accurate, she would thus only do so if her referees identified an error and requested that she remedy it. Similarly, a prudentially rational academic who aims to publish as much and as good as possible would be disinclined to verify that she had quoted her sources accurately if nothing in her arguments turn on the precise phrasing used.[19] And to increase her publication rate, she might eschew providing sources altogether, simply asserting that an argument that she addresses is one that is "widely held" or "common in the literature."[20]

Academics who are working to publish as much as possible thus have little incentive to make sure that their work is exegetically accurate. And there is no reason to think that the peer review process will identify exegetically inaccurate work and preclude its publication. Referees are themselves academics whose success is judged by the number and quality of their publications. They are thus faced with incentives to avoid engaging in scholarly activities that will not sufficiently repay them with an increased number or quality of publications. To carefully referee a work for possible publication is time-consuming. The author's references would need to be checked both for accuracy and to ensure that she accurately characterizes the work of those she cites, her use of quotation would need to be checked, and her arguments would need to be evaluated. But none of this work will redound to the advantage of the conscientious referee who performs it. As J. Angelo Corlett has noted: "Universities and their faculties typically do not recognize journal or book refereeing as important enough to even mention in RTP committee meetings."[21] To show just how time-consuming such refereeing could be, consider the work that needed to be done to determine if Stanley Aronowitz's claim that Herbert Marcuse first used the term "scholarshit" was correct.[22] Aronowitz provided no source for this claim, nor did he respond to an inquiry asking where this term appeared in Marcuse's work.[23] The only recourse to check this claim was to read all of Marcuse's work—in English, French, and German.[24]

Academics thus have a considerable disincentive to review the work of their peers properly. Since it is considerably less time-consuming (and more fun!) to evaluate a paper's arguments than it is to check its exegetical accuracy, referees will focus on the former aspect of refereeing and skimp on the latter. This preference for evaluating a work based on its arguments while skimping on checking that it is exegetically accurate is reinforced by the cultural preference (in contemporary American academia) for innovative work.[25] As Gerardo Patriotta wrote in his capacity as the General Editor for the *Journal of Management Studies*: "[j]ournals (and their reviewers) encourage originality and single out novelty as a major criterion for assessing the value of a contribution."[26] This view was echoed by Jason Brennan, who noted in his advice to aspiring academics that "[i]n economics or philosophy, your task is to come up with an original argument."[27] This preference for "surprising, innovative results" is also "strong" in science.[28] This preference for innovation over accuracy further undermines academics' motivation to fact-check the work that they engage with. Identifying the argumentative flaws in a published work is more likely to result in a publication than is identifying its exegetical inaccuracies.

It is thus not surprising that work that contains significant exegetical errors will be published—and published even in top venues.[29] For the same reasons it is similarly unsurprising that plagiarized work—sometimes almost entire books—or hoax articles will be published in top venues.[30] This is often overlooked by those perpetrators of academic hoaxes who believe that the publication of hoax articles casts doubt on the intellectual quality of the discipline in which they appeared. To establish that a discipline is intellectually problematic (e.g., it publishes work primarily because it conforms to a particular ideological standpoint), one would have to publish multiple hoax articles that put forward unsound arguments that adhered to the "correct" viewpoint. One would also have to establish via a control group of submitted articles (i.e., those that offered the same type of unsound arguments as the "test" articles but in favor of what was taken to be the "incorrect" viewpoint) that the "hoax" articles were likely accepted on ideological grounds. Both sets of articles would need to be submitted to refereed journals that did not charge authors publication fees; they would also need to be submitted to the same journals under the same editors. (And, ideally, reviewed by the same referees. But this is unlikely to occur—and in any case is not under the control of the would-be hoaxers. There will thus inevitably be noise in any data that a hoax produces.) Furthermore, to establish ideological bias, the content of the hoax (and test) articles would need to focus on offering spurious argumentation rather than falsified research. This would better establish that the acceptance in the literature of the hoax articles was a result of motivated reasoning rather than the difficulty of replicating experiments or fieldwork. However, even the publication of the first set of hoax articles but not the second (i.e., the control group) would merely establish that *some* referees and journal editors might be biased, *not* that the *discipline* in which they worked was. To establish that a *discipline* was biased, the hoax articles would have to become prominent within the field with frequent positive citations and few if any published articles criticizing the spurious reasoning in them. To date, no academic hoax has met these conditions and so none have demonstrated that the discipline that they targeted is biased.

But, leaving to one side plagiarized work and hoaxes, given the external incentives that academics face, we should expect some academic work to be filled with errors.[31] Some of these errors will be minor. These include misquotations or fabricated quotations that play no role in the argument the misquoting author develops (and that could be attributed simply to misremembering what one had read), erroneous factual claims that play no role in the argument developed, reference errors, misspelling of names, and misattributed authorship.[32] But some might be more serious. They might, for example, include failure to cite any sources at all, making it difficult or impossible to verify the claims that are made.[33] Or they might include misrepresentation of the views being criticized. Such misrepresentation might range from simply an uncharitable interpretation of another's work to the attribution of a position to her that she explicitly rejects.[34] Such misrepresentations might be supported by misquoting the misrepresented work,[35] providing quotations that are taken out of context,[36] or simply asserting that the author whose work one is addressing held a certain view without any attempt to support its attribution to her.[37]

Propagating Woozles

Given that academics have little external incentive to check the references in the work of others and so are likely to accept at face value published exegetical and empirical claims that are presented as being true, it is to be expected that errors that appear in one academic publication will be repeated in others.[38] This is especially so if those claims appear to be supported by proper scholarly references or if they appear to confirm what their readers already believe.[39] Moreover, if these claims would lend credence to the work of the academics who encounter them (and hence increase its chance of publication), they would have an incentive to repeat them.[40] It is thus to be expected that academics will repeat claims without checking their veracity, justifying this merely by citing the source where they found them.[41] The more frequently that a claim is cited, the more likely it is that it will be accepted as being true without anyone checking it; its repetition alone will have provided it with a veneer of veracity. And the more that a claim is repeated without being verified, the more likely it is that it will become subtly altered through repetition, much as the original phrase used in the child's game of "Telephone" will morph into something quite different at the conclusion of the game.[42] In this way a false claim might become widely accepted within an academic community.

A false claim that becomes accepted in this way is termed a "woozle" after the animal that Winnie-the-Pooh believes he is tracking in Chapter 3 of A.A. Milne's story, *Winnie-the-Pooh*. Pooh is following tracks in the snow of an unknown animal.[43] The tracks circle a spinney, and as Pooh follows them he sees that more tracks have joined the first set. Pooh believes that this indicates that a second animal has joined the first. Piglet then joins the hunt, suggesting that the animal they are pursuing is a "woozle." When he and Pooh have completed another circuit of the spinney Pooh realizes that a new set of tracks has appeared. From this he concludes that a second type of animal has joined the woozles. At this point Piglet departs, frightened that they are tracking too many animals which may be of Hostile Intent. After Piglet's departure, Christopher Robin prompts Pooh to realize that he and Piglet have simply been tracking their own footprints. Academics who fail to verify the truth of the claims they repeat but instead accept them based on their repetition within the academic literature might thus transpire to be just as Foolish and Deluded as Pooh.

That this occurs can be seen from the fact that several examples of academic woozles have been documented.

In 1938, Clifford Dobell recorded the "death" of Dr. O. Uplavici, a Czech physician who had apparently published a well-cited paper on dysentery.[44] Dobell explained that "O. Uplavici" had never lived. He had been brought into existence as a result of a transcription error. In 1887, the physician Jaroslav Hlava wrote a paper on his research into dysentery in cats, entitled (in Czech) "O uplavici. Predbezne sdeleni" ("On Dysentery. Preliminary Communication"). A review of this work was then published in German. Hlava's name was omitted by error and the author given as "O. Uplavici." Since German is more widely read than Czech, subsequent references to Hlava's paper also erroneously attributed Hlava's work to the fictitious O. Uplavici—although in one case Dobell reports that *both* Hlava and Uplavici were mentioned.[45]

Two other woozles that involve misattributed authorship have arisen in the medical literature as a result of mistaking an author's degree for the name of another author. In a letter to *Nature*, Dennis A. Brunning noted that a paper by T. Ghose and S. P. Nigam has been erroneously cited by "several writers" as being by "Ghose, Path, and Nigam."[46] Brunning explains that the reason for this error was that Ghose's post-nominal letters "M.R.C. Path" (identifying him as a Member of the Royal College of Pathologists) appeared in the same font as his name and after his degrees ("MBBS, PhD"). This led them to be mistaken for a second co-author called "M.R.C. Path."[47] Subsequent to Brunning's letter, Ghose and Nigam's paper has been erroneously cited as also being authored by "Path" several times, most recently (in 2019) by Katia Maso, Antonella Grigoletto, Maria J. Vicent, and Gianfranco Pasut.[48] Spurred by Brunning's letter, Dorothy A. Lunt also wrote to *Nature* to note that Martin Rushton had published an article with his degree "M.A. Cantab" appended to his name.[49] She noted that this was mistaken for a co-author and the article was subsequently cited as being by "Rushton and Cantab."[50] Unfortunately Lunt's account of this is inaccurate for she did not check her source before writing to *Nature*. The degrees that were appended to Rushton's name were "M.B., B. Ch. Cantab., L.D.S. Eng" and *not* "M.A. Cantab."[51] Rushton's "M.B." was correctly attributed to him. However, his "B. Ch." from Cambridge University (Latinized as "Cantab.") was taken to be the initials of his spurious co-author "B. C. Cantab" to whom the degree "L. D.S. Eng." was (presumably) attributed. Since Lunt's letter, Rushton's paper has been cited as being by "M. H. Rushton and B. C. Cantab" several times, most recently by Kamichika Hayashi et al. in 2020.[52] Ironically, Lunt's false claim that Rushton's spurious co-author was "M. A. Cantab" has generated a small woozle of its own, with this claim being repeated in academic papers whose authors draw on Lunt's letter to impress on their readers the importance of accurate references.[53]

It is possible that the original error of taking Ghose's and Rushton's post-nominal letters for the names of co-authors has been repeated by each person who mis-attributes their work in this way. However, it is more likely that many of those who mis-cite them have never read their work and are merely parroting an earlier incorrect citation that they found in the work of someone else.[54] And it is also possible that *this* person also never read the original papers but similarly merely parroted their citation. Thus are woozles born.

But woozles are not limited to misattributed authorship. Two woozles associated with the cartoon character Popeye have been extensively documented by Mike Sutton. The first is that

> biochemists, nutrition experts and E. Segar, the creator of Popeye, were misled in the 1920s and 1930s by a misplaced decimal point in nineteenth century calculations of the amount of iron in spinach; or else by a misunderstanding of the meaning of nineteenth century findings of the percentage iron content of dried rather than fresh spinach.[55]

The second is that Segar chose spinach as the "source of Popeye's superhuman powers" because he erroneously believed that it was especially rich in iron.[56] Laura Martin and Geoffrey K. Pullum have documented the "scholarly sloppiness" behind the woozle that Eskimos have "hundreds of words for different grades and types of snow."[57] And Hallie Lieberman and Eric Schatzberg have identified as a woozle Rachel Maines' widely-repeated claim that "Victorian physicians routinely used electromechanical vibrators to stimulate female patients to orgasm as a treatment for hysteria."[58] And three major new woozles—all of which owe their origins to *Markets Without Limits*—are now taking hold in the debates over the moral limits of markets.[59] The first of these (rebutted in Chapter 1, and addressed further in Chapter 7) is that discussion of the Asymmetry Thesis is where "the action" is in these debates.[60] The second (rebutted in Chapters 2, 3, 4 and 5 and addressed further in Chapter 6) is that semiotic objections to markets are the most common anti-market objection in the literature on the morality of markets.[61] The last (which I will discuss in Chapter 9) is that in Madagascar the Merina people consider it appropriate for men to give their wives cash in exchange for sex.[62]

Since academic woozles owe their existence to poor scholarship, their propagation could be taken to be indicative of "scholarshit"—a failure on the part both of those who generate them and those who subsequently propagate them to have done their due diligence in verifying the claims that they repeat.[63] Ironically, the term "scholarshit" provides yet another example of a woozle. The origin of this term is often attributed to Herbert Marcuse but, as I noted above, a careful reading of his corpus provides no evidence that he ever used it.[64]

Academic Incentives, Market Norms, and Academic Excellence

A Note on Norms

The external incentives faced by academics not only motivate the taking of shortcuts that are likely to lead to inaccurate work. They also motivate the production of academic work in accord with the norms of the market. In the context of this discussion a norm identifies what type of behavior (or which particular behaviors) would be appropriate to perform in a particular situation. Characterizing norms in terms of appropriateness rather than obligation allows for the possibility that in certain situations more than one type of behavior could be appropriate. In contemporary American society, it would, for example, be appropriate for a store owner to ask a customer to reduce the number of items that he was buying if he was unable to afford all of them. The norms of the market would be appropriate in that situation and would permit her to do this. But it would also be appropriate for her to guide her actions in accord with the norms of charity and allow her customer to take more than he could pay for.

This way of characterizing norms also makes room for there to be intelligible discussion of market norms. As Anderson characterizes these, "they are impersonal, egoistic, exclusive, want-regarding, and orientated to 'exit' rather than 'voice'."[65] These would be the norms to which the acts of *homo economicus* would conform when he is motivated to act "by the prospect of future rewards."[66] It might seem strange to describe self-interested actions as conforming to norms for they are simply the product of the exercise of instrumental rationality. Indeed, as Jon Elster notes, the acts of *homo economicus* are sometimes *contrasted* with those of *homo sociologicus*—a being whose behavior *is* "dictated by social norms" (as these are, perhaps, properly understood—more on this below).[67] These points are well taken. But describing the self-interested behavior of *homo economicus* in terms of conformity to norms is a helpful way to frame the issue at hand. Framing the question of how persons should behave in certain situations (e.g., when conducting academic research) in terms of asking to which set of norms they should conform their behavior avoids the implication that the default setting for human behavior is that of rational self-interest and that this setting must (in certain situations) be reined in by social norms. While this characterization of human behavior might be accurate, it might not. It is possible, for example, that in certain situations persons tend to default to behave in accord with pro-social norms rather than those of the market.[68] Asking to which set(s) of norms persons' behavior should (or could) conform (e.g., those of the market, the polity, or a profession) in any given situation thus avoids pre-judging whether any set of norms is descriptively prior (in the sense of being a "default setting") to others.

The understanding of norms that is adopted here is considerably broader than that used in some other contexts. It includes, for example, not only what Cristina Bicchieri would term "descriptive norms" and "social norms," but also what she would refer to as "moral rules" and "custom."[69] If one wishes to retain the narrower denotation of the term "norm," nothing in the following discussion will be lost if one simply substitutes the phrase "guideline for appropriate behavior" for the term "norm."

Norms in Academia

As Anderson notes, the norms of the market "are impersonal, egoistic, exclusive, want-regarding, and orientated to 'exit' rather than 'voice'."[70] An academic whose primary concern is simply to publish as much and as good as possible to secure the external rewards associated with this will view publication primarily (if not exclusively) as a means to satisfy her own ends.[71] Her pursuit of her own interests indicates that she is motivated by the egoistic norms of the market. Since her goal is not to enhance either her own or others' understanding of her subject, she will conduct her research impersonally, without consideration for the intellectual goals of her fellow academics.[72] The rewards that she is aiming to secure through publication will be those governed by market norms, for they will be both exclusive and rivalrous. They will be exclusive insofar as their benefits (of, for example, a summer research bonus or a speaking honorarium) will be limited to her. They will be rivalrous insofar as her receipt of them reduces the amount of that good that is available to others: There is only so much money available to pay out summer bonuses or speaking honoraria.

The academic who has responded to the external incentives that she is faced with by embracing the norms of the market will also not care about the reasons that others have for publishing her work or engaging with it. She will have no preference about whether they use it to advance their understanding of the subject, cite it merely to demonstrate their familiarity with the current literature, or engage with it as she engages with the work of others—as a means to advance their own interests in securing the market-orientated goods.[73] As such, its accuracy or otherwise is immaterial to her. If it is inaccurate and misleads others (even to the extent of generating woozles), that is of no concern to her.

In contrast to the norms of the market, Anderson observes that "[e]xcellent performance in professional roles is judged by the standards of goods internal to the practice rather than by external criteria such as profitability."[74] It is plausible to hold, with Anderson, that the good internal to academic work is that of understanding.[75] (I will defend this view more fully in Chapter 9.) To aim at furthering understanding of a subject (both one's own understanding at that of others) is not the same as aiming to publish as much as one can in top venues. Indeed, for the reasons outlined above, it is likely that aiming to publish as much as one can in top venues will *conflict* with furthering understanding.

Furthering understanding of one's subject might require significant creativity. But it also requires that one understands the work of those who have previously addressed the subject at hand. This does not require that one master everything that has been written on it prior to one's own research. That would clearly be absurd. But it does require that at a minimum one actively engages with the work that has been done by those who are already prominent scholars in the subject—and that one does so with the aim of enhancing understanding of it. To this end, one should make sure that one understands the terminology that is used in the debate.[76] One should also take care to represent others' views accurately. To make it more likely that one will do so, one should address them in the context of their overall projects. This will reduce the possibility of inadvertent misrepresentation that might occur as a result of treating a passage or a work in isolation. One should also view one's academic work as part of a collaborative project that is being undertaken by those writing on the subject. This requires ensuring that one's citations are accurate to enable others to check one's work. It also requires that one provides citations to the work of others when one attributes views to them. And it requires the recognition that others' citations and their characterizations of the work they engage with might be inaccurate and so should be verified.

This painstaking *academic* approach to academic work will likely result in fewer publications than the adoption of a more market-orientated approach. But it will also likely increase the quality of the work produced. Work produced by academics who direct their actions in accord with academic norms is more likely to be exegetically accurate than the work of more market-orientated academics. This, in turn, will make it more likely that their criticisms of others' work will be sounder than those of their more market-orientated counterparts. They will thus be more likely than them to produce work that contributes to—rather than derails—the debates that they engage in.

Conclusion

One might conclude from the above discussion that the norms of the market should never govern academic research.[77] But this conclusion would be too hasty. To establish that this would be a legitimate restriction on the scope of market norms, one must establish that it would always be better were academic work always to be conducted in accord with academic, rather than market, norms. But this will not always be true. Indeed, as I will note in Chapter 9, it could, under certain circumstances, be *better* for academic research to be conducted in accord with market norms. But the circumstances in which this would be true are not those in which we currently find ourselves. In our circumstances it would be better were academic research to be governed primarily by the norms of the academy rather than the norms of the market. This, I argue, will help scholarship to prevail over scholarshit. It is to this issue that I now turn.

Notes

1 Orin S. Kerr, "A Theory of Law," *Green Bag* 16, 1 (2012), 111.
2 This is widely recognized. See, for example, Benjamin Davies and Giulia Felappi, "Publish or Perish," *Metaphilosophy* 48, 5 (2017), 745; Athanassios Pitsoulis and Jan Schnellenbach, "On Property Rights and Incentives in Academic Publishing," *Research Policy* 41, 8 (2012), 1441; Virginia Barbour, "Perverse Incentives and Perverse Publishing Practices," *Science Bulletin* 60, 14 (2015), 1225. The phrase "top venues" is owed to Jason Brennan and Peter M. Jaworski, *Markets Without Limits* (New York: Routledge, 2016), 227, note 3.
3 Jason Brennan and Phillip Magness, *Cracks in the Ivory Tower: The Moral Mess of Higher Education* (New York: Oxford University Press, 2019), 27.
4 I owe this phrase to R.G. Frey.
5 As David Lodge puts it:

> Morris was shown into a well-appointed suite on the second floor … He felt sure he was going to enjoy his stay here. Not the least of its attractions was that it was entirely free. All you had to do, to come and stay in this idyllic retreat, pampered by servants and lavishly provided with food and drink, given every facility for reflection and creation, was to apply. Of course, you had to be distinguished—by, for instance, having applied successfully for other, similar handouts, grants, fellowships, and so on, in the past. That was the beauty of academic life, as Morris saw it. To them that had had, more would be given.
>
> *(1984, 172)*

6 Brennan and Jaworski, *Markets Without Limits*, 227, note 3. Georgetown, of course, expects its "rock star researchers" to "hit the best presses" to earn their bonuses. Brennan and Magness, *Cracks in the Ivory Tower*, 26.
7 Brennan and Jaworski, *Markets Without Limits*, 227, note 3. Note that the adjective "good" in this context means one published in a top venue.
8 Nuria Bautista-Puig, Luis Moreno Lorente, and Elías Sanz-Casado, "Proposed Methodology for Measuring the Effectiveness of Policies Designed to Further Research," *Research Evaluation* (2020), 2–4.
9 Lotte Bøgh Andersen and Thomas Pallesen, "'Not Just for the Money?' How Financial Incentives Affect the Number of Publications at Danish Research Institutions," *International Public Management Journal* 11, 1 (2008), 34.
10 See, for example, Chiara Franzoni, Giuseppe Scellato, and Paula Stephan, "Changing Incentives to Publish," *Science* 333 (2011): 702–703.
11 Not all academics are primarily motivated by the possibility of securing such rewards. Some are primarily motivated by the desire to understand the issues that they address and view publication as a means by which they can secure feedback on their ideas from their peers. And others are content to enjoy the benefits of tenure without feeling the need to publish at all. Jason Brennan, for example, notes that some of his colleagues at Georgetown "haven't published any peer-reviewed research in a decade" and "aren't even *trying* to publish" (*Good Work if You Can Get It* [Baltimore, MD: Johns Hopkins University Press, 2020], 19). It is also likely that most academics engaged in research will have mixed motives for doing so; the academy is not neatly divided into careerists and scholars. With these observations in hand, two points are worth noting. First, the truth of the explanation for why good academics will do bad research that I outline in this chapter is independent of how widespread the careerist motivation is within the academy. However—and, second—I acknowledge that the *interest* that this explanation will hold for persons concerned with how the academy functions *will* depend on how widespread this careerist motivation is.

12 The time pressure that academics face in a competitive academic system is neatly outlined by Bruno S. Frey, "Publishing as Prostitution? – Choosing Between One's Own Ideas and Academic Success," *Public Choice* 116 (2003), 210.
13 That ambitious academics have a disincentive to spend time on teaching was made clear in the stark pronouncement of Yale that:

> [a]n insistence on excellent undergraduate teaching as a condition for tenure, without a rigorous adherence to scholarly criteria, could lead to a deterioration in Yale's scholarly contribution and hence its national and international stature as a university ... The Committee received a number of suggestions for the establishment of Teaching Professorships. It rejected these because it is convinced that original scholarly work is the surest proof of intellectual distinction and the surest guarantee that intellectual activity will not cease.
> *(Hexter, 1969, 61)*

14 For the sake of simplicity, I am holding the discipline and subfield that this idealized academic is working in constant. I thus ignore complications (e.g., the strategic switching of fields) that would result from the possibility that it is easier to publish in some disciplines (e.g., English) than it is in others (e.g., philosophy) as well as from the possibility that it is easier to publish in some sub-fields of a discipline (e.g., within philosophy, business ethics) than others (e.g., within philosophy, metaphysics).
15 Alas for me, given that this is one of the foci of this volume.
16 See Chapter 7, note 53. Of course, a careerist academic might not care if the secondary sources that she relies upon are accurate or not.
17 Kerr, "A Theory of Law," 111. Alas, as the following discussion of woozles shows, that a claim is "made up or false" is no bar to its appearance in the academic literature.
18 See, for example, my discussion in Chapter 5 of Brennan and Jaworski's mistaken attribution of semiotic essentialism to Archard.
19 See, for example, Chapter 9, note 19.
20 The quotation marks here are used merely to identify generic phrases that might be used by such an academic. For an example, see Jason Brennan: "Here is a common argument against vote selling: Your right to vote is inalienable, just as your rights to basic personal liberty or to free speech are inalienable. The right to vote is not like a property right to a guitar or house." Brennan provides no citations in support of this claim. *The Ethics of Voting* (Princeton, NJ: Princeton University Press, 2011), 137.
21 J. Angelo Corlett, "Ethical Issues in Journal Peer-Review," *Journal of Academic Ethics* 2 (2004), 362–363. The acronym "RTP" stands for "Retention, Tenure, Promotion."
22 Stanley Aronowitz, "The Unknown Herbert Marcuse," *Social Text* 58 (1999), 139.
23 Henry A. Giroux also attributed this term to Marcuse without citation. He too failed to respond to an inquiry as to where it appears in Marcuse's work. See note 64.
24 Yes, I did this. And it was just as tedious and time-consuming as you would imagine. But it bore fruit! See note 64.
25 The preference was noted in William Hubbard, "Inventing Norms," *Connecticut Law Review* 44, 2 (2011), 373.
26 Gerardo Patriotta, "Crafting Papers for Publication: Novelty and Convention in Academic Writing," *Journal of Management Studies* 54, 5 (2017), 748.
27 Brennan, *Good Work If You Can Get It*, 100. Brennan also advises that aspiring academics work on "big ideas" rather than on "routine, boring normal science" (ibid., 96). He advises this because such an approach is likely to result in "higher citation counts—which matters for tenure and promotion ... [and] means you're likelier to get paid speaking invitations or be able to turn your journal articles into a royalty-producing book" (ibid., 97). This advice is expressly aimed at encouraging a market-orientated approach to academic research.

28 Brian A. Nosek, Jeffrey R. Spies, and Matt Motyl, "Scientific Utopia: II: Restructuring Incentives and Practices to Promote Truth over Publishability," *Perspectives on Psychological Science* 7, 6 (2012), 616.
29 The lack of incentives that referees have for refereeing well also explains why even errors that could be identified without the need to consult secondary sources often go undetected. For evidence of this unfortunate state of affairs, see Magne Nylenna, Povl Riis, and Yngve Karlsson, "Multiple Blinded Reviews of the Same Two Manuscripts: Effects of Referee Characteristics and Publication Language," *The Journal of the American Medical Association* 272, 2 (1994): 149–151; Sara Schroter et al., "What Errors Do Peer Reviewers Detect, and Does Training Improve Their Ability to Detect Them?," *Journal of the Royal Society of Medicine* 101, 10 (2008): 507–514.
30 See M.V. Dougherty, *Correcting the Scholarly Record for Research Integrity in the Aftermath of Plagiarism* (Dordrecht: Springer, 2018) for cases of plagiarized articles, chapters, and even (almost) whole books that have been published in top venues. For discussions of academic hoaxes, see Alan Sokal, *Beyond the Hoax: Science, Philosophy and Culture* (New York: Oxford University Press, 2008), and Maria Hynes, Scott Sharpe, and Alastair Grieg "Appearing True in the Social Sciences: Reflections on an Academic Hoax," *Journal of Sociology* 48, 3 (2011): 287–303.
31 The degree to which errors will occur in academic work will depend in part on the degree to which academics are motivated by careerism. See note 11.
32 I provide examples of such errors below.
33 See, for example, Brennan and Jaworski's attribution of the anti-commodification position (i.e., the Asymmetry Thesis) to Ruth Grant, Robert Skidelsky, Benjamin Barber, and George Ritzer in *Markets Without Limits*, 7. (As I noted in Chapter 1, they attribute to these authors the anti-expansion criticism of markets, although it appears that they intended to attribute to them the Asymmetry Thesis. In any case, none of these authors endorse either the anti-expansion criticism of markets or the Asymmetry Thesis.) Brennan and Jaworski *do* include in their bibliography a reference to Barber's *Consumed* (New York: W. W. Norton and [sic] Company, 2008) but they include no references at all to Grant, Skidelsky, or Ritzer. But in *Consumed*, Barber does not argue for the Asymmetry Thesis. Instead, he argues that "many of our primary business, educational, and governmental institutions are consciously and purposefully engaged in infantilization and as a consequence … we are vulnerable to such associated practices as privatization and branding" (ibid., 12). Barber's objection is thus not to the sale of certain goods or services but to certain practices that he believes institutions engage in—in part, in pursuit of sales. There is also no reason to believe that Grant, Skidelsky, or Ritzer endorse the Asymmetry Thesis. While the absence of citations makes it impossible to determine in which works Brennan and Jaworski believe these authors defend this thesis, none defend it in their major works in which they criticize capitalism or market processes. Grant discusses the morality of using incentives (including financial incentives) to encourage persons to become medical research subjects and to motivate children to learn in *Strings Attached: Untangling the Ethics of Incentives* (Princeton, NJ: Princeton University Press, 2012), 94–101, 111–122. Although it is odd to think of motivating a child to learn by the use of incentives as purchasing a "service" from her, Grant could be understood as discussing whether it is ethically appropriate to exchange cash for these services. But in neither case does Grant endorse the Asymmetry Thesis. With respect to the use of incentives to encourage people to become research subjects, she writes that "incentives themselves are not the ethical problem here"; they only become problematic when they reinforce or exploit existing inequalities of power or are likely to harm the participant in certain ways (ibid., 98–99). She similarly notes that in certain circumstances "even cash payments" could be both efficacious and ethically appropriate as incentives to encourage children to pursue education (ibid., 121). Rather than endorsing the Asymmetry Thesis, then, in *Strings*

Attached, Grant agrees with Brennan and Jaworski that objections to paying research subjects and children to learn should be understood as objections to particular uses of such payments, rather than the use of payments itself (Brennan and Jaworski, *Markets Without Limits*, 35). Robert Skidelsky (writing with Edward Skidelsky) offers his most extended criticisms of markets in *In How Much Is Enough?: Money and the Good Life* (New York: Other Press, 2012). But rather than addressing which goods or services should be market-inalienable, they argue that capitalism in general should be reined in to enable persons to live the "good life" (ibid., 3). The closest that they come to addressing the question of whether certain goods or services should be free from commodification is the claim that capitalism "enlarges the sphere of monetary measurement and thus the ease" of directly comparing goods that were previously unpriced (ibid., 41). But this is a far cry from endorsing the Asymmetry Thesis—and in any case is closer to a Walzerian concern than to one that holds that certain goods and services should be inherently market-inalienable. (Note that Sidelsky's concern is also compatible with objecting to the legitimation of existing but illicit markets, and so he is not committed to the anti-expansion criticism, either.) Finally, Ritzer's concern in his major works on the "McDonaldization" of society is not primarily a critique of markets at all (although he does criticize the pursuit of profit for being partially responsible for the phenomenon he decries). Instead, he argues that the "rationalization" of American society ("which emphasizes *efficiency, predictability, calculability, substitution of non-human for human technology*, and *control over uncertainty*") is leading to people becoming dehumanized and disenchanted as well as to other negative effects, such as adverse health consequences. "The 'McDonaldization' of Society," *Journal of American Culture* 6, 1 (1983), 100, 106.

34 See, for example, my discussion in Chapter 5 of Brennan and Jaworski's attribution of essentialist semiotics to Walzer.
35 See, for example, Daniel Sperling's attribution to David Hillel-Rubin of the position that "a subject cannot have properties if she does not exist in reality." Sperling attributes this position to Hillel-Rubin on the basis of his writing that "if a property is true of some object at *t*, then surely the object of which the property is true at *t* must itself exist at *t*, just in order to display or exemplify that property at that time" (Daniel Sperling, *Posthumous Interests: Legal and Ethical Perspectives* [New York: Cambridge University Press, 2008], 31). Sperling here is quoting David Hillel-Rubin, *Action and Its Explanation* (New York: Oxford University Press, 2003), 11. But what Sperling fails to realize is that Hillel-Rubin is outlining a position that he *rejects*. Two sentences prior to the sentence quoted by Sperling, Hillel-Rubin writes "[t]he thought that generates the puzzle of posthumous predication seems to me to be deep and initially convincing, *even though finally wrong*" (ibid., 11; emphasis added).
36 See the examples I provide of this in James Stacey Taylor, "The Myth of Semiotic Arguments in Democratic Theory and How This Exposes Problems with Peer Review" (*International Journal of Applied Philosophy*, forthcoming).
37 See Chapter 4, note 72.
38 This observation is not original to me. See, for example, Edward F. Hartree, "Ethics for Authors: A Case History of Acrosin," *Perspectives in Biology and Medicine* 20, 1 (1976), 82. Hartree discusses the woozle that J. Yamane studied canine spermatozoa (ibid., 84–87).
39 For an overview of recent literature on politically motivated cognition, see Uwe Peters, "An Argument for Egalitarian Confirmation Bias and Against Political Diversity in Academia," *Synthese* (2020). Available at: https://link.springer.com/article/10.1007/s11229-020-02846-2
40 A claim could lend credence to an argument by helping to establish that it is an important one in the debate to which it is intended to contribute. For example, if one wishes to criticize or defend a particular view, one's argument would be strengthened

if one could cite sources that claim that the view in question is widely held or held by prominent participants in the debate. Alternatively, a claim could lend credence to an argument by providing empirical evidence in its support.
41 Or, worse, by merely citing the original source that the secondary source cited in support of the claim it repeated without either checking the original source or citing the secondary source in which the citation to the original was discovered. This type of citation could be termed "cut-out citation." For examples, see Chapter 7, note 53, and Chapter 9, note 19.
42 See the discussion of "The Woozle Effect" in Richard J. Gelles, "Violence in the Family: A Review of Research in the Seventies," *Journal of Marriage and Family* 42, 4 (1980), 880.
43 A. A. Milne, *Winnie-the-Pooh* (London: E. P. Dutton, 1926), Chapter 3.
44 While this is a woozle since its propagation was owed to a translation error, its propagation is more understandable than that of the other woozles discussed below, especially since Czech was not as widely spoken as other languages in the late nineteenth and early twentieth centuries. This does not, though, excuse George Dunea's description of Czech as being "plain gibberish to the rest of the world"—although that date on which this article was published—and its general tone—might! "Uplavici Syndrome," *British Medical Journal* 1 (April 1, 1978), 846.
45 Clifford Dobell, "Dr O. Uplavici (1887–1938)," *Parasitology* 30 (1938): 239–241.
46 Dennis A. Brunning, "Beware the Ghost Writer," *Nature* 252, December 6 (1974): 437. The paper referred to by Brunning was T. Ghose and S.P. Nigam, "Antibody as a Carrier of Chlorambucil," *Cancer* 29, 5 (1972): 1398–1400.
47 Although Brunning provides no citation to any of the "several writers" who mis-cited Ghose and Nigam, it seems that he was referring to Christian de Duve, Thierry de Barsy, Brian Poole, Andre Trouet, Paul Tulkens, and François van Hoof, "Lysosomotropic Agents," *Biochemical Pharmacology* 23, 18 (1974), 2531, reference 155.
48 Katia Maso, Antonella Grigoletto, Maria J. Vicent, and Gianfranco Pasut, "Molecular Platforms for Targeted Drug Delivery," *International Review of Cell and Molecular Biology* (2019), 41. doi:10.1016/bs.ircmb.2019.03.001.
49 Dorothy A. Lunt, "Ghost Authors," *Nature* 252, December 20/27 (1974): 629. Although Lunt does not cite Rushton's paper, it is Martin A. Rushton, "Solitary Bone Cysts in the Mandible," *British Dental Journal* 81, 2 (1946): 37–49.
50 It seems that the first time this was done was by Kurt H. Thoma, "Case Report of a So-Called Latent Bone Cyst," *Oral Surgery, Oral Medicine, Oral Pathology* 8, 9 (1955), 966. Its authorship was cited as "Rushton and Cantab" (referred to as "their paper" by Thoma, at a time when this was used only in its plural form; ibid., 963). Thoma was a Professor Emeritus at Harvard and might not have been familiar with the English degree system. This error was then repeated by Eli Olech and Balraj K. Arora, "Lingual Mandibular Bone Cavity," *Oral Surgery, Oral Medicine, Oral Pathology* 14, 11 (1961), 1361, 1364, 1366.
51 Rushton, "Solitary Bone Cysts in the Mandible," 37.
52 Kamichika Hayashi, Takeshi Onda, Takahiro Iwasaki, Mitsuru Takata, Kiyotaka Mori, Hiroyuki Matsuda, Shinya Watanabe, Hidetoshi Tamura, Takahiko Shibahara, and Masayuki Takano, "A Case of a Stafne Bone Defect Associated with Sublingual Glands in the Lingual Side of the Mandible," *Case Studies in Dentistry* (December 18, 2020), 3, 4. Available at: https://doi.org/10.1155/2020/8851174.
53 See, for example, Hartree, "Ethics for Authors," 83, and James H. Sweetland, "Errors in Bibliographic Citations: A Continuing Problem," *The Library Quarterly* 59, 4 (1989), 294.
54 Olech and Arora, for example, referred to Thoma's paper immediately after referring to "Rushton and Cantab" and their account of the work of "Rushton and Cantab" followed closely the account that had been given by Thoma. It is thus likely that Olech and Arora never read Rushton's original paper.

55 Mike Sutton, "SPINACH, IRON and POPEYE: Ironic Lessons from Biochemistry and History on the Importance of Healthy Eating, Healthy Scepticism and Adequate Citation," *Internet Journal of Criminology* (2010), 3. Available at: https://botanologia.gr/wp-content/uploads/2020/02/spinach.pdf.
56 Ibid., 14. Segar chose spinach because he believed that it was a good source of Vitamin A. See also Ole Bjørn Rekda, "Academic Urban Legends," *Social Studies of Science* 44, 4 (2014): 638–654. I thank Neil Levy for reminding me about this paper!
57 Laura Martin, "'Eskimo Words for Snow': A Case Study in the Genesis and Decay of an Anthropological Example," *American Anthropologist* 88, 2 (1986): 418–423. Geoffrey K. Pullum, "The Great Eskimo Vocabulary Hoax," *Natural Language and Linguistic Theory* 7 (1989), 276, 275. For more recent discussion of this and related issues, see Willem J. de Reuse, "Primitivism in Hunter and Gatherer Languages: The Case of Eskimo Words for Snow," in Tom Guldemann, Patrick McConvell, and Richard A. Rhodes (Eds.), *The Language of Hunter-Gatherers* (Cambridge: Cambridge University Press, 2020): 523–551; Igor Krupnik and Ludger Müller-Wille, "Franz Boas and Inuktitut Terminology for Ice and Snow: From the Emergence of the Field to the 'Great Eskimo Vocabulary Hoax'," in Igor Krupnik, Claudio Aporta, Shari Gearhead, Gita Laidler, and Lene Kielsen Holm (Eds.), *SIKU: Knowing Our Ice: Documenting Inuit Sea Ice Knowledge and Use* (Dordrecht: Springer, 2010), 377–400, and Piotr Cichocki and Marcin Kilarski. "On 'Eskimo Words for Snow': The Life Cycle of Linguistic Misconception," *Historiographia Linguistica* XXXVII, 3 (2010): 341–377.
58 Hallie Lieberman and Eric Schatzberg, "A Failure of Academic Quality Control: *The Technology of Orgasm*," *Journal of Positive Sexuality* 4, 2 (2018), 24; Rachel Maines, *The Technology of Orgasm: "Hysteria," the Vibrator, and Women's Sexual Satisfaction* (Baltimore, MD: Johns Hopkins University Press. 1999).
59 These are in addition to the minor woozle of the misquotation of Hayek, discussed in Chapter 9, note 19.
60 See the Introduction to this volume, note 1, and Chapter 1, note 2.
61 See Chapter 6, note 2, for examples of persons who have accepted and propagated this woozle.
62 Brennan and Jaworski, *Markets Without Limits*, 65. In fairness to Brennan and Jaworski, this is perhaps only a medium-sized woozle; of more import than a misquotation, but not serious enough to derail a debate.
63 Such failures of verification can occur even when the claim that goes unverified is obviously erroneous. See, for example, Joan Stevens' discussion of the erroneous substitution of "snowstorm" for "thunderstorm" in a 1900 printing of Charlotte Brontë's letter to Mary Taylor of 4th September 1848. In this letter, Brontë referred to the weather conditions that she experienced in Yorkshire in *July*—a month not known for its snowstorms! "Woozles in Brontëland: A Cautionary Tale," *Studies in Bibliography* 24 (1971), 101–102.
64 The origin of this term is attributed to Marcuse by, for example, Tara Star Johnson and sj Miller, "Honoring Our History, Envisioning Our Future," *English Education* 48, 1 (2015), 9. Johnson and Miller cite Henry A. Giroux, *Impure Acts: The Practical Politics of Cultural Studies* (New York: Routledge, 2000), 14, as their source for this claim, but Giroux provides no citation to support his attribution of this term to Marcuse. sj Miller repeats the claim that Marcuse coined this term in "Ubuntu: Calling *in* the Field," *English Education* 48, 3 (2016), 192 (this time with no citation). This claim is also repeated by Daniel Albino Airasca, "La igualdad como punto de partida," *Praxis Pedagógica* (2018), 135 (again with no citation). The first time this term was attributed to Marcuse was Stanley Aronowitz, "The Unknown Herbert Marcuse," *Social Text* 58 (1999), 139—again, with no citation to any of Marcuse's work to support this claim. I have contacted both Henry Giroux and Stanley Aronowitz asking for the origin of this term in Marcuse's work but have received no response. It appears that Aronowitz is

responsible for starting this woozle. The earliest printed use of this term that I could find is in an anonymous letter to *Folklore Forum* in 1971 (Anonymous, "Letter," *Folklore Forum* 4, 5 (1971), 127). I thank Ben Bridges, the Editor-in-Chief of *Folklore Forum*, for his archival work that enabled me to identify this letter.

65 Elizabeth Anderson, *Value in Ethics and Economics* (Cambridge, MA: Harvard University Press, 1993), 145.

66 Jon Elster, *The Cement of Society: A Study of Social Order* (New York: Cambridge University Press, 1989), 97.

67 Ibid., 97.

68 It is also possible that it would be better were they to behave more in accord with market norms in those situations.

69 Cristina Bicchieri, *Norms in the Wild: How to Diagnose, Measure, and Change Social Norms* (New York: Oxford University Press, 2017), 41.

70 Anderson, *Value in Ethics and Economics*, 145.

71 See note 27.

72 The norm of impersonality is appropriate in some academic settings. As Barry Maguire and Brookes Brown note, the process of peer review is supposed to be impersonal. "Markets, Interpersonal Practices, and Signal Distortion," *Philosophers' Imprint* 19 (2019), 12.

73 As well as drawing on these four market norms to direct her research, the truly market-orientated academic will also eschew using her voice in faculty governance. Rather than spending time on academic politics to improve her current institution of employment—which she would view as a distraction from the pursuit of publication—she would draw on her publication record to threaten exit if the working conditions that it offered her were not to her satisfaction.

74 Anderson, *Value in Ethics and Economics*, 147.

75 Ibid., 147.

76 Hence my clarification, above, of how the term "norm" is being used here. See the discussion (in Chapter 4) of Brennan and Jaworski's misunderstanding of how Anderson uses the term "commodification."

77 To claim that academic research should not be governed by the norms of the market is not to claim that the spheres of the academy and the market should be completely segregated; it is not counter to the norms of the academy that academics sell their services. (See Anderson, *Value in Ethics and Economics*, 147–150.) Note too that to claim that academic research should not be governed by the norms of the market is not to claim that academic research should never lead to external rewards, just as to claim that sex should not be bought and sold according to the norms of the market is not to claim that it should never be exchanged for money (ibid., 156; see also Russell Keat, "Market Limits and Their Limits," *Economics and Philosophy* 28, 2 [2012], 156).

9
MARKET NORMS AND ACADEMIC NORMS

Introduction

In Chapter 8, I argued that academics have significant external incentives to publish as much as they can in top venues. I also argued that they thus have considerable incentives to take scholarly short-cuts to increase their publication rates. Checking references, for example, is time-consuming.[1] Since checking references will increase the time that it takes to complete an academic work, academics have an incentive to skimp on this. They similarly have an incentive not to spend much time on making sure that their characterizations of the work of others is accurate—an incentive that is compounded if they have access to a published secondary source that (they might believe) outlines the work they wish to address.[2] I argued that if academics respond to these incentives,, it is likely that their work will provide a distorted account of the issues that it addresses owing to the exegetical inaccuracy of its foundation. The process of peer review is unlikely to correct these adverse effects of producing academic work in accord with market norms. Referees will face the same external incentives as authors, for they, too, are judged by their publication rates and not by the quality of their academic gatekeeping. The effects of having academic work guided by market norms are thus likely to be baleful.

Since this is so, I will argue in this chapter that academic research as it is practiced today should *not* primarily be directed by the norms of the market. I will argue that the purpose of academic research lies in its potential for furthering understanding. This will be more likely achieved if academic researchers direct their efforts to this end rather than seeing their research as being of mainly instrumental value as a means to secure their own professional success, where this success is judged by the standards of the market. I will begin by outlining some

DOI: 10.4324/9781003251996-13

responses that could be offered by defenders of market norms to the concern that their use in the academy would be likely to lead to error. (In brief, these responses will note that these errors will be relatively harmless, and that any harm that they might lead to would likely be outweighed by the benefits that they could provide to market-orientated academic researchers.) I will argue that these responses are only plausible if one accepts a view of academia in which its primary purpose is as a system for providing extrinsic benefits to academics. I will argue that this view of the primary purpose of academic research is self-defeating. I then argue in favor of (largely) replacing the norms of the market with the norms of the academy. In Chapter 10, I will suggest how this could be achieved.

A Clarification: Markets Norms as Academic Admixture

Before continuing, I should clarify that I will argue that academic research *as it is currently practiced* should not *primarily* be directed in accord with the norms of the market. My argument is *not* that market norms are inherently inappropriate to direct academic research. (Indeed, I will argue below that market incentives could be harnessed to further the adoption of academic norms. Like Anderson, I believe that there are significant advantages to be gained from the partial commodification of the academy.[3]) Nor do I argue that academic research cannot excel if it is not conducted in accord with academic norms. Instead, my argument is merely that given the (contingent) beliefs and desires of *current* academics, academic research conducted in accord with market norms will be more prone to error than that conducted in accord with the norms of the academy. Since this is so, academic research should not be primarily driven by the norms of the market.

To see that academic research could excel even when guided by the norms of the market, consider again the Alternative America of Chapter 3. Assume that in Alternative America published academic research is the most desirable form of entertainment and accordingly commands high prices. Academic books are regularly best-sellers and academic journals are sold at supermarket check-out lines instead of magazines featuring celebrity gossip. It is widely accepted in Alternative America that the primary aim of academic research is and should be to make money for academic researchers. Academic research is expressly a commodity and academics direct their research in accord with market norms. There is nothing in the nature of academic research that precludes the research conducted in Alternative America from being genuine academic research. (Unlike, for example, sex, academic research is not one of those goods whose nature is partially constituted by the reasons that guide its production or distribution.[4]) Indeed, depending on the type of academic research that was desired in Alternative America, one who believes that (in Actual America) academic research should not be conducted in accord with market norms might even praise the academics of Alternative America for the excellence of their research. This would be the case if the consumers in Alternative America had strong desires for exegetical accuracy and were willing to pay significant premiums for this. The market-led producers of academic research in Alternative America would thus have an incentive to take the time to make sure that their work was accurate. They would accordingly produce fewer but more accurate publications rather than publications that were more numerous but less accurate.

Alas, we are not in Alternative America. My arguments thus apply to academia as it is currently practiced, taking academics as they are and not as we might wish them to be. But even when applied to academic research as it is conducted in Actual America (or Actual Academia in general), I do not claim that academic research should never be conducted in accord with market norms. It is possible that understanding would be best furthered were academic research to be conducted in accord with some mix of market and academic norms. If academics were to work in accord with such a mix of norms, it is likely that more academic research would be produced than would be produced if they were only to work in accord with academic norms, with the accuracy of this work being checked (both pre- and post-publication) in accord with the norms of the academy. However, it is likely that if market norms were to dominate the production of academic research, its overall quality would suffer owing to the tendency of work produced in this way (in Actual Academia) to be inaccurate. Academic research should thus be guided primarily (but not necessarily exclusively) by the norms of the academy.[5] The norms of the market should not be allowed to dominate the academic realm.

A Market-Based Defense of the Status Quo

Even though the effects of allowing market norms to guide academic research appear baleful, it is not obvious that any attempt should be made to change the status quo. The likely adverse effects of errors in some disciplines (or sub-fields) will be greater than errors in others. Errors in disciplines (or sub-fields) that are likely to have influence outside the academy would be of more concern to persons than errors in disciplines whose influence is largely relegated to the ivory tower. Errors in medical journals, for example, will be more likely to have adverse effects than errors in philosophy journals. (False claims about vaccinations, for example, are more likely to lead to harm than are false claims about vagueness.) And within those disciplines where published work could be expected to have an influence outside the academy, not all errors are equally problematic. Errors in references (e.g., spelling authors' names incorrectly, or providing erroneous page references) can be expected to have less adverse effects than certain factual errors (e.g., publishing LD50 levels of substance toxicity that are lower than the actual levels).[6] When a published claim could lead to adverse effects if it were acted upon, those who would act upon it have an incentive either to verify it themselves or else to encourage others to verify it for them. The likelihood that such verification would take place will depend on the combination of how significant the adverse effects were expected to be, together with the likelihood of their expected occurrence. In approaching academic work in this way, its consumers accept the principle of *caveat emptor* and respond to it just as they would any other product whose use had the potential to harm.

This response exemplifies the acceptance of market norms. It treats the relationship between the producers of academic work and its consumers as an impersonal one with each treating the other "as merely a means to the satisfaction of ends defined independently of the relationship and of the other party's ends."[7] As such, both the producers and consumers of academic work will behave egoistically, seeking to satisfy their own desires in their respective production and consumption of the work. And if a prospective consumer of academic work believes that she has incentive not to accept its recommendations, she could simply fail to do so, exercising her right to exit rather than believing that she has a duty to correct what she believes to be error.[8] Thus, while the adoption of market norms by the producers of academic work might lead to subpar research, the adverse effects of this would be mitigated by its consumers similarly adopting market norms to guide their behavior. Moreover, since the adoption of market norms by academics would be likely to increase the production of academic work while mitigating the adverse effects of its production under their direction, this should be encouraged rather than decried.

This is an elegant argument. But it should be noted that the operation of market norms will not be expected to mitigate all the errors that their adoption to direct academic research is expected to generate. Instead, they will only be expected to mitigate the costs of accepting erroneous claims made by researchers when the expected costs of consuming such claims will outweigh those of verifying them. False claims that, if accepted, would impose little cost would remain. This cost is assumed to be acceptable given the likely increase in the amount of academic work that would be produced if the norms of the market were widely accepted by its academic researchers. The method by which costs and benefits are being assessed in this argument is thus itself implicitly directed by the norms of the market. The value of information (and the disvalue of misinformation) are determined by the effective demand for them.[9] Whether one accepts the soundness of this argument defending the use of market norms in academic research will thus depend (in part) on whether one already accepts the appropriateness of market norms to evaluate academic research. This defense thus begs the question in favor of this use of those norms.

Academic Errors and a Defense of Market Norms

At this point one might expect someone who believes that academic research should be primarily (if not exclusively) governed by market norms to develop an alternative defense of this practice to respond to the criticism that academic research that has been produced in accord with the norms of the market is likely to contain more exegetical and factual errors than that which is produced in accord with the norms of the academy. But this might not occur. Instead, the defender of market norms might simply transfer the burden of proof back to her critics by asking: "So what?"

Reference Errors

This burden-shifting defense of the use of market norms to guide academic research is most plausible when applied to errors in academic references. A reference to a published article might, for example, misspell the author's name,[10] attribute incorrect initials to an author, get the name of the journal the article was published in wrong, provide a mistaken volume or issue number, or get the page numbers of the article wrong. They might get the year that the article was published wrong, or (in the case of books) provide the name of the wrong publisher. References might be "Frankenstein's monster" references with bibliographic information for two published works being combined in one reference. Such "Frankenstein" references might provide the title of one work by an author with the page numbers of another of her works.[11] Or they might combine the titles of two works by different authors into one.[12]

Such errors are to be expected if academics attempt to increase their publication rates by reducing the time that they spend checking their references so that they can focus on work that they expect to be more likely to result in publication. Persons concerned with these reference errors assert that they are problematic because they make it more difficult to find the sources that are cited. This, they claim, makes it more difficult for readers to check that the author has reported the views or information contained within them accurately. They also assert that readers who identify these errors are less likely to trust the work in which they occur.

But the defenders of the use of market norms to guide academic research have ready responses to these charges. First, these are empirical claims and so before being accepted, they should be supported by empirical evidence—and they are frequently offered without this. With respect to the first of these claims, it is plausible that incorrect references would make it more difficult for a reader to identify the work referred to and hence more difficult for her to verify that the author's account of it was correct. But this increase in difficulty is likely to be marginal. Even in "Frankenstein's monster" cases, correct references can often be readily identified with online search engines. And, in any case, given that academics have incentives *not* to check references, any possible increase in cost associated with this would likely be moot. With respect to the second of these claims, no evidence is provided for the claim that readers would be less likely to trust an author's work if they found mistakes such as these in her references. Worse, this claim is implausible on its face. In data-driven fields (such as medicine, marine biology, and veterinary science), it is unlikely that reference errors of the sort outlined above will lead a reader to call into question the legitimacy of the data that is being presented.[13] And in fields that are argument-driven (such as philosophy), a reader's assessment of the author's arguments will be unaffected by the knowledge that some of her references are erroneous. One concerned with reference errors might reply that if a reader recognizes that an author's references have *widespread* problems, her trust in his work would be undermined. She would infer that he has been similarly careless in recording or reporting his data or in representing the views of those that he engages with. But, the defender of market norms might respond, in this case the reference errors would signal that the work should not be trusted—and someone concerned with accuracy of academic exegesis should *welcome* such a signal rather than attempt to mute it.

Substantial Errors and Market Norms

The "So what?" defense of the use of market norms as the primary guide to direct academic research has considerable intuitive force when applied to the claim that this approach is likely to lead to an increase in reference errors. But poor scholarship manifests itself in more substantive ways than errors in references. It could lead the attribution of views to persons that they expressly deny endorsing.[14] It could also lead to factual errors and quotation errors (both in the form of fabricated quotations and in the less-worrisome form of simple misquotation).[15] Examples of such errors abound in the literature on the moral limits of markets. And since these are considerably more serious than mere reference errors, they cannot be so readily dismissed as inconsequential by the defenders of the use of market norms to direct academic research.

Since I have already outlined in this volume several examples of authors misrepresenting the views of others by attributing to them positions that they have explicitly disavowed, I will focus here on examples of the other two types of poor scholarship.

Factual Errors

I will begin with examples of factual errors. In his discussion of the concept of exploitation, Alan Wertheimer drew on the case of the *Port Caledonia* and the *Anna*. In this case a drifting vessel (*Port Caledonia*) required the aid of a tug. The tug agreed to aid—but only for an exceptionally high price. In his discussion, Wertheimer identified the tug as the *Anna*.[16] But this was incorrect. The *Anna* was the vessel that the *Port Caledonia* was in danger of fouling; the tug was the *Sarah Jolliffe*.[17] Similarly, in discussing the merits of economic inequality, Yew-Kwang Ng asserted that

> when the Rubik's cube was first available in the market around 1980, a cube was selling for many hundreds of US dollars at present prices. The price fell

very rapidly over the years and has cost less than a dollar for the past two decades or so.[18]

Ng was attempting to illustrate the point that inequality of wealth could work to the benefit of the poor. The rich would be the first to purchase new consumer items when they are expensive. The profits secured from their purchasers could then be reinvested to enable the manufacturers to discover how to make the items more cheaply and hence make them more available to the poor.[19] But it is not true that the Rubik's Cube initially cost "many hundreds of dollars at present prices." Nor is it true that such cubes "cost less than a dollar for the past two decades or so." The Rubik's Cube debuted in the United States at $1.99—roughly $3.40 "at present prices."[20] And Rubik's Cubes similar to the original now (in 2021) sell for $9.99.[21]

One of Brennan and Jaworski's much-cited empirical examples also appears to be based on a factual error—one that has now become a woozle.[22] Brennan and Jaworski claim that the Merina people of Madagascar have a "practice of men paying their wives for sex."[23] They claim that, among the Merina, a failure to give cash after sex would be seen as disrespectful.[24] They hold that the "Merina do distinguish between marital relationships and prostitution, and they do not believe cash exchanges for sex treat wives like prostitutes."[25] For the Merina, claim Brennan and Jaworski, "the thing that separates wives from prostitutes is *not* the exchange of money for sex, but whether the relationship is formal or informal, loving or impersonal, serious or casual."[26] They use this example to support their (correct) claim that how money is used can have different meanings in different cultures and so there is no "logically essential meaning" associated with its use.[27] (This is the crux of their objection to what they take to be semiotic objections to markets.) But Merina men do *not* pay their wives for sex, as Brennan and Jaworski claim.[28]

Brennan and Jaworski claim that Merina men buy sex from their wives to express respect for them.[29] But the sociological and anthropological work that they cite in support of their attribution of this practice to the Merina does not support their view that this is a Merina practice. Brennan and Jaworski cite the work of the sociologist Viviana A. Zelizer to support their claim that the Merina consider the exchange of money for sex to be required of men to express respect for their wives. They write that "[f]or Zelizer, the Merina men are in a sense buying sex, but they do so in order to express respect for their wives."[30] But Zelizer makes neither of these claims. Her *sole* reference to the Merina consists of the observation that among them "modern money often circulates as a legitimate personal or ritual gift."[31] She makes no reference to Merina men buying sex from their wives, nor does she claim that they do so to express respect for them.

The misattribution to Zelizer of the view that Merina men buy sex from their wives to express respect for them is not the only way in which Brennan and Jaworski misuse their sources. After wrongly ascribing this view to Zelizer, they go on to explain that the (putative) Merina practice of men paying their wives for sex is not "just an expression of patriarchy."[32] "On the contrary," they claim, the work of Gillian Feeley-Harnik (as summarized by the sociologist Kirsten Stoebenau) portrays

> [certain Madagascan] sexual relations as open and easy: a young man will propose to have sex with a young woman who, if interested, allows the man into her home/living quarters. Traditionally, the man will place a small amount of money under the pillow to show respect to her for giving the power of her body (as representation of fertility) to him.[33]

But (as Stoebenau notes) Feeley-Harnik is not writing here of the Merina's sexual practices but those of the Sakalava, a group from the coastal northwest of Madagascar.[34] Stoebenau notes that the practice of leaving money after sex also occurs among the Betsimisaraka on the east coast of Madagascar and the Tandroy of the southern (coastal) region of Androy, Madagascar.[35] She makes no mention of this being a Merina practice. Her work thus does not support the claim that *Merina* men engage in this practice.[36] Moreover, Stoebenau provides reason to *doubt* that this is a Merina practice. She notes that in Madagascar the elite urban Merina distinguish between the people of the central highland plateau (the Merina and the Betsileo) and the *côtiers*, the people of the coast.[37] From her conversations with elite urban Merina, she learned that they consider ideal Merina women to be "chaste and prudish" when compared with *côtier* women and that those who "allow or encourage their young women to engage in sexual activity at their leisure" are met with disapprobation.[38] The Sakalava, the Betsimisaraka, and the Tandroy are all coastal people—*côtiers*, in the terminology of the urban elite Merina. Stoebenau's summary of Feeley-Harnik's claims concerning the sexual mores of the Sakalava thus refers to a group whose sexual customs *differ* from the Merina. Thus, while leaving gifts of money after sex might be a *Madagascan* custom, it is not clearly one practiced by the Merina.[39]

Similar points can be made with respect to the other sources that Brennan and Jaworski cite in support of their attribution of this practice to the Merina. Brennan and Jaworski support their attribution of this practice to the Merina by citing the anthropologists Bruce G. Carruthers and Laura Ariovich.[40] Carruthers and Ariovich, in turn, cite Maurice Bloch as the source of their claims.[41] But Bloch does not expressly claim that a man's leaving money after sex is a *Merina* practice. Instead, he writes:

> [i]n Europe the linking of monetary exchange and sexual or familial exchange is seen as either typically immoral or as a source of humour and dissonance. By contrast, *in Madagascar* the need to keep the two areas separate is not present. The right thing for a man to do is to give his lover a present of money or goods after sexual intercourse. This applies not only to pre-

marital or extra-marital sex, but also to marital relations, though on a less regular basis.[42]

There is nothing in Bloch's discussion that commits him to the claim that post-coital gifts of money are common among the *Merina*, only that they are not unusual in *Madagascar*. One might respond on Brennan and Jaworski's behalf that since what Bloch claims here occurs in the context of his discussion of the Merina understanding of money, it is reasonable to assume that he was writing of the Merina. This is a fair point. But it is notable that in his discussion of this custom he referred to it as a *Madagascan* custom while in the rest of this discussion in this paper he referred more precisely to *Merina* practices.[43]

This reply to the above response that was offered above on Brennan and Jaworski's behalf places a lot of weight on Bloch's use of a general rather than a more specific term—weight that his use of this terminological distinction might not be able to bear. To clarify Bloch's views on specifically Merina practices, it would thus be sensible to engage with his work beyond that which was cited by Carruthers and Ariovich (and which was, in turn, cited by Brennan and Jaworski). In his New Foreword to the 1990 English version of Octave Mannoni's *Psychologie de la Colonisation*, Bloch observes that Merina people who stand in egalitarian relationships continually demand small presents from each other, "such as tobacco or food."[44] By contrast, they consider unsolicited gifts to be indicative of a hierarchical relationship.[45] Bloch notes that such demands for gifts occur continually between Merina of equal status. If they were to cease, then the relationship would change from one of solidarity between equals to a hierarchical relationship between a superior and an inferior.[46] Against this background it is conceivable that a Merina woman might demand a small gift after sex.[47] It is also conceivable that this demand might be satisfied by a gift of money (although it could also be satisfied by something else, "such as tobacco or food"). But in the context of this Merina practice, that this demand came *after sex* would be merely incidental. It would simply be a token of a type of demand that both parties understood should be made frequently—*and hence at any time*—between people of equal status. (Accepting that such monetary gifts might be bestowed by Merina men after sex is thus not to assimilate this practice to the outwardly similar practice of the Sakalava.) A Merina man's bestowal of a small gift of money to his wife after sex in response to her post-coital demand for a present should thus not be understood as him "buying sex," as Brennan and Jaworski claim.[48] Instead, in the context of Merina practice, it would be better understood as his continuing a relationship of equality with his wife in a way that was both "the right thing to do" and *entirely independent* of their having just had sex.[49]

None of the sociological and anthropological work that Brennan and Jaworski cite in support of their claim that Merina men pay their wives for sex supports their view that this is a Merina practice. But before moving to provide examples of other types of substantive errors that have occurred in academic work, three important points relevant to the discussion of the moral limits of markets should be made concerning their claim that this is a Merina practice. First, while Brennan and Jaworski might have mistakenly identified the Madagascan practice of men giving money to their sexual partners as a Merina custom, the sociological and anthropological work that they cite does support the claim that men of *other* Madagascan groups (e.g., the Sakalava, the Betsimisaraka, and the Tandroy) might bestow gifts of money on their sexual partners without implying that the relationship between them is one of prostitution.[50] However—and, second—this practice does *not* entail that these men are thereby engaging in "cash exchanges for sex" as Brennan and Jaworski claim.[51] While Feeley-Harnik notes that (e.g.) Sakalava men are expected to give women money to express their desire for them and persuade them to have sex, this does not establish that the participants in this practice consider their interaction to involve the exchange of money for sex.[52] Consider an analogy: In American heterosexual dating, the man traditionally pays for the activities the couple engages in during the date. But the couple does not (typically) understand their date as one in which the man is exchanging the goods of these activities for his partner's company or her sexual favors.[53] Indeed, in holding that a flow of goods from B to A that is consequent to a temporally proximate flow of goods from A to B *must* be understood as an exchange between trading partners, Brennan and Jaworski have overlooked the very point that their discussion of Madagascan sexual mores is intended to make:[54] That "the nature of an action, its meaning, is simply the conventional understanding of it" and so persons might not "conceive of these kinds of choices as 'trades'."[55] Thus, while Brennan and Jaworski are correct to draw on sociological and anthropological work to ensure that their philosophical claims are empirically grounded in their discussion of them, they should not substitute their understanding of the practices they consider for that which is held by their participants.[56]

Finally, note that even if we accept (as we should not) that the (e.g.) Sakalava practice of a man bestowing a gift of money on his sexual partners is to be understood in transactional terms, nothing of import for the debates over the moral limits of markets follows. To be sure, this observation does establish what Brennan and Jaworski want it to establish: That exchanges of goods and services for money have no essential meaning, and so the exchange of (e.g.) sex for money could occur without this being accompanied by "whatever deplorable or amoral attitudes some anti-commodification theorists want to say are essential to markets."[57] But (as I noted in Chapters 3–5), the critics of markets whose work Brennan and Jaworski address do not deny either of these claims. None believe that the act of exchanging goods or services for money (or the goods or services thus exchanged) has an essential meaning, and none believe that the exchange of (e.g.) sex for money must be accompanied by "deplorable or amoral attitudes."[58] Thus, even if Brennan and Jaworski were correct to claim that Merina men pay their wives for sex (and they are not), this would contribute nothing to the debate over the moral limits of markets.

Quotation Errors

Examples of both types of quotation errors noted above (fabricated quotations and simple misquotation) can be found in Brennan and Jaworski's work.[59] In discussing Anderson's views of surrogacy, they write that she worries that commercial surrogacy arrangements communicate the view that women are merely "incubation machines," citing her "Is Women's Labor a Commodity?," in support.[60] But Anderson makes no mention of women as "incubation machines" in that article—nor does she use this term anywhere else in her work. This quotation appears to be fabricated.[61] Similarly, they assert that Satz "refers to those markets that generate 'extreme revulsion' as noxious markets."[62] But the phrase "extreme revulsion" does not appear in Satz's work. (She thus does not use it as a hallmark of "noxious markets" as Brennan and Jaworski claim.) Instead, Satz writes that certain markets "strike many people as noxious, toxic to important human values. These markets evoke widespread discomfort, and, in the extreme, revulsion."[63] Rather than "extreme revulsion" being, for Satz, a hallmark of "noxious markets," it would be more accurate to hold that she views markets that "evoke widespread discomfort" as being "noxious." And of these, only some (presumably, those regarded as being the most noxious) would evoke "revulsion" (but not necessarily "extreme revulsion").[64]

Do Substantial Errors Matter? Continuing the Defense of Market Norms

But even though these errors are more substantive than mere reference errors, none of them are likely to worry the defender of the use of market norms to guide academic research. She would begin her response by noting that (as argued above) persons would have an incentive to identify errors in academic work that could impose (non-academic) costs on them if they were accepted uncritically. The errors that persons would lack this incentive to identify would thus be those whose verification would be expected to be more costly than their unverified acceptance—they would be *relatively cheap errors*. The errors above exemplify this. Brennan and Jaworski's misattribution of quotations to Anderson and Satz makes no difference to the objections that they level against their views. None of their arguments hinge on these quotations and they both come close to capturing the spirit (if not the letter) of Anderson's and Satz's views. Nor do these misattributions appear to have made a difference to anyone else engaged in the debate over the moral limits of markets. (They have, so far, gone unremarked in the literature. Until now.) The adverse effects of these errors are thus minimal or non-existent. Similar remarks can be made about the errors made by Wertheimer and Ng. Neither of these errors undermine their arguments. It does not matter for Wertheimer's discussion whether the *Anna* or the *Sarah Jolliffe* exploited the *Port Caledonia*. Only the terms of the contract between the parties that made it are relevant to his argument. Nor does it matter that Ng got the cost of Rubik's Cubes horribly wrong. His point could easily be made by appeal to another consumer good, such as computers.[65] And it does not matter for Brennan and Jaworski's argument whether it is the Merina or another Madagascan group that considers it socially acceptable for a man to give a woman money after sex.[66] In response to noting these errors, the defender of the use of market norms to guide academic research might thus again simply say: "So what?"

This response to concerns about factual errors and errors in quotation is implicitly based on the view that such errors are immaterial so long as they do not matter to the arguments in which they occur. But this response does not seem open to the defender of the use of market norms to guide academic research with respect to the concern that those who adopt such norms will be more likely than those who do not to misrepresent the views of those whose work they engage with. A failure to understand how Anderson defines "commodification," for example, matters if one's criticism of her view is based on her use of this term.[67] And it matters to one's argument if the views that one attributes to the targets of one's criticisms are views that they do not hold.[68]

But the defender of the use of market norms to guide academic research has a response even to this concern: The claim that an error "matters to one's argument" is ambiguous. It could be understood as the claim that the error in question should lead to the argument being rejected *tout court*. Alternatively, it could be understood as the claim that the error in question should lead to the argument being rejected *as an argument with a particular target*. Consider Brennan and Jaworski's critique of essentialist semiotic criticisms of commodification. This argument is sound. They are correct that we cannot "determine, a priori, that certain markets essentially signal disrespect."[69] That none of the philosophers whose work they identify as being the target of their critique endorse the semiotic essentialism that they attribute to them does not undermine its effectiveness against (any possible) arguments that are based on that position. That they have misrepresented the views of those they take to be the target of their criticisms should thus only lead to their argument being rejected *as an argument with a particular target* rather than being rejected *tout court*. Since it is not rejected *tout court*, it is still viable as a publishable argument for it could contribute to the literature by staking out a new position. Thus, an academic's misrepresentation of another's position would not matter (in the relevant sense) to her argument if this did not preclude it from contributing to the literature in a way that could justify its publication.

The Benefits of Error

But not only do errors of these sorts not matter to a defender of the use of market norms to guide academic research—she could move beyond her "So what?" shifting of the burden of proof onto the defenders of academic norms and go on the offensive: She could argue that they could *benefit* the wider academic community.

Errors in academic work provide an opportunity for others to publish work correcting them.[70] The more serious or widespread the error, the more likely it is that work written to correct it will be published. By increasing publication opportunities errors benefit academics by increasing their opportunities for professional advancement. Moreover, these benefits are likely to outweigh their costs. I have already noted that many published errors impose little to no costs on third parties. In such cases the only costs at issue will be the professional costs that might be imposed on the author whose errors are exposed. These costs will be low, likely involving only a small loss of professional prestige. (And she would secure some compensation for this through securing an additional citation to her work when they are corrected.[71]) By contrast, the author of the corrective work will be likely to benefit (relatively) significantly from its publication. Her professional prestige is likely to increase. And (in some cases) the publication of her work correcting that of others might result in her receiving further tangible rewards, such as increased monetary compensation, promotion, or course release.

Even if error goes undetected, it might still increase academics' opportunities for professional advancement through publication by stimulating new lines of inquiry. This could further understanding of the issues to which the errors related. An academic researcher might, for example, outline a view that no-one holds and (mistakenly) present it as a standard position within the literature.[72] This need not be done with the intention to deceive. Such a view might have been introduced by someone who misunderstood the views of those she cited, or by someone who genuinely believed that it was a position that was common in the literature. Alternatively, an academic researcher might mischaracterize a position that she is attempting to criticize so egregiously that she inadvertently develops a new position (albeit one that she criticizes) and hence opens up a new topic for discussion.[73] Both errors will introduce new views into the literature. Given their genesis, the new positions that were inadvertently introduced will resemble (however superficially) views current in the literature. This will give them a degree of superficial plausibility. This resemblance will also lead them to attract the attention of persons working on the (extant) positions that they resemble. Since the newly (and inadvertently) introduced positions will differ from the views that they were intended to represent, they will provide opportunities for discussion that were previously absent. Persons might attempt to defend them from the critiques that were leveled at them by those who (inadvertently) introduced them.[74] Others might then respond to these attempted defenses.[75] Such errors will thus not only provide academics with further publication opportunities. They might also advance understanding of the issues to which they are related. These reasons thus support both accepting the norms of the market and welcoming the errors that are likely to accompany this.

Defending the Primacy of Academic Norms

The above argument in favor of the use of market norms to guide academic research against the objection that this will likely result in the generation and propagation of error is plausible. It might be tempting to criticize it on the grounds that it is grounded on a debased approach to academic research. But there is no need to offer an external objection to the importation of market norms into academic research. The view that academic research (as this is currently practiced) should primarily be governed by market norms is self-defeating.

The plausibility of the above defense of the use of market norms to guide academic research is implicitly based on the view that the aim of academic research is the production of academic publications.[76] As this defense makes clear, the exegetical accuracy of these publications is, on the view of academic research that the proponents of this defense accept, immaterial to the primary reason for their production. The primary purpose of these publications is not to advance understanding of the issues that they address. Instead, it is to secure professional advancement (e.g., tenure, promotion, speaking invitations, or summer research grants) for their authors.

But the primary purpose of academic research *cannot* be to function as a sorting mechanism to allocate the extrinsic rewards of academic research. The primary reason for an activity to be performed cannot be to determine who should receive the rewards of performing it. Offering this as a reason for its performance would not answer the question of why the activity was judged valuable to perform in the first place. The purpose of encouraging the performance of an activity must thus lie in either its perceived consequential value (where this is independent of the extrinsic incentives that could be offered to encourage its performance) or in the value that it is judged to have for its own sake.

Some academic research is clearly conducted for the sake of the benefits that it could generate outside the academy. Some research conducted by faculty members of medical schools is the most obvious example here. But not all academic research has obvious benefits outside the academy. There seems to be little practical benefit to persons outside the academy to, for example, philosophical research on the nature of time or modal realism. This does not entail that such research must therefore be valued for its own sake. It too can be valued for the consequences to which it can lead, the most obvious of which is its ability to enhance our understanding of the issues that it addresses.

If the proper aim of academic research is to enhance understanding, then it should be directed by norms that would make this more likely to be achieved. Unlike market norms, such norms would be interpersonal, enjoining academics to enhance not only their understanding of the issues that they are working on but others' also. Since their goal would thus be partially (if not largely) other-directed, the norms governing their research would not be egoistic. What should matter to an academic is not that *she* enhances understanding through illuminating an issue but that understanding is enhanced through *someone* illuminating it. This focus on the work rather than on individual egos also follows from the recognition that the good that she is pursuing *qua* an academic researcher is a shared good. Her understanding of an issue will not be reduced but likely enhanced through her sharing her views and discoveries with others. And given that she is working in concert with others to enhance understanding, an academic would be expected to exercise voice both by participating in framing the questions that she and her fellow academics address rather than simply exiting a field of research if she disagrees with its direction.

This set of academic norms will (ideally) manifest themselves in a specifically *academic* approach to academic research. It will require that academic researchers (and referees) do their best to understand the views of those whose work they engage with. In the case of researchers, this requires that they engage with those views directly rather than with secondary accounts of them. (If they must engage with them in translation, then they would be required to determine from others familiar with the languages used which translations are authoritative.) It requires that they interpret the work that they engage with as charitably as possible, placing it in the context of other related work by its author. (Archard's work on meaning in the context of his work on the commodification of blood should, for example, be read in conjunction with his work on expressive action.[77]) It also requires that (where possible) academics submit their work to those whose views they criticize with a request that they verify that their views have been presented correctly—and that academics who receive such requests comply with them with the aim of improving their colleagues' work. This sharing of work should occur prior to the work in question being submitted for publication, for this will make it easier for any exegetical errors that it might contain to be corrected.

The aim of enhancing understanding also requires that academics take care to avoid the introduction and propagation of false claims. (And, of course, it requires that they avoid fabricating evidence to support their claims.[78]) This supports the norm that they verify not only their own claims but also the exegetical and factual claims made by others. This requires that they check the references that are provided by those with whose work they engage. It also requires that they then check the references provided in *those* references if the author whose work they are engaging with did not engage directly with a primary source. (This will reduce the possibility of woozles.) Academic researchers should also verify the claims that others make if there are no references provided in support of them.[79] And they should provide in their own work accurate references to the work that they either mention or engage with so that their claims about it can be readily verified.

Once an academic who has produced work in accordance with these norms believes that she can no longer improve upon it—or that any attempt to do so will merely result in diminishing marginal returns—then she should submit it for publication.[80] The primary purpose of publication will not, however, be the author's professional advancement. Instead, it would be to disseminate her work as widely as possible, both so that others might enhance their understanding of the issues addressed through engaging with it and that her understanding could also be enhanced when others who engage with it improve upon it. On this approach to academic research an academic's success will not be judged by the sheer number of publications that she has, or by her salary, or by the prestige of the institution where she works. Instead, it will be judged by how well her work has contributed to the understanding of the issues that she addresses.[81]

Conclusion

I noted in Chapter 8 that most academics will engage in research for a mixture of careerist and more purely academic motives, with the degree of each varying from person to person. The degree to which academic researchers conduct their work in accord with the norms of the market or the norms of the academy will similarly vary. To the degree that an academic researcher conducts her work in accord with academic norms, it is likely to have fewer exegetical errors than that produced in accord with market norms—including fewer misrepresentations of others' views. Since such misrepresentations will impede (or even derail) productive debate, avoiding them is a consummation devoutly to be wish'd. Thus, given that the internal aim of the practice of academic research is to further understanding, academics should primarily (if not exclusively) direct their research in accord with academic, rather than market, norms. I outline how they could be encouraged to do so in Chapter 10.

Notes

1. Did you, dear reader, check this one?
2. See Chapter 7, note 53.
3. Elizabeth Anderson, *Value in Ethics and Economics* (Cambridge, MA: Harvard University Press, 1993), 147–148.
4. See the discussion in Chapter 7.
5. Not *necessarily* exclusively. It is possible that the production of academic research guided by the norms of the market would be so disruptive to the furtherance of understanding that it would have an overall adverse effect on this. If this is the case, then academic research *should* be guided exclusively by the norms of the academy.
6. Less dangerously but also worryingly LD50 levels of toxicity can sometimes be reported as being higher than they actually are. See, for example, Bernd Mayer, "How Much Nicotine Kills a Human? Tracing Back the Generally Accepted Lethal Dose to Dubious Self-Experiments in the Nineteenth Century," *Archives of Toxicology* 88, 1 (2014): 5–7. The widely reported high level of toxicity of nicotine appears to be yet another woozle.
7. Anderson, *Value in Ethics and Economics*, 145.
8. Ibid., 145–146.
9. Ibid., 146.
10. Often mine. See, for example, Gerald Dworkin, "Review of James Stacy Taylor, *Practical Autonomy and Bioethics*," *Notre Dame Philosophical Reviews* 9 (2009); J.R. Kuntz,

"A Litmus Test for Exploitation: James Stacey Taylor's *Stakes and Kidneys*," *Journal of Medicine and Philosophy* 34, 6 (2009), 552; Alexandru Volacu, "Electoral Quid Pro Quo: A Defence of Barter Markets in Votes," *Journal of Applied Philosophy* 36, 5 (2019), 769. And (of course!) Jason Brennan and Peter M. Jaworski, *Markets Without Limits* (New York: Routledge, 2016), 234, and in Jason Brennan and Peter M. Jaworski, "If You Can Reply for Money, You Can Reply for Free," *Journal of Value Inquiry* 51 (2017), 657. In fairness, some of these errors might have been introduced during typesetting or even after proofs have been corrected. See, for example, James Stacy [*sic*] Taylor, "Logrolling, Earmarking, and Vote Buying," *Philosophia* 44 (2016): 905–913. Note that I am not miffed at this—I just find it amusing that "Stacey" is apparently so difficult to spell!

11 See Chapter 4, note 12.
12 See, for example, Luke Semrau's citation of the nonexistent work, James Stacey Taylor, "Selling a Kidney Fails to Rescue Indians from Poverty," in *Stakes and Kidneys: Why Markets in Human Body Parts Are Morally Imperative* (Luke Semrau, "Kidneys Save Lives: Markets Would Probably Help," *Public Affairs Quarterly* 27, 4 [2013], 391). This is the combination of Taylor, *Stakes and Kidneys*, and Deborah Josefson, "Selling a Kidney Fails to Rescue Indians from Poverty," *British Medical Journal* 325, 7368 (2002): 795.
13 Indeed, that references are frequently inaccurate in many data-driven fields is well established. For a helpful overview of this information, see Neal Smith and Aaron Cumberledge, "Quotation Errors in General Science Journals," *Proceedings of the Royal Society A* 476, 2242 (2020): 1–7. https://doi.org/10.1098/rspa.2020.0538. But there is no evidence that this has led to any decrease in the degree to which academics in the fields affected trust in the work of their peers.
14 See, for example, Chapter 5, note 8.
15 See, for example, notes 19, 61, and 64. These types of errors are obviously not clearly differentiated; both the misrepresentation of another's views and misquotation will be types of factual error.
16 Alan Wertheimer, *Exploitation* (Princeton, NJ: Princeton University Press, 1996), 69, 233. Wertheimer cites as his source S.M. Waddams, "Unconscionability in Contracts," *Modern Law Review* 39, 4 (1976). But Waddams only cited the case when quoting the judge's opinion, providing no further details. The error here is thus Wertheimer's. This error has been repeated in the exploitation literature by persons who address Wertheimer's work. See, for example, Denis G. Arnold, "Review: 'Exploitation' and 'The Sweatshop Quandary'," *Business Ethics Quarterly* 13, 2 (2003), 244; Ricardo Andrés Guzmán and Michael C. Munger, "A Theory of Just Market Exchange," *Journal of Value Inquiry* 54, 1 (2020), 108, note 11. Wertheimer is thus responsible for a minor woozle.
17 House of Lords, *The Law Times Reports*, vol. 89, September 1903 to February 1904 (London: Horace Cox, 1904), 216.
18 Yew-Kwang Ng, *Markets and Morals* (New York: Cambridge University Press, 2019), 30.
19 Ibid., 30. In support of this view, Ng offers an extended passage from F.A. Hayek's *The Constitution of Liberty* which (as quoted by Ng) begins with the claims, "Our rapid economic advancement is in large part a result of inequality and is impossible without it. Progress at a fast rate cannot proceed on a uniform front, but must take place in an echelon fashion … ." (ibid., 30). While Ng cites Hayek as the author, he notes that he did not quote this passage directly from Hayek's work. Instead, he quoted it from Brennan and Jaworski (*Markets Without Limits*, 171), who in turn cited F.A. Hayek, *The Constitution of Liberty* (Chicago: University of Chicago Press, 1960), 42–44 as its source. Ng did not check the accuracy of Brennan and Jaworski's quotation of Hayek for he failed to recognize that they misquoted him. The correct quotation is:

The rapid economic advance that we have come to expect seems in a large measure to be the result of this inequality and to be impossible without it. Progress at such a fast rate cannot proceed on a uniform front but must take place in echelon fashion ...

(Hayek, 1960, 42)

Ng also replicates Brennan and Jaworski's other misquotations of this passage. Brennan and Jaworski write "there will always be many things we already know how to produce but which are too expensive to provide for more than the few ..." (*Markets Without Limits*, 171; replicated by Ng, *Markets and Morals*, 30) for Hayek's "there will always be many things we already know how to produce but which are still too expensive to provide for more than a few" (*The Constitution of Liberty*, 43). They write: "All of the conveniences of a comfortable home ..." (*Markets Without Limits*, 171; replicated by Ng, *Markets and Morals*, 30) for Hayek's "All the conveniences of a comfortable home ..." (*The Constitution of Liberty*, 43). They write: "we gradually learned to make them or similar things at a much smaller outlay of resources and thus began to supply them to the great majority" (*Markets Without Limits*, 171; replicated in Ng, *Markets and Morals*, 30) for Hayek's "we gradually learned to make them or similar things at a much smaller outlay of resources and thus became able to supply them to the great majority" (*The Constitution of Liberty*, 43). And they write: "A large part of the expenditure of the rich, though not intended for that end, thus serves to defray experimentation with the new things that, as a result, can later be made available to the poor" (*Markets Without Limits*, 171; replicated in Ng, *Markets and Morals*, 30) for Hayek's "A large part of the expenditure of the rich, though not intended for that end, thus serves to defray the cost of the experimentation with the new things that, as a result, can later be made available to the poor" (*The Constitution of Liberty*, 43–44). Brennan replicates these misquotations of Hayek and (almost verbatim) the two paragraphs of commentary that follow it in *Markets Without Limits* (ibid., 171) in his *Why It's OK to Want to Be Rich* (New York: Routledge, 2021), 169–170. Brennan does not note in *Why It's OK to Want to Be Rich* that these two paragraphs were previously published. Assuming that he (and not Jaworski) was the original author of the two paragraphs that follow the (mis)quotation of Hayek, their appearance in *Why It's OK to Want to Be Rich* is an example of duplicate publication (and one that further propagates error!). (If Jaworski was the original author, this would be an example of plagiarism.) Brennan and Jaworski's misquotation of Hayek is also replicated by Katrin Paldan, Hanno Sauer, and Nils-Frederic Wagner, "Promoting Inequality? Self-Monitoring Applications and the Problem of Social Justice," *AI & SOCIETY* (2018): https://doi.org/10.1007/s00146-018-0835-7. Although Paldan et al. do not cite Brennan and Jaworski as their source of this passage from Hayek, they not only replicate their misquotations, but they also elide the passage in precisely the same way as do Brennan and Jaworski. (They also introduce further error, quoting Hayek as writing "Progress at a fist rate cannot proceed at a uniform front ... .") Like Ng, Paldan et al. seem to have taken this misquoted passage from Brennan and Jaworski without checking its accuracy—although unlike Ng, they do not acknowledge Brennan and Jaworski as their source. (They also fail to cite Hayek in their bibliography.) Brennan and Jaworski are thus responsible for yet another minor woozle—the misquotation of this passage from Hayek.

20 See www.firstversions.com/2015/08/rubiks-cube.html.
21 See www.amazon.com/Hasbro-A9312-Rubiks-Cube/dp/B00YBWOMRA.
22 It is, for example, repeated in Nir Eyal and Emma Tieffenbach, "Incommensurability and Trade," *The Monist* 99, 4 (2016), 399; Lamont Rodgers, "Book Review: Jason F. [*sic*] Brennan and Peter Jaworski, *Markets Without Limits: Moral virtues and commercial interests*," *Philosophy in Review* 37, 1 (2017), 9; John Danaher, "The Symbolic-Consequences

Argument in the Sex Robot Debate," in J. Danaher and N. McArthur (Eds.), *Robot Sex: Social and Ethical Implications* (Cambridge, MA: MIT Press, 2017), 116; Geoffrey M. Hodgson, "On the Limits of Markets," *Journal of Institutional Economics* 17, 1 (2020), 154; J. Flanigan, "Book Review: Michael J. Sandel, *What Money Can't Buy: The Moral Limits of Markets*," *Leadership and the Humanities* 3, 1 (2015), 75 (Flanigan refers to the Merina as a place, rather than a people), and James Stacey Taylor, "Sandel, Semiotics, and Money-Based Exchange: What We Can Learn from Brennan and Jaworski's Failed Critique," *Public Affairs Quarterly* 33, 2 (2019), 163. (Yes, I, too, fell prey to—and propagated—this woozle!) Brennan repeats this claim in *Why It's OK to Want to Be Rich*, 65.
23 Brennan and Jaworski, *Markets Without Limits*, 65.
24 Ibid., 65.
25 Ibid., 65.
26 Ibid., 65. Brennan and Jaworski support these claims by citing Bruce G. Carruthers and Laura Ariovich, *Money and Credit: A Sociological Approach* (London: Polity Press, 2010), 68. But Carruthers and Ariovich do not mention wives (or marriage) at all, referring only to "sexual relations" (ibid., 68). They also do not claim that (non-prostitute) sexual partners who receive money are distinguished from prostitutes by reference to the formality of the relationship in question, nor do they claim that they are distinguished by the emotional quality of the relationship. Instead, they simply cite Maurice Bloch's claim that these types of relationships are distinguished by how casual they are. See his "The Symbolism of Money in Imerina," in J. Parry and M. Bloch, *Money and the Morality of Exchange* (New York: Cambridge University Press, 1989), 166; cited by Carruthers and Ariovich, *Money and Credit*, 68.
27 Brennan and Jaworski, *Markets Without Limits*, 65. I focus here on Brennan and Jaworski's specific claim that Merina men pay their wives for sex as a sign of respect; I am *not* denying their general (and correct) claim that money has different symbolic meanings in different cultures. This latter claim is clearly supported by Maurice Bloch, "The Symbolism of Money in Imerina," 165–190. See too Supriya Singh, "The Cultural Distinctiveness of Money," *Sociological Bulletin* 45, 1 (1996): 55–85.
28 Or, more cautiously, there is no reason to believe that this is true. It is *possible* that it is common for Merina men to pay their wives for sex—just as it is *possible* that it is common for American men to pay their wives for sex. It is simply that there is no evidence that this is the case. Nothing I write below precludes the possibility that this occurs widely (in both cultures) and that everyone involved just keeps very quiet about it.
29 Brennan and Jaworski, *Markets Without Limits*, 65.
30 Ibid., 65. Brennan and Jaworski cite "Zelizer 1995, 84." (*Markets Without Limits*, 73, note 9). Their bibliography identifies this as "1995. *The Social Meaning of Money*, New York, Basic Books" (ibid., 235). (This appears to refer to a reprint version of *The Social Meaning of Money*; the original was published in 1994. The pagination and text of the reprint and the original are identical.) But Zelizer makes no mention of the Merina on p. 84 of *The Social Meaning of Money*. She does mention them on p. 83—but makes *none* of the claims there that Brennan and Jaworski attribute to her.
31 Viviana A. Zelizer, *The Social Meaning of Money* (New York: Basic Books, 1994), 83; note again that the text and pagination of the reprint version are identical to that of this original.
32 Brennan and Jaworski, *Markets Without Limits*, 65.
33 Kirsten Stoebenau, "'Côtier' Sexual Identity as Constructed by the Urban Merina of Antananarivo, Madagascar," *Études océan Indien* 45 (2010), 7. (The page numbers refer to the Open Access version of this article.) Quoted by Brennan and Jaworski, *Markets Without Limits*, 65. Stoebenau is here summarizing the work of Gillian Feeley-Harnik *A Green Estate: Restoring Independence in Madagascar* (Washington, DC: Smithsonian Institution Press, 1991). (Brennan and Jaworski also misspell "Feeley-Harnik" as

"Feeley-Harnick.") Although Stoebenau provides no page numbers in her citation, she is referring to Feeley-Harnik, *A Green Estate*, 290.
34 Stoebenau makes this clear in her summary; "'Côtier' Sexual Identity," 6–7. Feeley-Harnick also makes this clear; see *A Green Estate*, 21, 289–290.
35 Stoebenau, "'Côtier' Sexual Identity," 7, 15, note 8. In support of the first claim, Stoebenau cites E. Mangalaza, "Sous la moustiquaire: fidélité conjugale et libertinage chez les Betsimisaraka. L'amour," *Cahiers ethnologiques* 15 (1993): 61–71. In support of the second, she cites S. Fee, "Fisiky ty mahaondaty. Textiles and Social Life in Androy, Madagascar," PhD dissertation, 2003, INALCO, Paris.
36 And even among the Sakalava, the Betsimisaraka, and the Tandroy, it is not clear that the leaving of money should be understood as paying for sex, as Brennan and Jaworski claim. See the discussion below.
37 Stoebenau, "'Côtier' Sexual Identity," 2.
38 Ibid., 5.
39 Note again that I am not claiming that this is definitely *not* a Merina custom but that the relevant ethnographic literature fails clearly to support the claim that it is. One might further defend Brennan and Jaworski's attribution of the practice to the Merina by noting that Stoebenau was working with the Merina *urban* elite. It is thus possible that this practice could be a Merina practice in rural areas. (This speculation could support reading Bloch's mention of this practice as justifying its ascription to the Merina, as his anthropological research was performed in rural Madagascar—see the discussion of Bloch below.) But, as Stoebenau notes, in rural Madagascar persons are less likely to identify as Merina and more likely to identify as Malagasy (ibid., 3). There is thus still little reason to believe that this is a Merina custom
40 Brennan and Jaworski, *Markets Without Limits*, 65. Brennan and Jaworski cite Carruthers and Ariovich, *Money and Credit*, 68.
41 Bloch, "The Symbolism of Money in Imerina," 165–190. Cited by Carruthers and Ariovich, *Money and Credit*, 68.
42 Bloch, "The Symbolism of Money in Imerina," 166, emphasis added.
43 Moreover, Bloch expressly observes that some of the cultural practices of the Merina that concern money and its symbolism differ from those of other Madagascan groups. For example, he observes that while the Merina require a groom to provide a sum of money to the father of his bride, they see this practice as being different *in kind* from the bride price that other Madagascan groups expect of grooms, which the Merina view as "buying women." (See Maurice Bloch, "Marriage Amongst Equals: An Analysis of the Marriage Ceremony of the Merina of Madagascar," *Man* 13, 1 [1978], 25.) The ways in which other Madagascan groups understand and use money thus cannot automatically be generalized to the Merina. See Brennan and Jaworski, *Markets Without Limits*, 65.
44 Maurice Bloch, "New Foreword," in Octave Mannoni, trans. Pamela Powesland, *Prospero and Caliban: The Psychology of Colonization* (Ann Arbor, MI: University of Michigan Press, 1990), xvii. This is an English edition of Octave Mannoni, *Psychologie de la Colonisation* (Paris: Editions du Seuil, 1950).
45 Bloch, "New Foreword," xvii.
46 Ibid., xviii.
47 It is also unlikely that a Merina man would give his partner an *unsolicited* gift after sex, for rather than expressing respect, this would express that the relationship was not one between equals.
48 Brennan and Jaworski, *Markets Without Limits*, 65. See, also, the discussion below.
49 The Merina's view that money can be an appropriate gift within an egalitarian friendship, combined with their practice of continuously demanding such gifts from each other, appears to falsify Simmel's claim that "[m]oney is never an adequate mediator of personal relationships ... that are intended to be permanent and based on

the sincerity of the binding forces" (Georg Simmel, *The Philosophy of Money* [London: Routledge, 2004], 378). However, it seems that within this practice gifts of money are not gifts of money *qua* money but simply gifts of a "gifted object" whose nature is irrelevant to its function in the practice. This Merina practice thus does not undermine Simmel's claim that gifts of money *qua* money are inadequate mediators of personal relationships. This defense of Simmel's view is not intended to endorse it—see my discussion of the use of money as a gift in Alternative America, in Chapter 3.

50 Feeley-Harnik notes that "the commonest local word for a woman or women" is *manangy*, derived from "the money (*tangy*) men are expected to give women in expressing their desire and persuading them to agree" (*A Green Estate*, 295). This is distinct from other words for women which were associated with "trading for profit" (e.g., prostitution, the sale of sex in accord with market norms), such as *koetra* (ibid., 295).

51 Brennan and Jaworski, *Markets Without Limits*, 65.

52 Feeley-Harnik, *A Green Estate*, 289–295. Brennan and Jaworski's discussion here is thus doubly erroneous: They focus on a custom that is not clearly an exchange, and they attribute it to the wrong group of people in Madagascar.

53 In personal correspondence, Sarah Fee has noted that Tandroy women consider receiving gifts of money from their sexual partners to be no different from North American women receiving a "dinner and a movie" from their dates. (Indeed, they consider women who do *not* receive money to lack virtue, as the receipt of money is a way by which their male partners recognize their honor.) Thus, if dates in North American culture should not be understood as transactional, then this Tandroy practice should not be understood as transactional, either. Similarly, the financial and sexual relationships that hold between contemporary "sugar babies" and "sugar daddies" are often understood by their participants in a way that distinguishes them from being mere exchanges of cash for sex. See, for example, Kavita Ilona Nayar, "Sweetening the Deal: Dating for Compensation in the Digital Age," *Journal of Gender Studies* 26, 3 (2016): 335–346.

54 Brennan and Jaworski make it clear that they believe that every time goods flow between persons in this way, those persons are involved in buying and selling. *Markets Without Limits*, 65.

55 Margaret Jane Radin, *Contested Commodities* (Cambridge, MA: Harvard University Press, 1996), 12. It appears that Brennan and Jaworski not only endorse the worldview of universal commodification (*Markets Without Limits*, 3) but also (and without justification) take it to be normatively prior to competing views. I draw on Radin here to emphasize—once again—that the view of meaning that Brennan and Jaworski believe to have been overlooked by philosophers is not only philosophical orthodoxy but one that is explicitly endorsed by persons that Brennan and Jaworski claim reject it. (Radin is writing not of Madagascan practices but of a case in which a person takes a high-paying job in a distant city but does not understand this as trading the company of her spouse for the amount of her salary increase. See the discussion of this issue in Chapter 7.)

56 The possibility that a flow of goods or services from A to B in temporal proximity to a flow of goods from B to A would not be understood as an exchange by those party to it was recognized by F. M. Cornford and provided the basis of his lampooning of disguised academic favor-trading. See his *Microcosmographica Academica: Being a Guide for the Young Academic Politician* (Cambridge: Bowes & Bowes, 1908), Chapter IX.

57 Brennan and Jaworski, *Markets Without Limits*, 65.

58 Ibid., 65.

59 See, too, note 19.

60 Brennan and Jaworski, *Markets Without Limits*, 48. They cite Elizabeth Anderson, "Is Women's Labor a Commodity?" in ibid., 71.

61 In fairness to Brennan and Jaworski, it seems that this fabrication was unintentional. In an earlier work ("In Defense of Commodification," *Moral Philosophy and Politics* 2, 2 [2015]: 357–377), they use the term "incubation machines" without quotation marks in outlining Anderson's views on surrogacy, referring to her work in *Value in Ethics and Economics* ("In Defense of Commodification," 364). They then repeat this term *with* quotation marks later in this paper referring to "Is Women's Labor a Commodity?" ("In Defense of Commodification," 373). It thus appears that they initially introduced the phrase themselves and then mistakenly believed it to be a quotation later in their writing of the paper; this mistake was then replicated in *Markets Without Limits*.
62 Brennan and Jaworski, *Markets Without Limits*, 7. They cite "Satz 2012, 4" as the source of this claim. Their bibliography identifies "Satz 2012" as Satz, *Why Some Things Should Not Be for Sale*—although this was published in 2010 rather than 2012. She makes no mention of "revulsion" on p. 4; it appears that they intended to refer to p. 3.
63 Debra Satz. *Why Some Things Should Not Be for Sale* (Oxford: Oxford University Press, 2010), 3.
64 While the phrase "extreme revulsion" does not appear in Satz's work, it does appear in Momoi's account ("Satz to Graduates: Some Things Should Never Be for Sale," *Stanford Report*, June 12, 2010. Available at: https://news.stanford.edu/news/2010/june/class-day-lecture-061210.html) of the speech that Satz gave at Stanford that was published in the student newspaper. (See the discussion of this in Chapter 5.) It seems that Brennan and Jaworski not only attributed views to Satz based on this student newspaper report, but they also drew from it to attribute quotations to her.
65 See, for example, the price declines documented in William D. Nordhaus, "Two Centuries of Productivity Growth in Computing," *The Journal of Economic History* 67, 1 (2007): 128–159, esp. Table 10, p. 153.
66 Although getting this right might matter to the Merina.
67 See the discussion in Chapter 4.
68 See Chapters 1–5.
69 Brennan and Jaworski, *Markets Without Limits*, 68.
70 See, for example, the citations in the articles cited in Chapter 8 that identified and corrected woozles. And, of course, this book.
71 As George Ritzer notes, some works might be highly cited simply because they are filled with error! "The 'McDonaldization' of Society," *Journal of American Culture* 6, 1 (1983), 104.
72 See Chapters 1–5.
73 This is the case with Brennan and Jaworski's critique of semiotic essentialism.
74 See, for example, Jacob Sparks, "Can't Buy Me Love: A Reply to Brennan and Jaworski," *Journal of Philosophical Research* 42 (2017): 341–352 and Anthony Robert Booth, "The Real Symbolic Limits of Markets," *Analysis* 78, 2 (2018): 198–207.
75 See, for example, Julian Jonker, "The Meaning of a Market and the Meaning of 'Meaning'," *Journal of Ethics and Social Philosophy* 15, 2 (2019): 186–195.
76 That this is taken to be the aim of producing academic work is important for my argument. If the aim of academic work is taken to be something else—such as the production of academic work to entertain consumers, as in Alternative America—then its production in accord with market norms would not be self-defeating. The primary purpose of its production would not be to function as a sorting mechanism for the allocation of the extrinsic rewards of academic research.
77 See the discussion in Chapter 5.
78 For an extraordinary example of this, see William Meacham, "The Amazing Dr Kouznetsov," *Antiquity: A Review of World Archaeology* 81, 313 (2007): 779–783.
79 As was the case with Ng's example of the Rubik's Cube. See, too, Chapter 8, notes 24 and 64.

80 Even a complete adherence to academic norms would thus not result in the elimination of the errors outlined above in an academic work—and nor should it. Given time constraints, the optimal number of such errors in an academic text is unlikely to be zero, for identifying and correcting them will come at the cost of time that could be spent on furthering understanding through other research activities. Even an academic who adheres wholly to academic norms will thus have to decide how to balance the need for exegetical accuracy with the need to further understanding of her subject through making original contributions to the debates in which she participates. I am thus confident that, despite the care I have taken, there are exegetical errors in this text. Unfortunately, I do not know where they are.

81 See Anderson, *Value in Ethics and Economics*, 147. See, too, Russell Keat, "Ethics, Markets, and Cultural Goods," in Allyn Fives and Keith Breen (Eds.), *Philosophy and Political Engagement: Reflection in the Public Sphere* (London: Palgrave Macmillan, 2016), 122–125, and Alasdair MacIntyre's discussion of the good internal to a "practice," in *After Virtue: A Study in Moral Theory*, 3rd edn (Notre Dame, IN: University of Notre Dame Press, 2007), 187–194.

10
THE THEORY AND PRACTICE OF CHANGING NORMS

Introduction

As I noted in Chapter 8, contemporary academics have significant external incentives to conduct their research in accord with the norms of the market. I also noted that the presence of these incentives explains the publication of academic work that is marred by significant error, including (but not limited to) errors of fact, erroneous quotations, erroneous or absent citations, misrepresentations of the views that it addresses, and the propagation of woozles.

In this chapter, I will suggest ways to remedy this unfortunate situation by altering the incentives that academics face so that they will perform their duties as referees and researchers in conformity more to the norms of the academy rather than those of the market. I will also draw out a surprising implication that follows from accepting academic norms: Plagiarism is not as bad as it is widely held to be.

Changing Norms in Theory

From the discussions of Chapters 8 and 9 it might be tempting to endorse a form of academic Gresham's Law: Bad research will drive out the good. This is a superficially plausible view. The likelihood that market norms would supplant academic norms as the primary guides for conducting academic research might appear to be high. The painstaking approach to research that would be adopted by academics who adhere more to the norms of the academy than to the norms of the market ("academic academics") will likely result in their producing fewer publications than their more market-driven (and hence careless) colleagues. While the quality of their work would be likely to be higher (at least with respect to its accuracy), this could not be determined by third parties merely from looking at their publication records. The accuracy of a publication will not be the main determinant of the quality of the journal in which it will be published. Academic academics would thus be likely to have fewer publications than their more market-orientated colleagues. They would thus appear to be less productive and so less likely to receive professional advancement. Scholarshit will accordingly triumph over scholarship.

But this argument is mistaken. If academic norms are sufficiently widely accepted within an academic community, then they will be stable by default. If all (or almost all) academics in an academic community conduct their research primarily in accord with academic norms, then referees would be likely to check the exegetical claims that are made in the work they review. (For the purposes of this discussion, an academic community consists of academics who submit to the same set of journals and book publishers—a rough characterization, to be sure, but one that will suffice here.) Given their adherence to the view that academic work should aim at enhancing understanding, they would reject work submitted for publication that was exegetically inaccurate. They might also reject work that had errors of fact. (Although if nothing in the argument turned on the errors made, then they might simply require that these be corrected in a revised version of the work.) An academic "outlier" in this community who conducted her research in accord with the norms of the market would thus be motivated to ensure that her work was exegetically accurate. (Although she might still be willing to skimp on checking her references and her factual claims if these were not crucial to her argument, "outsourcing" these verifications to her referees in the belief that they would not reject her paper outright for these sorts of errors.) Her adherence to market norms to guide her academic research would not lead her to spend (much) less time on each publishable unit of her research than would be spent by an academic academic. Her adherence to market norms would thus secure her little (if any) competitive advantage. There would thus be no incentive for academics within this community to change from directing their research in conformity with the norms of the academy to directing it in accord with the norms of the market.

Just as the acceptance of academic norms would (*ceteris paribus*) be stable within an academic community if they were sufficiently widely accepted, so too would the acceptance of market norms be stable within an academic community, if they were sufficiently widely accepted. The reasons for this are obvious. Since the referees in such a community would be likely to accept the norms of the market, they would not bother to check the accuracy of work submitted for publication. This would be time-consuming and would take them away from working on publishable work of their own. Since inaccuracy would thus be no bar to publication, academic researchers within an academic community in which market norms were widely accepted would have no external incentive to spend time making sure that their work was accurate. Doing so would serve only to reduce their publication rates. They would thus have no external incentive to replace their acceptance of market norms as being appropriate to guide academic research with an acceptance of academic norms as being appropriate to guide it. The widespread acceptance of market norms as being appropriate to guide academic research would thus be stable.

Both normative systems for the direction of academic research could thus be stable. But even stable systems will change if the background conditions against which they operate change. For example, as Robert C. Ellickson has argued, an exogenous shock could provide an incentive for the members of a group to direct their behavior in accord with new norms. To illustrate this, Ellickson notes that norms directing people in the United States to be more visibly "patriotic" (and nativist) became more widely accepted in the 1950s as a result of the increasing threat of the Soviet Union.[1] Exogenous events that lead to the addition or subtraction of group members or that disrupt its boundaries could also lead to a revision of the group's norms. For example, Ellickson holds that the Civil Rights Acts of the 1960s led to more racial integration in workplaces. This disrupted the boundaries of groups that were previously segregated by race. As a result, African-Americans were able to impose informal sanctions and confer esteem upon Caucasians, which led to an increasing norm against the telling of racist jokes.[2] To illustrate how the subtraction of certain group members might lead to a change in norms, Ellickson observes that the exclusion of children from an apartment building might lead to "lessen the costs of a norm against noise making because fewer children would have to bear the burden of suppressing their high spirits."[3]

Finally, to illustrate how norms could change as a result of the addition of members to a group, consider this Just-So story about how academic norms could change.[4] Imagine that the number of people entering an academic discipline increases dramatically in a relatively short period of time without a correlative increase in the number of tenure-stream jobs. The resulting increase in competition for entry-level academic positions could lead to the increasing adoption of market norms to direct academic research. The new members of the group (i.e., graduate students and recent PhDs) might believe that their chance of a tenure-stream job would largely depend on their publication record. Each would thus have a strong incentive to publish as much and as good as she could. This alone would not lead to the widespread adoption of market norms in a situation where academic norms had previously dominated. If the pool of active referees consisted of established academics who endorsed academic norms as being those appropriate to govern research, the new members of the group would have an incentive to direct their work in accord with these norms to avoid its rejection. However, the new members of the group might also have incentive to distinguish themselves ways apart from (and in addition to) publishing—such as by serving as referees for journals.[5] More established academics would not only lack this incentive to referee but would know of graduate students or recent PhDs (such as those they supervised) to whom it applied. They would thus have incentive to pass the names of these younger academics to journal editors to serve as referees in their stead. The pool of referees would thus skew toward the new members of the group. These persons would be less acculturated to academic norms than would their more established colleagues. Conscientiously serving as a referee would take up time that they could otherwise spend on activities that would be geared toward publication. They would secure the (perceived) advantages of refereeing merely by serving as referees, independent of the quality of their refereeing. These persons would thus have incentive to skimp on their refereeing duties (e.g., by failing to check the references in the articles they referee). This would increase the chance that research conducted according to the norms of the market would be published. Academics (whether established or younger) who directed their research in accord with academic norms would check the references in the published academic work that they read. Over time, they would come to realize that inaccuracy in research was no bar to its publication and so this external incentive that they had to ensure that their work was accurate would diminish. They would also come to realize that, given this, they would be at a competitive disadvantage (with respect to securing the external rewards of academia) if they continued to strive to ensure that their work was accurate. The external incentive that all academics in this community had to adhere to academic norms in the production of research would thus lessen while the incentive that they had to adopt the norms of the market would increase. Assuming that the motivations that the academics in this community had for doing research were a mix of the careerist and the scholarly, over time the norms of the market would come to supplant those of the academy within this community.[6] This Just-So story further supports the view that even (formerly) stable systems of norms can change. This raises the possibility that changes in norms could be deliberately brought about.[7] It is now time to turn from theory to (possible) practice.

Changing Norms in Practice

I argued in Chapter 9 that academic research should primarily conform to the norms of the academy rather than the norms of the market. How could this be encouraged? Anderson suggests that this could, in part, be achieved through academics being employed by non-profit universities "whose defining aims are the promotion of goods internal to professional practice."[8] But this is false. Academics might not share the aims of their employers. And in any case, the incentives that they are faced with will not be determined by whether the rewards that they are offered originate from private or public sources, or from for-profit or non-profit organizations.[9] They will instead be determined by the nature of the rewards that they are offered, together with the actions that they need to take to secure them.

With this observation in place, I will suggest how to encourage academics to direct their research in conformity with the norms of the academy rather than those of the market. In offering these suggestions I am not assuming that most (or even many) academics draw on market norms to direct their research. If very few academics draw on market norms to direct their research but instead already direct their work by the norms of the academy, implementing these suggestions will simply reinforce this desirable *status quo* at little cost. If, however, market norms are prevalent within the academy (either as a whole, or within certain disciplines, or within certain sub-disciplines), then following these suggestions could serve as a welcome corrective.

Encourage Referees to Become Bounty Hunters

Academics need to be provided with incentives to encourage them to conduct their research in accord with academic norms. Since referees serve as the gatekeepers of the good of publication, they should be provided with incentives to identify and correct inaccuracies in the work that they referee.[10] One simple way to achieve this would be to encourage authors to hide the occasional "Easter Egg" in their footnotes to encourage referees to check them. These Easter Eggs could take the form of academic jokes that would become apparent once the referee checked the source located in the footnote.[11] Alas, it is unlikely that referees will sufficiently value these Easter Eggs to be motivated diligently to check the footnotes to find them.[12] Moreover, authors whose academic research was produced in accord with the norms of the market will have little incentive to encourage referees to check their references in this way.[13]

A more effective way to motivate referees to identify reference errors, exegetical errors, and factual inaccuracies in manuscripts is to pay them to do so. The idea that referees should be paid to encourage them to behave in ways that are considered desirable is not new. It has, for example, been suggested that academics should be paid to referee for journals, or paid to submit their referee reports in a timely fashion.[14] And many book publishers offer small honoraria to manuscript referees. The suggestion here, however, is different: It is that referees get paid to referee *well*. Rather than simply offer prospective referees a flat rate per manuscript, a publisher should instead offer them a financial bounty for each error that they discover in a manuscript. The amounts of these bounties could differ depending on the type of error discovered. The discovery and documentation of relatively trivial errors that are easy to detect (such as identifying erroneous page numbers in a reference or a misspelling of an author's name) could secure referees small bounties. Errors of fact that might require more checking on the part of the referee could secure the referees that detect and document them larger bounties. And errors in which an author (e.g.) misrepresents the view of a work that she is engaging with could secure the referees that detect and document them substantial bounties (where "substantial" is larger than "larger"!). The size of the bounties in this last set would recognize both the effort that would need to be taken to discover these errors and that their propagation is (of all the errors noted above) the most inimical to the furtherance of understanding.

If there was more than one referee for a manuscript, this system could be arranged either so that each referee would receive the full bounty if they detected and documented the same error, or so that the bounty in such cases was divided equally between them. The drawback of the latter approach might be that some referees would not bother to detect and document the "obvious" and low-paid errors as they assume that the other referee would do so and believe that the divided bounty would not be worth the work involved. This might lead to a situation where none of the referees for a manuscript document these errors. Alternatively, if one wished to encourage referees to submit their reports quickly as well as detect the errors in a manuscript, then the first referee to submit would receive the full bonus for any errors that were also documented by other referees while the referees who submitted their reports later would receive little or nothing for their identification of them. But this, too, might be a sub-optimal approach. On this system referees might be tempted to ignore checking references in order to detect higher-paying errors (e.g., those that misrepresented the view of an author whose work was being addressed). Reference-checking of this sort would be time-consuming, might not pay off, and would undermine their chance of being the first to submit their report and thus to secure the full bonus for the more obvious errors that they had detected.

The payments that are made to referees who detect and document errors should come from the authors in whose manuscripts the errors are detected. This would place the costs of detecting such errors where it belongs (i.e., on those who committed them). (The transaction costs that publishers would incur as a result of imposing this bounty-based system should be built into the costs borne by those authors in whose manuscripts errors were detected.) This would also provide a further incentive to academics to attempt to reduce the number of errors that they make in their work. Various means might be adopted to facilitate such payments. Authors could be required to place a certain amount of money in escrow at the time they submit their manuscripts. Alternatively (since this initial approach would disadvantage financially poorer academics), they could be required to sign an enforceable contract to pay any costs associated with error detection within a specified period of time after receiving the referees' reports.

This bounty-based approach is faced with the obvious problem of false negatives. If the bounties offered are too low, this might discourage referees from spending time checking for errors. Referees who previously spent time checking for errors as they believed that doing so was valuable might revise their opinion when offered only a small bounty for each error detected. Their intrinsic motivation to check for error would thus be diminished and the small size of the bounty might not provide a sufficient extrinsic motivation to make up for this.[15] Moreover, checking for errors is time-consuming. The referees might judge that the small bounty offered for the detection and documentation of error would be insufficient to compensate them for the time that they would spend on this.[16] To rectify this, the bounties offered—even for the detection and documentation of obvious errors—would need to be fairly substantial.

But the higher the bounty paid per error, the greater the incentive authors would have to avoid error in their work. This, in turn, would make it less likely that a referee would earn a bounty each time she checked the exegetical accuracy of an author's claims in a manuscript she was reviewing. Yet rather than supporting a *reduction* in the bounty paid per error, the increased carefulness of authors should support its *increase*. While the likelihood would be low that any given reference check by a referee would identify an error if bounties were high, the value of the bounty would still motivate some referees to check references despite the low chance of them earning a bounty by so doing. The knowledge that some referees would do this would motivate authors to avoid errors (and thus avoid the chance of having to pay a large bounty), even if they believed that few referees would be motivated by the (large but unlikely) bounty to check for errors. The exegetical accuracy of academic work could thus be expected to increase under this system (and the number of woozles decline).

It might seem perverse to suggest using financial incentives to motivate academics to eschew directing their research in conformity with market norms. But an exchange of services for payment does not entail that the service in question has been commodified.[17] The publishers who offer such payments to referees could make it clear that they (the publishers) will receive no commercial benefit from increasing accuracy through offering such bounties. They could make it clear (if this is true) that the accuracy or otherwise of the academic work that they publish has no effect on sales of journals or academic texts. Instead, they could note, they are offering this incentive to fact-check because, as publishers of *academic* work, they value accuracy in publication for the sake of its potential for furthering understanding. They could also offer non-financial incentives to referees. They could, for example, extend the current practice of offering books in lieu of financial payment, with the value of the books offered being (e.g.) double that of the financial bounty that would have otherwise been received. They could also offer their referees the option of donating the payments that they would have received to an academically orientated charity, such as a scholarship fund for underserved student populations.

Shifting Incentives for Academic Researchers

Providing referees with incentives to identify errors in the work that they referee would provide an incentive to academic researchers to be more concerned with the accuracy of their work. Not only would they have to pay bounties to the referees who had detected inaccuracy in their work, but it is likely that work that referees identify as being seriously inaccurate will not be published. Other changes could also be made to alter the incentives that are currently faced by academic researchers so that they become more concerned with the accuracy of their work.

As I discussed in Chapter 8, prudentially rational, ambitious academics who are moved primarily by the prospect of external rewards will currently be motivated to skimp on checking the accuracy of their work by the external incentives contemporary academia offers to publish as much and as good as possible. To increase their concern with the accuracy (and hence the quality) of their work, the incentives that academics face should be realigned so that the number of publications matters less than their quality.

This could be achieved in several ways. Most obviously, academic units that offer annual incentives to encourage productivity (such as Georgetown University's McDonough School of Business) should cease doing so. Such short-term incentives are likely to exacerbate the problem of a focus on increasing the number of publications at the expense of their accuracy. These short-term bonuses should be replaced by medium-term incentives (e.g., ones awarded every five years) which are presented to academics who produce a certain number of high-quality publications within the award period. To qualify for these incentives, eligible academics would be required to provide copies of the requisite number of publications to the award body. If these publications did not appear in outlets that used the bounty-hunting system of refereeing outlined above, then the award body would check them for accuracy. Academics who submit work that exceeds a certain pre-determined level of "excusable" inaccuracy would become ineligible to receive the incentive offered.[18]

Market-oriented academics who are eligible to apply for such internal awards might still submit work that has been produced in conformity with market (rather than academic) norms as they believe that the pursuit of professional success in academia is (and should be) governed by egoism. As a result, they are likely to believe that the members of the award body would have little incentive to vet their work thoroughly to detect inaccuracy. In this case they would believe that the cost of submitting their work (i.e., the possibility of becoming ineligible for the award) would be low, but the benefits of doing so (i.e., receipt of the proffered incentive) could be high. Such opportunistic submissions would consume the time of the award body. To preclude this, academics eligible to apply for such incentives should be faced with significant disincentives to submit inaccurate work. This could take the form of the bounty-hunting scheme outlined above, with the members of the award body serving as *de facto* referees. This scheme could also be coupled with the imposition of further penalties on academics who submit work that exceeds a certain pre-determined level of "excusable" inaccuracy. The amount of the bounty that would be earned by the detection of error could be translated into demerits, with penalties being imposed for work that earns above a certain number of demerits. An academic who submits work that exceeds the "permissible" number of demerits, for example, would not only fail to receive the incentive that she was applying for but also would be ineligible to apply for it the next time she would otherwise have been eligible to do so. A sliding scale of such disincentives could be designed to impose increasingly severe penalties according to the number of demerits earned.

This might lead some academics to game the system by producing a certain number of exegetically accurate publications for submission to internal award-making bodies while skimping on working to ensure that their other publications are similarly accurate. This would enable them both to be eligible for the internal awards while maintaining their publication rate to secure the benefits offered by external bodies (e.g., job offers or paid speaking invitations). From an academic perspective, this result would not be ideal. But, overall, it would still be likely to lead to the production of higher-quality work by such academics than they would otherwise have produced.

This approach to shifting focus from the *quantity* of publications produced to their *accuracy* and *quality* should also be adopted in other areas of academic assessment. Rather than providing copies of all of their published materials, candidates for tenure, promotion, and merit raises should, for example, instead be asked to provide a subset of these that are independently chosen by the academic bodies responsible for evaluating them. These publications should then be vetted for accuracy (perhaps using the bounty-hunting scheme outlined above) with the results of this playing a non-trivial role in determining the outcome of the assessment.

Revising Other Academic Incentives to Reinforce Academic Norms

The above suggestions have focused on shifting academic incentives to encourage academics to concentrate on the accuracy and quality of their publications rather than merely their number. Their aim was to encourage academics to conform the production of their research more to academic, rather than market, norms. This emphasis on academic norms could receive further support from other changes in the incentives that are offered to academics. Rather than offering honoraria for invited talks, for example, academic units could instead offer a prospective presenter payment of her expenses together with the opportunity to present her work in conjunction with a presentation made by another researcher in her field whose work she admires. This would shift the nature of the incentive from one that offers a financial benefit to one that offers intellectual benefit. That this was the incentive that was offered and accepted would be made clear at the resulting colloquium. This would communicate that both those who extended this offer and those who accepted it consider the proper rewards offered by academia to be primarily those of the wits rather than the wallet, with this communication being intended to encourage wider conformity to academic norms. This approach would also provide the members of the inviting institution with the opportunity to engage with a greater number of persons working on the issues that they are interested in.

This approach to reinforcing the norm that the primary value of academic work lies in its potential to further understanding rather than its potential to increase the income of academics could be supported by the making of a particular disjunctive offer: A prospective presenter could *either* have the opportunity to present with another researcher in her field *or* she could receive a market-orientated incentive of a financial honorarium. To make it clear that the latter incentive was one that was *market*-orientated, the amount of the honorarium would be commensurate with that which the invited academic could have earned had she sold tickets to her presentation. It would be impossible to determine how much this amount would be unless tickets were actually sold. However, a (very) rough approximation of how much a talk would have netted could be secured from distributing (prior to the speaker's presentation) a questionnaire to those who attend the talk. They would be asked to check off how much they would have been willing to pay from a list of possible ticket prices (e.g., $0, $5, $10, $20).[19] This information could then be used to determine the optimal ticket price that should have been charged to maximize revenue. The total revenue that would have been garnered from charging the attendees this ticket price, less the direct in-house costs associated with arranging the talk, would then be awarded to the presenter in lieu of travel expenses and honorarium.[20]

It is likely that the (quasi-)market value of most academic presentations would be low.[21] (Possible exceptions might include presentations by Nobel Prize-winners, by winners of MacArthur "Genius" grants, such as Elizabeth Anderson, or by academics such as Michael Sandel, who have authored best-selling books.) Most academics would thus refuse this market-orientated inducement to present their work. They would either decline the disjunctive offer to present outright, or else accept the alternative inducement of the opportunity to present in conjunction with another academic whose work they admire. Their decision to decline this market-orientated inducement should be noted at their colloquium to reinforce the view that the value of academic work does not lie primarily in its market value.

Plagiarism, Negligence, and Academic Norms

The above suggestions as to how to retrench academic norms might be controversial. But if we accept that the purpose of accepting academic norms is to facilitate the furthering of understanding through academic research, we should also accept two unexpected conclusions that are likely to be even *more* controversial. The first is that academics' plagiarism of previously published work is not a serious academic offence. The second (which is related to the first) is that to reinforce academic norms, we should condemn negligence in academic work far more harshly than we should condemn plagiarism.

Following M.V. Dougherty, I will hold that:

> academic plagiarism has been committed when there is: (1) a non-trivial appropriation of words, images, or formulas, (2) with inadequate credit, (3) that generates an appearance of original authorship, (4) in a discrete item belonging to the scholarly record.[22]

As Dougherty observes, plagiarism extends beyond the verbatim copying of another's words without attribution.[23] It includes not only literal plagiarism (e.g., copy-and-paste plagiarism) but also disguised plagiarism such as translation plagiarism, pawn sacrifice plagiarism (where a source is cited but it is not clear how much of the work to which is appended is taken from it), and structural plagiarism.[24]

No matter what form it takes, plagiarism is widely condemned within the academic literature. John Maddox holds that "[a]mong scholars plagiarism is the worst of bad behavior" and Ben Rosamond claims that it is "widely thought of as perhaps the most grievous academic crime."[25] Although these claims are almost certainly false (even allowing for changing views in the academy since their publication, it is likely that the fabrication of data was and is considered to be worse than plagiarism), plagiarism is considered a serious breach of academic ethics.

The reasons for the condemnation of plagiarism vary. Mathieu Bouville holds that a "common argument against plagiarism" is that "plagiarized authors do not receive what they would have deserved to receive" such as "citations and recognition."[26] These losses might lead them to lose "promotions or awards" or "market shares and royalties" if their books are plagiarized.[27] Bouville also holds that plagiarism is wrong as the plagiarist "steals citations, fame, royalties, etc. from the plagiarized."[28] These views are echoed by Dougherty who holds that plagiarism is wrong (in part) because it could lead to the authors of plagiarized work being denied "credit for their discoveries."[29]

Dougherty also objects to plagiarism as it could lead to "inefficiencies and redundancies in the body of published research."[30] When researchers unsuspectingly engage with plagiarized work, they might cite it as being the origin of the ideas that they engage with. It thus enters the relevant literature as being the source of those ideas. This, claims Dougherty, creates a redundancy in the literature as the plagiarism leads to two streams of engagement with the plagiarized idea: That which engages with the original author's work and that which engages with that of the plagiarizing author.[31] In turn, he argues, this "duplication generates subsequent inefficiencies for researchers working through the research literature in a field."[32] John W. Snapper similarly objects to plagiarism on the grounds that it "destroys the scholarly trails and causes significant harm to the scholarly effort itself. Like the creation of false data and false histories, plagiarism cheats the public by presenting claims with a misleading or hidden provenance."[33]

These differing reasons to condemn plagiarism variously appeal to market and academic norms. The view that plagiarism is wrongful as it would misappropriate academic credit, and hence the extrinsic rewards that could flow from this, appeals to the norms of the market. On this view, an academic's research output is her intellectual property with its value being primarily (if not exclusively) derived from the extrinsic rewards that it could secure for her. By contrast, to hold that plagiarism is wrongful as it would do "significant harm to the scholarly effort itself" is an appeal to academic norms. On this view, plagiarism is wrongful as it obfuscates rather than clarifies through making false claims to authorship.

Since I have argued that the conduct of academia should primarily be governed by academic norms rather than those of the market, I will put to one side the objections to plagiarism that stem from an acceptance of market norms to focus on those that stem from the norms of the academy. But the objections to plagiarism that appeal to academic norms are relatively weak. While plagiarized work does obfuscate understanding of the issues it addresses through concealing its origins, this merely leads the reader to an erroneous attribution of authorship. Indeed, if plagiarized work communicates the same ideas as the original work from which it was taken, then it would have the same potential to further its readers' understanding of the issues that it addresses as did the original. Furthermore, if a reader of a plagiarized work would not have engaged with the original (if, for example, it was published in a language that she does not read), then the publication of a plagiarized work would *increase* the possibility that her understanding of the issue it addresses would be furthered.[34] *Ceteris paribus*, then, in such a case plagiarism should be *prima facie welcomed* rather than decried.[35]

This conditional defense of plagiarism opposes Dougherty's charge that it is wrongful as "the plagiarizing article creates a redundancy in the published research literature."[36] Dougherty's objection rests on the assumption that the publication of plagiarized work would not contribute to the academic debate as it would simply replicate work that was already available, and hence would be redundant. But that a publication replicates work published elsewhere does not entail that it is redundant. It would not be redundant to publish a facsimile of a rare book that had long been out of print, for example, if this would make it available to a wider audience. The redundancy or otherwise of a publication thus depends in part on the degree to which the audience to whom it was relevant would have access to the work that it presents prior to its publication. But this is not the only consideration that matters when determining if a publication is redundant. A work that was accessible to an audience for whom it was relevant might not be read by them as they are unaware of its existence. It might, for example, have been published in an obscure journal, or long ago in a major journal and since forgotten, or in a journal whose primary audience was in another discipline. Or it might have originally appeared in an unpublished dissertation or in a journal published in another language.[37] The republication of this work in an outlet that would be read by an audience who would otherwise have been unaware of it would thus not be redundant as it would bring it to their attention.

The degree to which the republication of existing work would be redundant is thus determined both by the access that its expected audience would have otherwise had to it and, if accessible, the likelihood that they would avail themselves of this access. Plagiarizers prefer to remain undetected. They thus have an incentive only to publish plagiarized work to audiences that they have reason to believe would either lack access to the original, or else would not avail themselves of their access to it. Plagiarizers thus have an incentive only to publish plagiarized work when they have reason to believe that it would *not* be redundant.[38]

But while the publication of plagiarized work might not be redundant, it would be inefficient. An academic who legitimately engages with the work of another would either simply cite it or else briefly outline it to situate her response. This would efficiently bring the cited work to the attention of those who might also productively draw upon it in their work. A plagiarizer, however, would either duplicate another's work or else extensively replicate its content. She would thus consume significantly more publication space (e.g., pages in a print journal) than a non-plagiarizer would to convey the same information. It is plausible to assume that competition for publication space (especially in print journals) is a zero-sum game.[39] A plagiarizer's over-consumption of this space would thus reduce the amount of other (original) work that would be published. It is plausible to assume that (*ceteris paribus*) understanding of an issue is likely to be furthered if more original work on it is published rather than less. The publication of plagiarized work would thus reduce the possibility that the work that appeared in the (set) publication space would further the understanding of its readers when compared with how that space could have been used when the information conveyed by the plagiarizer was conveyed (more concisely) by a non-plagiarizer.

A person who believes that academic research should be pursued in conformity with academic norms should thus condemn plagiarism to the degree that it hinders the academic pursuit of understanding. But since this is so, plagiarism should be considered merely a minor academic sin rather than the grave offense that it is often taken to be. Each plagiarized work would consume only a small amount of the available publication space. The degree to which it would preclude the furtherance of understanding through the publication of original research is thus likely to be low. Indeed, the academic pursuit of understanding is more likely to be compromised by academics' *negligence* than by plagiarism. Academics who negligently misrepresent others' views, who fail to check their own and others' references, or who fail to cite their sources will not only undermine their own understanding of the issues they address, but also that of those who engage with their work and who are similarly negligent. Moreover, since plagiarism merely renders the academic enterprise less efficient while the effects of negligence can actively pervert its course (by, for example, the creation and propagation of woozles), plagiarism should be considered to be a *lesser* form of academic misconduct than negligence.

None of these comparative claims imply that plagiarism is acceptable. They show only that someone who adheres to academic norms should not consider it to be as wrongful as academic negligence. But this discussion of the wrong of plagiarism achieves something in addition to clarifying how an adherent of academic norms should assess the relative wrongness of plagiarism and academic negligence. It also emphasizes the point that a proper understanding of the purposes of our norms can help us to re-evaluate our practices—and that this can sometimes occur in surprising ways.[40]

Conclusion

I noted above that in offering suggestions as to how to motivate academics to conform more to the norms of the academy rather than to the norms of the market, I was not assuming that acceptance of market norms is widespread in the academy. The extent to which norms are so accepted within the academy is an empirical question and (as far as I know) one that is currently open. It is also an open question as to how effective implementing my suggestions would be in practice. But these are not the only empirical questions concerning the role and status of norms in contemporary academia that could be profitably addressed in future work: I will outline others in the Conclusion to this volume. But before turning to these issues, I would like to emphasize that the critics of market imperialism are correct to hold that the norms of the market should not dominate every sphere of human life. Academic research should be conducted primarily in conformity with the norms of the academy, not those of the market. Otherwise, we are more likely to produce scholarshit than scholarship.

Notes

1. Robert C. Ellickson, "The Market for Social Norms," *American Law and Economics Review* 3, 1 (2001), 24, citing Eric A. Posner, "Symbols, Signals, and Social Norms in Politics and the Law," *Journal of Legal Studies* 27 (1998), 775. Ellickson notes that scientific, technological, and environmental changes could also lead to changes in accepted norms.
2. Ellickson, "The Market for Social Norms," 25. Ellickson offers no evidence for any of these claims.
3. Ibid., 24.
4. Ellickson illustrates how the addition of new members to a group could lead to a change in its norms by noting that the addition of younger faculty members to a fading academic department could lead to its accepting norms that would encourage academic productivity. But unless there is a reason why the introduction of more productive academics into a department would lead to the established members changing their behavior, this example would be less of an example of norms changing within a group than it would be of the introduction of a different group with different norms into an area. Ibid., 24.
5. Recall—this is merely a Just-So story!
6. This mix of motivations would be exhibited both within individual academics and within the group as a whole.
7. See, for example, Cristina Bicchieri, *Norms in the Wild* (New York: Oxford University Press, 2017), Chapter 4.
8. Elizabeth Anderson, *Value in Ethics and Economics* (Cambridge, MA: Harvard University Press, 1993), 148.

9 The use of the former Research Assessment Exercise to assess the quality of academic work performed in the United Kingdom—which, in turn, played a role in determining how *public* funds were allocated—has been charged with the increasing commodification of academic research in the United Kingdom. See Sandra Harley, "Accountants Divided: Research Selectivity and Academic Accounting Labour in UK Universities," *Critical Perspectives on Accounting* 11, 5 (2000), 552. Similarly, it appears that the public and non-profit National Institutes of Health encouraged the production of academic research in accord with market norms while the private Howard Hughes Medical Institute was orientated to the norms of the academy. See Pierre Azoulay, Joshua S. Graff Zivin, and Gustavo Manso, "Incentives and Creativity: Evidence from the Academic Life Sciences," *RAND Journal of Economics* 42, 3 (2011): 527–554.

10 My focus here is on the question of how to encourage referees to attempt to identify exegetical errors in the manuscripts that they referee. A distinct but related question concerns whether the way in which peer review is structured can affect the quality of papers published. On this, see Justin Esarey, "Does Peer Review Identify the Best Papers? A Simulation Study of Editors, Reviewers, and the Scientific Publication Process," *PS: Political Science and Politics* 50, 4 (2017): 963–969.

11 See James Stacey Taylor, *Stakes and Kidneys* (Aldershot: Ashgate, 2005), 49, note 6. You will need to check the reference for the joke!

12 *Stakes and Kidneys* was published over 16 years ago and is now in its third printing—and as far as I know no-one has checked the note identified above. I am rather miffed.

13 Two other possible ways of encouraging academics to conduct their research in accord with academic, rather than market, norms are likely to be similarly inefficacious. Exhorting graduate students to conduct their research in accord with academic rather than market norms is unlikely to be efficacious, for those who already conduct their work in accord with market norms will be motivated by the type of incentives that such encouragement will lack. And, as Brian A. Nosek, Jeffrey R. Spies, and Matt Motyl argue, expanding opportunities for publishing work that corrects the exegetical errors of others is unlikely to encourage persons who do not already do this to begin to do so; "Scientific Utopia: II: Restructuring Incentives and Practices to Promote Truth over Publishability," *Perspectives on Psychological Science* 7, 6 (2012), 619.

14 See, for example, Derek Leslie, "Are Delays in Academic Publishing Necessary?," *American Economic Review* 95, 1 (2005), 412–413.

15 The possibility of such motivational crowding is discussed by Bruno S. Frey and Reto Jegen, "Motivation Crowding Theory," *Journal of Economic Surveys* 15, 5 (2001): 589–611.

16 I have developed an argument of this form to explain why blood donations might decline when donors are offered small amounts of compensation for their donations. See James Stacey Taylor, "Why Prohibiting Donor Compensation Can Prevent Plasma Donors from Giving Their Informed Consent to Donate," *Journal of Medicine and Philosophy* 44, 1 (2019): 10–32.

17 See the account of Anderson's discussion of commodification in Chapter 4.

18 As I noted in Chapter 9, the optimal number of exegetical errors in an academic work is unlikely to be zero. See Chapter 9, note 80.

19 The price of $0 should be included as some attendees would be students who only attend to secure the extra credit they had been bribed with. Some of these students would be willing to give up time to secure extra credit but would not be willing also to spend money for it.

20 Some might find asking attendees to put a price on academic talks to be inappropriate. I agree. That is precisely the point!

21 Consider a relatively large and academically engaged audience of 80 students and 20 faculty members. The faculty members would each be willing to pay $25 to attend the presentation while 50 students would pay $10, 15 would pay $5, and 15 would not be

willing to pay anything. The optimal ticket price would be $10. Assuming that the talk was accompanied with a small coffee reception that cost $100, this would net $600 for the presenter from which she would have to pay her own travel and accommodation expenses.
22 M.V. Dougherty, *Correcting the Scholarly Record for Research Integrity in the Aftermath of Plagiarism* (Dordrecht: Springer, 2018), 12. This definition precludes the possibility of self-plagiarism; this should thus be termed "duplicate publication." See Chapter 9, note 19 for a possible example.
23 M.V. Dougherty, *Disguised Academic Plagiarism: A Typology and Case Studies for Researchers and Editors* (Dordrecht: Springer, 2020), 2.
24 These types of plagiarism—among others—are outlined and discussed by Debora Weber-Wulff, *False Feathers: A Perspective on Academic Plagiarism* (Dordrecht: Springer, 2014). Cited by Dougherty, *Disguised Academic Plagiarism*, 2.
25 John Maddox, "Plagiarism Is Worse Than Mere Theft," *Nature* 376 (31 August 1995), 721; Ben Rosamond, "Plagiarism, Academic Norms, and the Governance of the Profession," *Politics* 22, 3 (2002), 167.
26 Mathieu Bouville, "Plagiarism: Words and Ideas," *Science and Engineering Ethics* 14, 3 (2008), 315. This justification for holding plagiarism to be wrong is also noted by John W. Snapper, although Snapper is skeptical that this would be a serious harm and notes that it would not apply to material plagiarized from entities that no longer exist, such as "a defunct C19th corporation." "On the Web, Plagiarism Matters More Than Copyright Piracy," *Ethics and Information Technology* 1 (1999), 128–129.
27 Bouville, "Plagiarism," 315.
28 Ibid., 316.
29 M.V. Dougherty, "The Pernicious Effects of Compression Plagiarism on Scholarly Argumentation," *Argumentation* 33 (2019), 391. This is a common view. See Laurie Stearns, "Copy Wrong: Plagiarism, Process, Property, and the Law," *California Law Review* 80, 2 (1992), 517, 519.
30 Dougherty, "The Pernicious Effects," 391.
31 Ibid., 394.
32 Ibid., 394.
33 Snapper, "On the Web," 129.
34 L.S. Caton's (fictitious) plagiarism of James Dixon's work on the "strangely neglected topic" of "The Economic Influence of the Development in Shipbuilding Techniques, 1450 to 1485" (*Journal of a Fictitious Italian Historical Society* 0, 0 (1954): 1450–1485) and its consequent publication in an Italian journal would thus have performed a useful service to Italian historians interested in this topic. (And also, if it were translated, to English historians in the world of *Lucky Jim*, given Dixon's fate.) Kingsley Amis, *Lucky Jim* (London: Penguin, 1991), 14–15.
35 There are two possible responses here. First, one might object that it would still have been better had the work been attributed to the original author. But it might be that this would have precluded publication as publishers desire to publish new material rather than present old material to new audiences. In such cases plagiarism might be the most straightforward way to communicate certain ideas to certain audiences. Second, one might hold that plagiarism is wrongful as it is dishonest—and that the wrong of dishonesty either outweighs the benefits of the plagiarism or else it is both incommensurable with them and trumps them.
36 Dougherty, *Disguised Academic Plagiarism*, 9.
37 Although Dougherty is a fierce opponent of plagiarism, he provides an example where a plagiarized work is published "in a high-profile international journal in medieval philosophy and theology" while the source from which it was plagiarized was "a revised dissertation published 6 years earlier by a small academic press in Finland." Dougherty held that "[t]he article was cited frequently in relevant literature that had

appeared in the nine nears [sic] between publication and retraction, but the published dissertation received comparatively few citations" (Dougherty, *Correcting the Scholarly Record for Research Integrity in the Aftermath of Plagiarism*, 236). Dougherty is referring here to Martin W.F. Stone's plagiarism (in his article, "The Origins of Probabilism in Late Scholastic Thought: A Prolegomenon to Further Study") of Ilkka Kantola's *Probability and Moral Uncertainty in Late Medieval and Early Modern Times* (Martin W.F. Stone, "The Origins of Probabilism in Late Scholastic Thought: A Prolegomenon to Further Study," *Recherches de Théologie et Philosophie médiévales* 67, 1 [2000]: 114–157; Ilkka Kantola, *Probability and Moral Uncertainty in Late Medieval and Early Modern Times* [Helsinki: Luther-Agricola-Society, 1994].) Stone's plagiarism of Kantola is extensively documented as Case 4, in M.V. Dougherty, Pernille Harsting, and Russell L. Friedman, "40 Cases of Plagiarism," *Bulletin de Philosophie médiévale* 51 [2009], 357). But Dougherty's claim is false. According to Google Scholar, Stone's article had been cited 5 times between its publication in 2000 and 2009 when its status as a plagiarized article was exposed. By contrast, Kantola's dissertation had been cited 21 times between its publication in 1994 and 2009—a greater rate of citation than Stone's article both in terms of raw numbers and per-year citation.

38 A successful plagiarizer might thus not merely be an unskilled repeater of others' views. Plagiarizers can be viewed as the inverse of forgers (Stearns, "Copy Wrong," 517). Forgers produce items and attribute their authorship to someone other than themselves, while plagiarizers appropriate others' work and claim it as their own. But just as a successful forger must have a significant amount of technical skill to reproduce others' work accurately enough to fool experts, so too must a plagiarist possess considerable technical skills. To be successful, a literal plagiarist would need to have considerable command of work that is being done in her discipline. She would have to be able to identify which issues are being actively debated to know where her chance of publication was greatest. She would have to have an extensive command of both primary and secondary academic literature in that area so that she could identify work that is both worth plagiarizing and that has been overlooked by her peers. A successful plagiarizer might thus be an accomplished scholar—just as a successful forger would be an accomplished practitioner of the artform she decides to forge.

39 The truth of this assumption is likely to depend on the publication medium in question. A plagiarized journal article in a print journal might preclude the publication of another article, given that journals often publish only a set number of pages each year. But a plagiarized chapter in an anthology might not have precluded the publication of an alternative chapter, and a plagiarized book might not have precluded the publication of an alternative volume. If so, then a person who believes that academic research should be pursued in conformity with academic norms should condemn plagiarized books and book chapters to a lesser degree than she condemns plagiarized journal articles. Indeed, if the publication of these works would raise awareness of the issues they address and hence further understanding of them, she might not, on balance, condemn them at all.

40 See Anderson, *Value in Ethics and Economics*, 97–103.

CONCLUSION

This volume appears in the middle of one research program and at the start of another. The on-going research program to which it contributes is that which encompasses the various debates that are concerned with the appropriate limits of markets. The new research program (that this volume might, in part, be responsible for initiating) concerns both the descriptive question of the nature of the norms that govern academic research—and the normative question of which norms *should* govern academic research.

With respect to the philosophical debates over the moral limits of markets, I argued that neither the Asymmetry Thesis nor the essentialist semiotic arguments that are purported to be widely offered in support of it are of primary concern to contemporary critics of markets. I argued both that the attribution of these views to many of the prominent critics of markets was mistaken and that these misattributions were doubly unfortunate. Not only were they themselves errors, but (as I noted in Chapter 8) they spawned two serious woozles that have started to redirect discussions of the moral limits of markets into misleading and unproductive avenues.[1] The first of these woozles is the claim that the Asymmetry Thesis is widely held by the critics of markets: That their focus is on establishing that there are some goods or services that can be given away freely but which should not be bought or sold. The second (and related) woozle is the claim that essentialist semiotic arguments are widely offered in favor of the Asymmetry Thesis.

This second woozle is especially pernicious. Not only is it becoming more widespread than the first, it is also generating more confusion. First, it tempts persons to treat all expressivist arguments as semiotic arguments. I argued in Chapter 6 that this is a serious mistake: While all (possible) semiotic arguments are expressivist arguments, not all expressivist arguments are semiotic arguments.

DOI: 10.4324/9781003251996-15

Second, it owes its existence to the claim that philosophers believe that "we can determine, a priori" the essential (necessary) meaning of certain actions.[2] But, as I argued in Chapter 2, rather than being widespread in philosophy, this essentialist view of meaning is widely rejected. (Including, as I argued in Chapters 3, 4, and 5, by the critics of the market to whom it has been attributed.) Moreover, (as I argued in Chapter 6) recognition of why this view is widely rejected will lead to the further recognition that essentialist semiotic arguments are necessarily doomed to fail.[3] Recognizing that the claim that semiotic arguments are widely offered is a woozle will bring a great deal of clarity to the debates over the moral limits of markets.

The positive contributions that this volume makes to the contemporary debates over the moral limits of markets in Part I and Part II are thus focused on getting these debates back on track. This volume identifies and slays the twin woozles that are currently obfuscating them. It then provides an account of the different roles that expressivist arguments can play in moral and political debate—including the debates over the moral limits of markets. This clarification of the roles that such arguments can play in these debates will enable them to progress more productively. And the outline of the different debates associated with the moral status of various markets (provided in Chapter 7) will further clarify the scope and nature of each. As with the clarificatory taxonomy of expressivist arguments (developed in Chapter 6), this will enable future debates over the moral limits of markets to be more productive.

I outlined in Chapters 8 and 9 how the adoption of market norms to govern the conduct of academic research is likely to compromise its quality, especially with respect to its exegetical and empirical accuracy. The need to clarify and reorientate the current debates over the moral limits of markets can hence be explained by the influence that market norms have had on their conduct. The current debates over the moral limits of markets—in particular, those that focus on the Asymmetry Thesis and semiotic objections to markets—thus provide a performative demonstration of why the influence of market norms should be restricted in academia.

But this volume does not merely diagnose the problems associated with the market's influence on academic work: It also provides solutions for this. In Chapter 10, I argued that to encourage the production of academic work in accord with academic norms, referees should be paid bounties to detect and document errors in manuscripts, that institutions should cease offering financial incentives to encourage rapid publication, and that invited presenters at academic colloquia should be rewarded with discussion rather than *denarii*.

This market-critical aspect of this volume raises a series of questions concerning both the nature and the role of the norms that govern academic research. These questions would need to begin by precisely specifying both the nature of the types of norms that could govern academic research and the means by which one would identify when each type was governing its conduct. An initial approach to this was offered in Chapters 8 and 9 where I outlined the distinction between market and academic norms and argued that (in contemporary academia) the prevalence of the former would be correlated with inaccurate research. With this distinction in hand, one could then begin to address further questions. One might, for example, consider whether researchers in some academic disciplines would be more likely than those in others to adhere to the norms of the market rather than to the norms of the academy. Would researchers in academic fields that could be expected to be more market-friendly (e.g., business, perhaps, or economics), be more likely to adhere to market norms than those in fields that might be more hostile to markets (e.g., gender studies, perhaps, or philosophy)? (And how would a discipline's "market friendliness" be measured?) Similarly, will academics within a particular discipline (e.g., philosophy) vary in the likelihood that they would adhere to the norms of the market according to the sub-discipline that they are in? Would, for example, philosophers in some sub-disciplines of philosophy (e.g., business ethics) be more likely than those in others (e.g., the history of philosophy) to direct their work in conformity to market norms?

The natural hypothesis is that faculty in more market-friendly disciplines (or sub-disciplines) would be more likely than faculty in less market-friendly disciplines (or sub-disciplines) to direct their research in conformity with market norms. This hypothesis will be complicated by the fact that faculty in some academic disciplines will have greater opportunities outside the academy than others. Faculty in economics and finance, for example, have far greater job opportunities outside the academy than faculty in (e.g.) gender studies or philosophy. An academic researcher in a field in which there are plenty of non-academic jobs available might thus have more self-consciously chosen to work in the academy than one in a discipline where non-academic jobs are rare. If so, then it might be that academic researchers in such in-demand fields would be *more*, rather than *less*, likely to adhere to academic rather than to market norms in conducting their research. A corollary to this hypothesis is that academics in disciplines (or sub-disciplines) that are more market-friendly but whose faculty lack significant job opportunities outside the academy (e.g., faculty in business ethics) would be the most likely to conduct their work in accord with market rather than academic norms.

These hypotheses are defeasible. And they are also testable. If my arguments in Chapters 8 and 9 are correct, then the greater the degree that an academic comports her research in conformity to market norms, the more likely it will be that her work is exegetically or empirically inaccurate.

To assess the above hypotheses, then, one will first need to identify a representative set of academic researchers in each field. (One might, for example, choose a certain number of researchers in each field with those eligible for inclusion being those who had published a certain number of articles in a certain number of years prior.) Then, the accuracy of their references would be tested for both minor errors (e.g., incorrect page numbers, misspelled authors' names) and major errors (e.g., clear misrepresentation of the positions outlined in referenced works, the propagation of woozles). The degree to which the commission of these errors correlates with work performed in certain disciplines or sub-disciplines could then be determined. This would allow (at least tentative) conclusions to be drawn about whether academic researchers in certain disciplines (or sub-disciplines) would be more likely than others to conduct their research in accordance with market norms.

The above method of testing hypotheses concerning the prevalence of market norms in academia could also be used to test hypotheses concerning (possible) changes in norms in academia. For example, the claim that academics shift the conduct of their research to conform more closely to market norms (and hence increase their productivity) in response to changing incentives could be tested. This could be done by identifying an event that clearly changes the incentives faced by academic researchers. (Such as, for example, the introduction of the former Research Assessment Exercise in the UK.) A set of academic researchers affected by this change would then need to be identified. Then, the exegetical and empirical accuracy of their work for several years both prior to and after the change would be measured to determine if its quality declined (even if its quantity increased) after their incentives changed. Similar approaches could be taken to determine the effects on academic research of any (new) internal incentives that academic institutions offer to their faculty, and whether different types of incentives have differing effects on how research is conducted.[4]

These suggestions require refinement. They are merely offered as possible avenues of investigation at the (possible) start of a research program and so they will require considerable improvement before meeting the standards required of social scientific research.

But refining these suggestions and implementing them as a research program that is both within and about the academy would be valuable. It would contribute to a greater understanding of the nature of the norms that govern academic research, as well as a greater understanding of which norms *should* govern academic research. It would also contribute to a greater understanding of how to organize academic incentives to encourage academic research to be conducted in accord with the norms that it should be governed by. And if my arguments in this volume are correct, this research program would also provide empirical support for my view that there are certain realms of human activity in which the influence of markets should be limited. We should be a market economy. But we should not be a wholly market society.

Notes

1 The woozle concerning Merina practices is only a relatively minor woozle as it does not derail the debate.
2 Jason Brennan and Peter M. Jaworski, *Markets Without Limits* (New York: Routledge, 2016), 68.

3 These are not, alas, highly original points. They could have been made by anyone with even a passing familiarity with philosophy of language or twentieth-century analytic philosophy.
4 Daniele Fanelli observes that it seems that financial incentives are more likely to result in academic misconduct (i.e., that which would justify the retraction of a paper) among scientists than other types of "pressures to publish" ("Pressures to Publish: What Effects Do We See?," in Mario Biagioli and Alexandra Lippman (Eds.), *Gaming the Metrics: Misconduct and Manipulation in Academic Research* [Cambridge, MA: The MIT Press, 2020], 114). It is unclear to what extent this observation could be generalized to the related but distinct questions associated with the relationship between accepting the norms of the market and the production of exegetically inaccurate research.

BIBLIOGRAPHY

Adams, Robert Merrihew, *Finite and Infinite Goods: A Framework for Ethics* (New York: Oxford University Press, 1999).
Airasca, Daniel Albino, "La igualdad como punto de partida," *Praxis Pedagógica* (2018) 18, 23: 130–138.
Alter, Torin, "Symbolic Meaning and the Confederate Battle Flag," *Philosophy in the Contemporary World* 7, 2–3 (2000): 1–4.
Amis, Kingsley, *Lucky Jim* (London: Penguin, 1991).
Anderson, Elizabeth, "Is Women's Labor a Commodity?," *Philosophy & Public Affairs* 19, 1 (1990): 71–92.
Anderson, Elizabeth, *Value in Ethics and Economics* (Cambridge, MA: Harvard University Press, 1993).
Anderson, Elizabeth, "Feminist Epistemology: An Interpretation and a Defense," *Hypatia* 10, 3 (1995): 50–84.
Anderson, Elizabeth, "Why Commercial Surrogate Motherhood Unethically Commodifies Women and Children: Reply to McLachlan," *Health Care Analysis* 8 (2000): 19–26.
Anderson, Elizabeth, "Reply," *Brown Electronic Article Review Service*. Available at: www.brown.edu/Departments/Philosophy/bears/9912ande.html.
Andersen, Lotte Bøgh, and Thomas Pallesen, "'Not Just for the Money?' How Financial Incentives Affect the Number of Publications at Danish Research Institutions," *International Public Management Journal* 11, 1 (2008): 28–47.
Andre, Judith, "Blocked Exchanges: A Taxonomy," *Ethics* 103, 1 (1992): 29–47.
Anomaly, Jonathan, "Review: *Markets Without Limits*," *Notre Dame Philosophical Reviews*. Available at: https://ndpr.nd.edu/news/markets-without-limits-moral-virtues-and-commercial-interests/.
Anonymous, "Letter," *Folklore Forum* 4, 5 (1971): 127.
Aquinas, Thomas, "Summa Theologica," in *The 'Summa Theologica' of St Thomas Aquinas Literally Translated by Fathers of the English Dominican Province* (Westminster, MA: Christian Classics, 1980).

Archard, David, "'A Nod's as Good as a Wink': Consent, Convention, and Reasonable Belief," *Legal Theory* 3 (1997): 273–290.
Archard, David, "Selling Yourself: Titmuss' Argument Against a Market in Blood," *The Journal of Ethics* 6, 1 (2002): 87–103.
Archard, David, "Insults, Free Speech, and Offensiveness," *Journal of Applied Philosophy* 31, 2 (2014): 127–141.
Archer, Alfred, Bart Engelen, and Viktor Ivankovic, "Effective Vote Markets and the Tyranny of Wealth," *Res Publica* 25, 1 (2019): 39–54.
Aristotle, *Categories and De Interpretatione*, trans. J.L. Ackrill (Oxford: Oxford University Press, 1975).
Arnold, Denis G., "Review: 'Exploitation' and 'The Sweatshop Quandary'," *Business Ethics Quarterly* 13, 2 (2003): 243–256.
Aronowitz, Stanley, "The Unknown Herbert Marcuse," *Social Text* 58 (1999): 133–154.
Austin, J.L., *How to Do Things with Words* (New York: Oxford University Press, 1965).
Azoulay, Pierre, Joshua S. Graff Zivin, and Gustavo Manso, "Incentives and Creativity: Evidence from the Academic Life Sciences," *RAND Journal of Economics* 42, 3 (2011): 527–554.
Baker, G.P., and P.M.S. Hacker, *Language, Sense, and Nonsense* (Oxford: Blackwell, 1984).
Barber, Benjamin R., *Consumed: How Markets Corrupt Children, Infantilize Adults, and Swallow Citizens Whole* (New York: W. W. Norton & Company, 2008).
Barbour, Virginia, "Perverse Incentives and Perverse Publishing Practices," *Science Bulletin* 60, 14 (2015): 1225–1226.
Bautista-Puig, Nuria, Luis Moreno Lorente, and Elias Sanz-Casado, "Proposed Methodology for Measuring the Effectiveness of Policies Designed to Further Research," *Research Evaluation* (2020): 1–15. doi:10.1093/reseval/rvaa021.
Ben-Ari, Eyal, "On Acknowledgements in Ethnographies," *Journal of Anthropological Research* 43, 1 (1987): 63–84.
Bentham, Jeremy, *The Rationale of Reward* (London: Robert Heward, 1830).
Bicchieri, Cristina, *Norms in the Wild: How to Diagnose, Measure, and Change Social Norms* (New York: Oxford University Press, 2017).
Blackburn, Simon, *Spreading the Word* (Oxford: Oxford University Press, 1984).
Bloch, Maurice, "Marriage Amongst Equals: An Analysis of the Marriage Ceremony of the Merina of Madagascar," *Man* 13, 1 (1978): 21–33.
Bloch, Maurice, "The Symbolism of Money in Imerina," in J. Parry and M. Bloch, *Money and the Morality of Exchange* (New York: Cambridge University Press, 1989): 165–190.
Bloch, Maurice, "New Foreword," in Octave Mannoni, trans. Pamela Powesland, *Prospero and Caliban: The Psychology of Colonization* (Ann Arbor, MI: University of Michigan Press, 1990): v–xx.
Booth, Anthony Robert, "The Real Symbolic Limits of Markets," *Analysis* 78, 2 (2018): 198–207.
Bouville, Mathieu, "Plagiarism: Words and Ideas," *Science and Engineering Ethics* 14, 3 (2008): 311–322.
Boxhill, Bernard R., "Self-Respect and Protest," *Philosophy & Public Affairs* 6, 1 (1976): 58–69.
Brennan, Jason, *The Ethics of Voting* (Princeton, NJ: Princeton University Press, 2011).
Brennan, Jason, *Against Democracy* (Princeton, NJ: Princeton University Press, 2016).
Brennan, Jason, *Good Work if You Can Get It: How to Succeed in Academia* (Baltimore, MD: Johns Hopkins University Press, 2020).
Brennan, Jason, *Why It's OK to Want to Be Rich* (New York: Routledge, 2021).

Brennan, Jason, and Peter M. Jaworski, "Markets Without Symbolic Limits," *Ethics* 125, 4 (2015a): 1053–1077.

Brennan, Jason, and Peter M. Jaworski, "In Defense of Commodification," *Moral Philosophy and Politics* 2, 2 (2015b): 357–377.

Brennan, Jason, and Peter M. Jaworski, "Klotzes and Glotzes, Semiotics and Embodying Normative Stances," *Business Ethics Journal Review* 4, 2 (2016a): 7–13.

Brennan, Jason, and Peter M. Jaworski, *Markets Without Limits: Moral Virtues and Commercial Interests* (New York: Routledge, 2016b).

Brennan, Jason, and Peter M. Jaworski, "If You Can Reply for Money, You Can Reply for Free," *Journal of Value Inquiry* 51 (2017): 655–661.

Brennan, Jason, and Phillip Magness, *Cracks in the Ivory Tower: The Moral Mess of Higher Education* (New York: Oxford University Press, 2019).

Brunning, Dennis A., "Beware the Ghost Writer," *Nature* 252, December 6 (1974): 437.

Carnegy-Arbuthnott, Hannah, "On a Promise or on the Game: What's Wrong with Selling Consent?," *Journal of Applied Philosophy* 37, 3 (2020): 408–427.

Carruthers, Bruce G., and Laura Ariovich, *Money and Credit: A Sociological Approach* (London: Polity Press, 2010).

Caton, L.S., "The Economic Influence of the Development in Shipbuilding Techniques, 1450 to 1485," *Journal of a Fictitious Italian Historical Society* 0, 0 (1954): 1450–1485.

Caulfield, Matthew, "The Expressive Functions of Pay," *Business Ethics Journal Review* 6, 1 (2016): 1–6.

Chang, Ruth, "The Possibility of Parity," *Ethics* 112, 4 (2002): 659–688.

Choi, Ginny Seung, and Virgil Henry Storr, *Do Markets Corrupt Our Morals?* (Basingstoke: Palgrave Macmillan, 2019).

Chomanski, Bartek, "What's Wrong with Designing People to Serve?," *Ethical Theory and Moral Practice* 22, 4 (2019): 993–1015.

Cichocki, Piotr, and Marcin Kilarski, "On 'Eskimo Words for Snow': The Life Cycle of Linguistic Misconception," *Historiographia Linguistica* XXXVII, 3 (2010): 341–377.

Cohen, Lloyd, *Increasing the Supply of Transplant Organs: The Virtues of an Options Market* (Berlin: Springer, 1995).

Corlett, J. Angelo, "Ethical Issues in Journal Peer-Review," *Journal of Academic Ethics* 2 (2004): 355–366.

Cornford, F.M., *Microcosmographica Academica: Being a Guide for the Young Academic Politician* (Cambridge: Bowes & Bowes, 1908).

Cowen, Nick, and Rachela Colosi, "Sex Work and Online Platforms: What Should Regulation Do?," *Journal of Entrepreneurship and Public Policy* 10, 2 (2021): 284–303.

Crummett, Dustin, "Expression and Indication in Ethics and Political Philosophy," *Res Publica* 25, 3 (2019): 387–406.

Danaher, John, "The Symbolic-Consequences Argument in the Sex Robot Debate," in J. Danaher and N. McArthur (Eds.), *Robot Sex: Social and Ethical Implications* (Cambridge, MA: MIT Press, 2017): 103–132.

Davidson, Donald, *Inquiries into Truth and Interpretation* (Oxford: Oxford University Press, 2001).

Davies, Benjamin, and Giulia Felappi, "Publish or Perish," *Metaphilosophy* 48, 5 (2017): 745–761.

Davis, Ryan W., "Symbolic Values," *Journal of the American Philosophical Association* 5, 4 (2019): 449–467.

Davis, Wayne A., "Grice's Meaning Project," *Teorema: Revista Internacional de Filosofía* 26, 2 (2007): 41–58.

de Duve, Christian, Thierry de Barsy, Brian Poole, Andre Trouet, Paul Tulkens, and François van Hoof, "Lysosomotropic Agents," *Biochemical Pharmacology* 23, 18 (1974): 2495–2531.
de Reuse, Willem J., "Primitivism in Hunter and Gatherer Languages: The Case of Eskimo Words for Snow," in Tom Guldemann, Patrick McConvell, and Richard A. Rhodes (Eds.), *The Language of Hunter-Gatherers* (Cambridge: Cambridge University Press, 2020): 523–551.
Dick, David G., "Transformable Goods and the Limits of What Money Can Buy," *Moral Philosophy and Politics* 4, 1 (2017): 121–140.
Dick, David G., "Impure Semiotic Objections to Markets," *Public Affairs Quarterly* 32, 3 (2018): 227–246.
Dobell, Clifford, "Dr O. Uplavici (1887–1938)," *Parasitology* 30 (1938): 239–241.
Dougherty, M.V., *Correcting the Scholarly Record for Research Integrity in the Aftermath of Plagiarism* (Dordrecht: Springer, 2018).
Dougherty, M.V., "The Pernicious Effects of Compression Plagiarism on Scholarly Argumentation," *Argumentation* 33 (2019): 391–412.
Dougherty, M.V., *Disguised Academic Plagiarism: A Typology and Case Studies for Researchers and Editors* (Dordrecht: Springer, 2020).
Dougherty, M.V., Pernille Harsting, and Russell L. Friedman, "40 Cases of Plagiarism," *Bulletin de Philosophie médiévale* 51 (2009): 350–391.
Dubner, Stephen, and Steven Levitt, "The Gift Card Economy," *New York Times*, January 7, 2007.
Dummett, Michael, *The Seas of Language* (Oxford: Oxford University Press, 1993).
Dunea, George, "Uplavici Syndrome," *British Medical Journal* 1 (April 1, 1978): 846–847.
Dworkin, Gerald, "Review of James Stacy Taylor, *Practical Autonomy and Bioethics*," *Notre Dame Philosophical Reviews* 9 (2009). Available at: https://ndpr.nd.edu/reviews/practical-autonomy-and-bioethics/.
Dworkin, Ronald, *Sovereign Virtue: The Theory and Practice of Equality* (Cambridge, MA: Harvard University Press, 2000).
Ellickson, Robert C., "The Market for Social Norms," *American Law and Economics Review* 3, 1 (2001):1–49.
Elster, Jon, *The Cement of Society: A Study of Social Order* (New York: Cambridge University Press, 1989).
Emblidge, David, "The Sick/Healthy Humor of Lenny Bruce," *Revue française d'études américaines* 4 (1977): 103–114.
Esarey, Justin, "Does Peer Review Identify the Best Papers? A Simulation Study of Editors, Reviewers, and the Scientific Publication Process," *PS: Political Science and Politics* 50, 4 (2017): 963–969.
Eyal, Nir, and Emma Tieffenbach, "Incommensurability and Trade," *The Monist* 99, 4 (2016): 387–405.
Fanelli, Daniele, "Pressures to Publish: What Effects Do We See?," in Mario Biagioli and Alexandra Lippman (Eds.), *Gaming the Metrics: Misconduct and Manipulation in Academic Research* (Cambridge, MA: MIT Press, 2020): 111–122.
Fee, S., "Fisiky ty mahaondaty. Textiles and Social Life in Androy, Madagascar," PhD dissertation, INALCO, Paris, 2003.
Feeley-Harnik, Gillian, *A Green Estate: Restoring Independence in Madagascar* (Washington, DC: Smithsonian Institution Press, 1991).
Feinberg, Joel, "The Expressive Function of Punishment," *The Monist* 49, 3 (1965): 397–423.

Flanigan, J., "Book Review: Michael J. Sandel, *What Money Can't Buy: The Moral Limits of Markets*," *Leadership and the Humanities* 3, 1 (2015): 73–78.
Foucault, Michel, *The Archaeology of Knowledge* (London: Tavistock, 1974).
Foucault, Michel, *The Order of Things* (London: Tavistock, 1970).
Franzoni, Chiara, Giuseppe Scellato, and Paula Stephan, "Changing Incentives to Publish," *Science* 333 (2011): 702–703.
Frey, Bruno S., "Publishing as Prostitution? – Choosing Between One's Own Ideas and Academic Success," *Public Choice* 116 (2003): 205–223.
Frey, Bruno S., and Reto Jegen, "Motivation Crowding Theory," *Journal of Economic Surveys* 15, 5 (2001): 589–611.
Gelles, Richard J., "Violence in the Family: A Review of Research in the Seventies," *Journal of Marriage and Family* 42, 4 (1980): 873–885.
Ghose, T., and S.P. Nigam, "Antibody as a Carrier of Chlorambucil," *Cancer* 29, 5 (1972): 1398–1400.
Giroux, Henry A., *Impure Acts: The Practical Politics of Cultural Studies* (New York: Routledge, 2000).
Gombrich, Ernst H., *The Image and the Eye: Further Studies in the Psychology of Pictorial Representation* (Ithaca, NY: Cornell University Press, 1982).
Grant, Ruth W., *Strings Attached: Untangling the Ethics of Incentives* (Princeton, NJ: Princeton University Press, 2012).
Grice, H.P., "Meaning," *The Philosophical Review* 66, 3 (1957): 377–388.
Guzmán, Ricardo Andrés, and Michael C. Munger, "A Theory of Just Market Exchange," *Journal of Value Inquiry* 54, 1 (2020): 91–188.
Harley, Sandra, "Accountants Divided: Research Selectivity and Academic Accounting Labour in UK Universities," *Critical Perspectives on Accounting* 11, 5 (2000): 549–582.
Hartree, Edward F., "Ethics for Authors: A Case History of Acrosin," *Perspectives in Biology and Medicine* 20, 1 (1976): 82–91.
Hayashi, Kamichika, Takeshi Onda, Takahiro Iwasaki, Mitsuru Takata, Kiyotaka Mori, Hiroyuki Matsuda, Shinya Watanabe, Hidetoshi Tamura, Takahiko Shibahara, and Masayuki Takano, "A Case of a Stafne Bone Defect Associated with Sublingual Glands in the Lingual Side of the Mandible," *Case Studies in Dentistry* (December 18, 2020): 1–4. Available at: https://doi.org/10.1155/2020/8851174.
Hayek, F.A., *The Constitution of Liberty* (Chicago: University of Chicago Press, 1960).
Henry, O., "A Blackjack Bargainer," in O. Henry, *O. Henry Stories* (New York: Platt & Munk, 1962): 167–188.
Herodotus, *The Histories*, trans. A.D. Godley (Cambridge, MA: Harvard University Press, 1920).
Hexter, J.P., "Publish or Perish—A Defense," *The Public Interest* 17 (1969): 60–77.
Hillel-Rubin, David, *Action and Its Explanation* (New York: Oxford University Press, 2003).
Hodgson, Geoffrey M., "On the Limits of Markets," *Journal of Institutional Economics* 17, 1 (2020): 153–170.
House of Lords, *The Law Times Reports*, vol. 89, *September 1903 to February 1904* (London: Horace Cox, 1904).
Hubbard, William, "Inventing Norms," *Connecticut Law Review* 44, 2 (2011): 369–414.
Hughes, Paul, "Exploitation, Autonomy, and the Case for Organ Sales," *International Journal of Applied Philosophy* 12, 1 (1998): 89–95.
Hume, David, *Treatise on Human Nature* (Oxford: Oxford University Press, 1978).
Hynes, Maria, Scott Sharpe, and Alastair Grieg, "Appearing True in the Social Sciences: Reflections on an Academic Hoax," *Journal of Sociology* 48, 3 (2011): 287–303.

Jevons, W. Stanley, *Money and the Mechanism of Exchange* (New York: D. Appleton & Co., 1896).
Johnson, Tara Star, and sj Miller, "Honoring Our History, Envisioning Our Future," *English Education* 48, 1 (2015): 4–10.
Jonker, Julian, "The Meaning of a Market and the Meaning of 'Meaning'," *Journal of Ethics and Social Philosophy* 15, 2 (2019): 186–195.
Josefson, Deborah, "Selling a Kidney Fails to Rescue Indians from Poverty," *British Medical Journal* 325, 7368 (2002): 795.
Kant, Immanuel, *Lectures on Ethics*, Eds. Peter Heath and J.B. Schneewind, trans. Peter Heath (Cambridge: Cambridge University Press, 2001).
Kant, Immanuel, *Groundwork of the Metaphysics of Morals* trans. and Eds. Mary Gregor and Jens Timmerman (Cambridge: Cambridge University Press, 2012).
Kantola, Ilkka, *Probability and Moral Uncertainty in Late Medieval and Early Modern Times* (Helsinki: Luther-Agricola-Society, 1994).
Keat, Russell, "Market Limits and Their Limits," *Economics and Philosophy* 28, 2 (2012): 251–263.
Keat, Russell, "Ethics, Markets, and Cultural Goods," in Allyn Fives and Keith Breen (Eds.), *Philosophy and Political Engagement: Reflection in the Public Sphere* (London: Palgrave Macmillan, 2016): 117–136.
Kerr, Orin S., "A Theory of Law," *Green Bag* 16, 1 (2012): 111.
Keynes, John Maynard, *A Treatise on Money* (London: Macmillan & Co. Ltd, [1930] 1965).
Kline, Jesse, "Read Any Good Books Lately? Post Editors and Columnists Submit Their Picks for Your Holiday Reading: *Markets Without Limits*," *National Post* (December 26,2016). Available at: https://nationalpost.com/opinion/read-any-good-books-lately-post-editors-and-columnists-submit-their-picks-for-your-holiday-reading.
Kolodny, Niko, "Love as Valuing a Relationship," *The Philosophical Review* 112, 2 (2003): 135–189.
Konigs, P., "Two Types of Debunking Arguments," *Philosophical Psychology* 31, 3 (2018): 383–402.
Koplin, Julian J., "Commodification and Human Interests," *Journal of Bioethical Inquiry* 15, 3 (2018): 429–440.
Kopytoff, Igor, "The Cultural Biography of Things: Commoditization as Process," in Arjun Appadurai (Ed.), *The Social Life of Things: Commodities in Cultural Perspective* (Cambridge: Cambridge University Press, 1986): 64–91.
Krupnik, Igor, and Ludger Müller-Wille, "Franz Boas and Inuktitut Terminology for Ice and Snow: From the Emergence of the Field to the 'Great Eskimo Vocabulary Hoax'," in Igor Krupnik, Claudio Aporta, Shari Gearhead, Gita Laidler, and Lene Kielsen Holm (Eds.), *SIKU: Knowing Our Ice: Documenting Inuit Sea Ice Knowledge and Use* (Dordrecht: Springer, 2010): 377–400.
Kuntz, J.R., "A Litmus Test for Exploitation: James Stacey Taylor's *Stakes and Kidneys*," *Journal of Medicine and Philosophy* 34, 6 (2009): 552–572.
Layman, Daniel, "Review: *Markets Without Limits*," *Business Ethics Quarterly* 26, 4 (2016a): 561–564.
Layman, Daniel, "Expressive Objections to Markets: Normative, Not Symbolic," *Business Ethics Journal Review* 4, 1 (2016b): 1–6.
Leef, George, "What's Really Disgusting?," *Regulation* (Spring 2016): 62–64.
Leslie, Derek, "Are Delays in Academic Publishing Necessary?," *American Economic Review* 95, 1 (2005): 407–413.
Lessig, Lawrence, "The Regulation of Social Meaning," *University of Chicago Law Review* 62, 3 (1995): 943–1045.

Lewis, David, *Convention* (Cambridge, MA: Harvard University Press, 1969).
Lewison, Martin, "Conflicts of Interest? The Ethics of Usury," *Journal of Business Ethics* 22, 4 (1999): 327–339.
Lieberman, Hallie, and Eric Schatzberg, "A Failure of Academic Quality Control: *The Technology of Orgasm*," *Journal of Positive Sexuality* 4, 2 (2018): 24–47.
Lodge, David, *Small World* (New York: Warner Books, 1984).
Lunt, Dorothy A., "Ghost Authors," *Nature* 252, December 20/27 (1974): 629.
Maddox, John, "Plagiarism Is Worse Than Mere Theft," *Nature* 376 August 31(1995): 721.
Maguire, Barry, and Brookes Brown, "Markets, Interpersonal Practices, and Signal Distortion," *Philosophers' Imprint* 19 (2019): 1–16.
Maines, Rachel, *The Technology of Orgasm: "Hysteria," the Vibrator, and Women's Sexual Satisfaction* (Baltimore, MD: Johns Hopkins University Press. 1999).
Mangalaza, W., "Sous la moustiquaire: fidélité conjugale et libertinage chez les Betsimisaraka. L'amour," *Cahiers ethnologiques* 15 (1993): 61–71.
Mannoni, Octave, *Psychologie de la Colonisation* (Paris: Editions du Seuil, 1950).
Martin, Laura, "'Eskimo Words for Snow': A Case Study in the Genesis and Decay of an Anthropological Example," *American Anthropologist* 88, 2 (1986): 418–423.
Maso, Katia, Antonella Grigoletto, Maria J. Vicent, and Gianfranco Pasut, "Molecular Platforms for Targeted Drug Delivery," *International Review of Cell and Molecular Biology* (2019): 1–50. doi:10.1016/bs.ircmb.2019.03.001.
Mayer, Bernd, "How Much Nicotine Kills a Human? Tracing Back the Generally Accepted Lethal Dose to Dubious Self-Experiments in the Nineteenth Century," *Archives of Toxicology* 88, 1 (2014): 5–7.
McGinn, Thomas A.K., "The Expressive Function of Law and the *Lex Imperfecta*," *Roman Legal Tradition* 11 (2015): 1–41.
McIntyre, Alasdair, *After Virtue: A Study in Moral Theory*, 3rd edn (Notre Dame, IN: University of Notre Dame Press, 2007).
Meacham, William, "The Amazing Dr Kouznetsov," *Antiquity: A Review of World Archaeology* 81, 313 (2007): 779–783.
Miller, sj, "Ubuntu: Calling *in* the Field," *English Education* 48, 3 (2016): 192–200.
Milne, A.A., *Winnie-the-Pooh* (London: E. P. Dutton, 1926).
Mogensen, Andreas L., "Meaning, Medicine, and Merit," *Utilitas* 32, 1 (2020): 90–107.
Momoi, Beverly, "Satz to Graduates: Some Things Should Never Be for Sale," *Stanford Report*, June 12, 2010. Available at: https://news.stanford.edu/news/2010/june/class-day-lecture-061210.html.
Morrison, Richard, "Book Review: *Markets Without Limits: Moral Virtues and Commercial Interests*," *Cato Journal* 36, 3 (2016): 721–725.
Nayar, Kavita Illona, "Sweetening the Deal: Dating for Compensation in the Digital Age," *Journal of Gender Studies* 26, 3 (2016): 335–346.
Ng, Yew-Kwang, *Markets and Morals: Justifying Kidney Sales and Legalizing Prostitution* (New York: Cambridge University Press, 2019).
Nordhaus, William D., "Two Centuries of Productivity Growth in Computing," *The Journal of Economic History* 67, 1 (2007): 128–159.
Nosek, Brian A., Jeffrey R. Spies, and Matt Motyl, "Scientific Utopia: II. Restructuring Incentives and Practices to Promote Truth Over Publishability," *Perspectives on Psychological Science* 7, 6 (2012): 615–631.
Nozick, Robert, *The Examined Life: Philosophical Meditations* (New York: Simon & Schuster, 1989).

Nozick, Robert, *The Nature of Rationality* (Princeton, NJ: Princeton University Press, 1993).
Nylenna, Magne, Povl Riis, and Yngve Karlsson, "Multiple Blinded Reviews of the Same Two Manuscripts: Effects of Referee Characteristics and Publication Language," *The Journal of the American Medical Association* 272, 2 (1994): 149–151.
Olech, Eli, and Balraj K. Arora, "Lingual Mandibular Bone Cavity," *Oral Surgery, Oral Medicine, Oral Pathology* 14, 11 (1961): 1360–1366.
Paldan, Katrin, Hanno Sauer, and Nils-Frederic Wagner, "Promoting Inequality? Self-Monitoring Applications and the Problem of Social Justice," *AI & SOCIETY* (2018): https://doi.org/10.1007/s00146-018-0835-7.
Panitch, Vida, "Liberalism, Commodification, and Justice," *Politics, Philosophy & Economics* 19, 1 (2020): 62–82.
Pateman, Carole, *The Sexual Contract* (Stanford, CA: Stanford University Press, 1988).
Patriotta, Gerado, "Crafting Papers for Publication: Novelty and Convention in Academic Writing," *Journal of Management Studies* 54, 5 (2017): 747–759.
Peters, Uwe, "An Argument for Egalitarian Confirmation Bias and Against Political Diversity in Academia," *Synthese* (2020). Available at: https://link.springer.com/article/10.1007/s11229-020-02846-2.
Phillips, Anne, *Our Bodies, Whose Property?* (Princeton, NJ: Princeton University Press, 2013).
Pitsoulis, Athanassios, and Jan Schnellenbach, "On Property Rights and Incentives in Academic Publishing," *Research Policy* 41, 8 (2012): 1440–1447.
Plato, "Cratylus," in Plato, *Cratylus. Parmenides. Greater Hippias. Lesser Hippias*, trans. H.N. Fowler (Cambridge, MA: Harvard University Press, 1926): 1–192.
Posner, Eric A., "Symbols, Signals, and Social Norms in Politics and the Law," *Journal of Legal Studies* 27 (1998): 765–797.
Pullum, Geoffrey K., "The Great Eskimo Vocabulary Hoax," *Natural Language and Linguistic Theory* 7 (1989): 275–281.
Putnam, Hilary, *Mind, Language, and Reality: Philosophical Papers*, vol. 2 (Cambridge: Cambridge University Press, 1975).
Quine, W.V.O., *Word and Object* (Cambridge, MA: MIT Press, 1960).
Radin, Margaret Jane, "Market-Inalienability," *Harvard Law Review* 100, 8 (1987): 1849–1937.
Radin, Margaret Jane, *Contested Commodities: The Trouble with Trade in Sex, Children, Body Parts, and Other Things* (Cambridge, MA: Harvard University Press, 1996).
Rand, Erin J., *Reclaiming Queer: Activist and Academic Rhetorics of Resistance* (Birmingham, AL: University of Alabama Press, 2014).
Raz, Joseph, *The Morality of Freedom* (Oxford: Oxford University Press, 1986).
Rekda, Ole Bjørn, "Academic Urban Legends," *Social Studies of Science* 44, 4 (2014): 638–654.
Ritzer, George, "The 'McDonaldization' of Society," *Journal of American Culture* 6, 1 (1983): 100–107.
Rivlin, Ram, "The Puzzle of Intra-Familial Commodification," *University of Toronto Law Review* 67, 1 (2017): 68–95.
Rodgers, Lamont, "Book Review: Jason F. Brennan and Peter Jaworski, *Markets Without Limits: Moral virtues and commercial interests*," *Philosophy in Review* 37, 1 (2017): 8–10.
Rosamond, Ben, "Plagiarism, Academic Norms, and the Governance of the Profession," *Politics* 22, 3 (2002): 167–174.

Ross, W.D., *The Right and the Good*, Ed. Philip Stratton-Lake (Oxford: Clarendon Press, [1930] 2002).
Rushton, Martin A., "Solitary Bone Cysts in the Mandible," *British Dental Journal* 81, 2 (1946): 37–49.
Sandel, Michael J., *What Money Can't Buy: The Moral Limits of Markets* (New York: Farrar, Straus and Giroux, 2012).
Satz, Debra, *Why Some Things Should Not Be for Sale: The Moral Limits of Markets* (Oxford: Oxford University Press, 2010).
Saussure, Ferdinand de., *Course in General Linguistics*, Eds. Charles Bally and Albert Sechehaye, trans. Roy Harris (La Salle, IL: Open Court. 1983).
Schroter, Sara, Nick Black, Stephen Evans, Fiona Godlee, Lyda Osorio, and Richard Smith, "What Errors Do Peer Reviewers Detect, and Does Training Improve Their Ability to Detect Them?," *Journal of the Royal Society of Medicine* 101, 10 (2008): 507–514.
Semrau, Luke, "Kidneys Save Lives: Markets Would Probably Help," *Public Affairs Quarterly* 27, 4 (2013): 369–391.
Semrau, Luke, "Review: *Markets Without Limits*," *Economics and Philosophy* 33, 2 (2017): 326–332.
Silk, Alex, "Theories of Vagueness and Theories of Law," *Legal Theory* 25, 2 (2019): 132–152.
Simmel, Georg, *The Philosophy of Money*, Ed. David Frisby, trans. Tom Bottomore and David Frisby, 3rd edn (London: Routledge, 2004).
Singh, Supriya, "The Cultural Distinctiveness of Money," *Sociological Bulletin* 45, 1 (1996): 55–85.
Skidelsky, Robert, and Edward Skidelsky, *How Much Is Enough? Money and the Good Life* (New York: Other Press, 2012).
Skorupski, John, *Symbol and Theory: A Philosophical Study of Theories of Religion in Social Anthropology* (Cambridge: Cambridge University Press, 1976).
Smith, Neal, and Aaron Cumberledge, "Quotation Errors in General Science Journals," *Proceedings of the Royal Society A* 476, 2242 (2020): 1–7.
Snapper, John W., "On the Web, Plagiarism Matters More Than Copyright Piracy," *Ethics and Information Technology* 1 (1999): 127–135.
Sokal, Alan, *Beyond the Hoax: Science, Philosophy and Culture* (New York: Oxford University Press, 2008).
Somin, Ilya, "Opinion: Brennan and Jaworski's 'Markets Without Limits'," *The Washington Post*, November 13 (2015). Available at: www.washingtonpost.com/news/volokh-conspiracy/wp/2015/11/13/brennan-and-jaworskis-markets-without-limits/.
Sparks, Jacob, "Can't Buy Me Love: A Reply to Brennan and Jaworski," *Journal of Philosophical Research* 42 (2017): 341–352.
Sparks, Jacob, "You Give Love a Bad Name," *Business Ethics Journal Review* 7, 2 (2019): 7–13.
Sparling, Robert, "Blocked Exchanges and the Constitution: Montesquieu on the Moral and Constitutional Limits of Markets," *Polity* 51, 3 (2019): 532–558.
Sperling, Daniel, *Posthumous Interests: Legal and Ethical Perspectives* (New York: Cambridge University Press, 2008).
Stearns, Laurie, "Copy Wrong: Plagiarism, Process, Property, and the Law," *California Law Review* 80, 2 (1992): 513–553.
Stevens, Joan, "Woozles in Brontëland: A Cautionary Tale," *Studies in Bibliography* 24 (1971): 99–108.
Stoebenau, Kristen, "'Côtier' Sexual Identity as Constructed by the Urban Merina of Antananarivo, Madagascar," *Études océan Indien* 45 (2010): 1–16.

Stone, Martin W.F., "The Origins of Probabilism in Late Scholastic Thought: A Prolegomenon to Further Study," *Recherches de Théologie et Philosophie médiévales* 67, 1 (2000): 114–157.

Suárez, Francisco, "De virtute et statu religionis," in C. Berton (Ed.), *Opera Omnia* (Paris: Lodovicus Vives, 1859).

Sunstein, Cass R., "On the Expressive Function of Law," *University of Pennsylvania Law Review* 144, 5 (1996): 2021–2053.

Sutton, Mike, "SPINACH, IRON and POPEYE: Ironic Lessons from Biochemistry and History on the Importance of Healthy Eating, Healthy Scepticism and Adequate Citation," *Internet Journal of Criminology* (2010): 1–34. Available at: https://botanologia.gr/wp-content/uploads/2020/02/spinach.pdf.

Sweetland, James H., "Errors in Bibliographic Citations: A Continuing Problem," *The Library Quarterly* 59, 4 (1989): 291–304.

Taylor, James Stacey, *Stakes and Kidneys: Why Markets in Human Body Parts Are Morally Imperative* (Aldershot: Ashgate, 2005).

Taylor, James Stacey, "Book Note: Jason Brennan and Peter M. Jaworski, *Markets Without Limits: Moral virtues and commercial interests*," *Choice Reviews* 54, 1 (2016a). Available at: www.choicereviews.org/review/10.5860/CHOICE.198180.

Taylor, James Stacey, "What Limits Should Markets Be Without?," *Business Ethics Journal Review* 4, 7 (2016b): 41–46.

Taylor, James Stacey, "Logrolling, Earmarking, and Vote Buying," *Philosophia* 44 (2016c): 905–913.

Taylor, James Stacey, "Markets in Votes and the Tyranny of Wealth," *Res Publica* 23, 3 (2017a): 313–328.

Taylor, James Stacey, "Autonomy, Vote Buying, and Constraining Options," *Journal of Applied Philosophy*, 34, 5 (2017b): 711–723.

Taylor, James Stacey, "Markets in Votes, Voter Liberty, and the Burden of Justification," *Journal of Philosophical Research* 42 (2017c): 325–340.

Taylor, James Stacey, "What Can't Money Buy?," *Public Affairs Quarterly* 32, 1 (2018a): 45–66.

Taylor, James Stacey, "Two (Weak) Cheers for Markets in Votes," *Philosophia* 46 (2018b): 223–239.

Taylor, James Stacey, "Why Prohibiting Donor Compensation Can Prevent Plasma Donors from Giving Their Informed Consent to Donate," *Journal of Medicine and Philosophy* 44, 1 (2019a): 10–32.

Taylor, James Stacey, "Sandel, Semiotics, and Money-Based Exchange: What We Can Learn from Brennan and Jaworski's Failed Critique," *Public Affairs Quarterly* 33, 2 (2019b): 159–176.

Taylor, James Stacey, "Buying and Selling Friendship," *American Philosophical Quarterly* 56, 2 (2019c): 187–202.

Taylor, James Stacey, "The Myth of Semiotic Arguments in Democratic Theory and How This Exposes Problems with Peer Review," *International Journal of Applied Philosophy*, forthcoming.

Thoma, Kurt H., "Case Report of a So-Called Latent Bone Cyst," *Oral Surgery, Oral Medicine, Oral Pathology* 8, 9 (1955): 963–966.

Tyler, Tom R., and Renee Weber, "Support for the Death Penalty: Instrumental Response to Crime, or Symbolic Attitude?," *Law and Society Review* 17, 1 (1982): 21–46.

Velthuis, Olav, *Talking Prices: Symbolic Meanings of Prices on the Market for Contemporary Art* (Princeton, NJ: Princeton University Press, 2005).

Volacu, Alexandru, "Electoral Quid Pro Quo: A Defence of Barter Markets in Votes," *Journal of Applied Philosophy* 36, 5 (2019): 769–784.

von Platz, Jeppe, "Person to Person: A Note on the Ethics of Commodification," *Journal of Value Inquiry* 51, 4 (2017): 647–653.

Waddams, S.M., "Unconscionability in Contracts," *Modern Law Review* 39, 4 (1976): 369–393.

Waldfogel, Joel, "The Deadweight Loss of Christmas," *American Economic Review* 83, 5 (1993): 1328–1336.

Waldfogel, Joel, *Scroogenomics: Why You Shouldn't Buy Presents for the Holidays* (Princeton, NJ: Princeton University Press, 2009).

Walzer, Michael, *Spheres of Justice: A Defense of Pluralism and Equality* (New York: Basic Books, 1983).

Waugh, Evelyn, *Decline and Fall* (London: Chapman & Hall, 1955).

Weber-Wulff, Debora, *False Feathers: A Perspective on Academic Plagiarism* (Dordrecht: Springer, 2014).

Wertheimer, Alan, *Exploitation* (Princeton, NJ: Princeton University Press, 1996).

Wittgenstein, Ludwig, *Philosophical Investigations*, 3rd edn, trans. G.E.M. Anscombe (Harlow: Pearson, 1973).

Wolterstorff, Nicholas, "Would You Stomp on a Picture of Your Mother? Would You Kiss an Icon?," *Faith and Philosophy* 32, 1 (2015): 3–24.

Zelizer, Viviana A., *The Social Meaning of Money: Pin Money, Paychecks, Poor Relief, and Other Currencies* (New York: Basic Books, 1994; reprinted 1995).

INDEX

academic referees, *see* referees
Adams, Robert Merrihew, 99–101, 101, 102, 113n30, 113n32
adoption auctions, 49
Alice's Adventures in Wonderland, 121
Alternative America, 53, 54, 108, 109, 160, 161, 178–179n49, 180n76
altruism, 25
Anderson, Elizabeth, 2, 5, 11, 19–25, 29n2, 30n18, 32n67, 32n80–81, 33n96, 33n100–101, 34n122, 40, 43, 44n9, 45n41, 57n9, 61–71, 71n1, 71n6, 72n12–15, 73n32, 73n43–44, 73n49, 74n51, 74n66, 86, 88n33, 89n67, 89n72, 101, 111n2, 118, 119, 122, 123, 128, 136n39, 149, 150, 158n76–77, 160, 169, 170, 185, 191, 196n17
anti-expansion criticism of markets, 15, 16, 30n24, 154–155n33
Aquinas, Thomas, 29, 119
Archard, David, 2, 5, 11, 25, 27–28, 33n102, 34n118, 34n124, 40, 43, 46n49, 74n65–66, 75, 83–86, 89n71–74, 89n77, 112n2, 118, 153n18, 173
Ariovich, Laura, 166, 167, 177n26
Aristotle, 46n53
Aronowitz, Stanley, 144, 157–158n64
art, 37, 39, 60–61n43
Asymmetry Thesis, 2–5, 11–34, 37, 43, 48, 57, 62, 63, 66, 71, 75, 89n73, 93, 111, 115n72, 118, 134n2, 148, 154n33, 199

Austin, J. L., 40
authorship, misattributed, 145, 147, 148, 156n50, 163, 198n38
autonomy, 20–23, 23–25, 63, 67, 72n13, 128

Baker, G. P., 40
Barber, Benjamin, 30n24, 154–155n33
bare wrong, 11, 29n1, 36, 42, 43
bets, 49, 57n8, 58n11
Betsileo, the, 166
Betsimisaraka, the, 166, 168, 178n36
Bicchieri, Cristina, 116n86, 149–150
Blackburn, Simon, 40
blood, 25, 27–28, 34n118, 40, 83–86, 89n73, 173, 196n16
  See also gift, blood as a
body parts, markets in, 39, 98, 112n2, 119–120, 135n13
  See also kidneys, markets in
  See also organs, markets in
bonded labor, 16, 31n33
Booth, Anthony Robert, 95, 103–105, 107–110, 115n72, 116n80, 116n91, 116n94, 136n46
bounty hunters, *see* referees, as bounty hunters
Bouville, Mathieu, 192
Brennan, Jason, 44n6, 142, 144–145, 152n11, 153n20, 153n27, 175–176n19
Brennan, Jason, and Peter M. Jaworski, attribution of the Asymmetry Thesis to

critics of markets, 2, 3, 11, 11–12, 16, 18, 19–20, 25, 27, 28–29, 29n2, 30n24, 31n46, 33n101, 33n102, 34n126, 43, 63, 71, 75, 134n2; attribution of semiotic objections to critics of markets, 2, 3, 5, 15, 26, 35–37, 42–43, 44n9, 49, 51, 53, 55, 61–63, 66–68, 75, 79, 83, 86; careless in identifying their own thesis, 30n12, 30n25; orthodox view of market scope, 33n88, 51
bribery, 75, 76
Brown, Brookes, 97–98, 107, 158n72
Brunning, Dennis A., 147, 156n46
business ethics, 153n14, 201

careerism, 154n31
careerists, *see* careerism
Carlos III University of Madrid, 142
Carruthers, Bruce G., 166, 167, 177n26
caucus-race, 121
chess, 121–122
children, markets in, 49–50, 50–51, 57, 60n45
See also adoption auctions
citation, absent, 16, 20, 33n100, 57n9, 71n7, 72n9, 72n26, 79, 144, 146, 153n20, 153n23, 154–155n33, 156n47, 157–158n64, 182; "cut-out," 156n41; inaccurate, 6, 72n12, 74n66, 136–137n53, 144, 148, 151, 177–178n33, 182
Civil Rights Act, 99, 184
commensurable values, 56, 103–104, 114n48, 116n84, 130
commodity, Anderson's understanding of, 21–23, 24–25, 32–33n81, 61–62, 66–71, 73n32, 73n43, 170
commodification, Anderson's understanding of, *see* commodity, Anderson's understanding of
commodification-resistant goods, *see* ontological limits to markets
comparable values, 103–104, 136n46
Confederate battle flag, 40
Congress, 13–14, 15
consent, 24, 40, 85–86, 126, 127
Contamination of Meaning argument, 27–28, 83–84
contracts, 23–25, 33n96, 33n100, 63, 107, 169, 187
conventionalism (action), 64–65
conventionalist view of meaning, 39–41, 46n53, 76, 87n13, 89n74, 96, 97,

102, 103, 110, 112n3, 113n30, 115n49, 115n52, 168
Corlett, J. Angelo, 144
corruption, 37–38, 44n18, 50, 56, 58n14–15, 69
crowding out, 123–124
Crummett, Dustin, 112n2, 127

Davidson, Donald, 40
death, financial speculation concerning, 49, 50–51, 57n8, 58n11, 60n45
death penalty, 114n44
democracy, 18–19, 31–32n57
Dick, David J., 47n65, 89n83
dignity, 23, 24, 37, 48, 58n10, 69, 120, 128
Dobell, Clifford, 147
dominant good, 26–27, 78
domino arguments, 27, 83–84
Dougherty, M. V., 191–193, 197–198n37
drugs, 22
Dubner, Stephen, 51, 59n27
Dummett, Michael, 40
duplicate publication, 175–176n19, 197n22
See also plagiarism
Dworkin, Ronald, 101–102

Easter Eggs, hidden ?; mentioned, 6–7, 18
ecclesiastical office, *see* ecclesiastical privilege
See also offices
ecclesiastical privilege, 26, 75, 76, 87n15, 87n16
See also offices
economic coercion, 126
economics, 3, 141, 145, 201
Ellickson, Robert C., 184, 195n1–2, 195n4
Elster, Jon, 149
equality, 18, 65, 101–102, 168; complex, 26, 78, 128; of opportunity, 21; simple, 26, 78
Erosion of Motivation argument, 27, 34n118
Eskimo words for snow, 148, 157n57
ethic of the market, 12
ethic of the queue, 12
See also queuing
etiquette, 65
exploitation, 37, 41, 69, 82, 95, 164, 175n16
expressive theory of rational action, 63
expressivist arguments, 5, 81, 88n41, 94–95, 95–96, 103–105, 110, 111, 111n1, 118, 199, 200; consequentialist

prescriptive, 97–99; descriptive, 95, 96–97; non-consequentialist prescriptivist justifications of individual action, 99–101; non-consequentialist prescriptivist justifications of law and policy, 101–103, 103–105

Feeley-Harnik, Gillian, 166, 168, 177–178n33, 179n50
Feinberg, Joel, 96–97, 112n8, 112–113n11
feuding, 121, 135n17
freedom, 20–23, 24, 28, 34n122, 62–63, 68–71, 72n13, 74n66, 84, 89n67, 120, 123, 128
Frey, R.G., 152n4
friendship, 15, 32n66, 52–55, 57, 58n10, 77, 80–81, 104, 120–121, 122, 127, 128, 129, 131, 135n17, 178–179n49
See also norms, friendship
gambling, *see* bets
games, 7, 121–122
See also Telephone, child's game
Georgetown University, 142, 189; derelict faculty, 152n11; "rock star researchers," 152
"ghost authors," *see* authorship, misattributed
Ghose, T., 147–148
gift, 28, 29n2, 73n43, 83, 109, 165–168, 178n47; blood as a, 28, 83–84; gift certificate as a, 49, 50, 51–52, 52–55, 57, 58n10, 59n29; money as a, 38, 46n54, 49, 50, 51–52, 52–55, 57, 58n10, 59n29, 178–179n49, 1789n53; sex as a, 68, 70; votes as a, 108, 116n87
Grant, Ruth, 30n24, 154–155n33
Gresham's Law, 102
Grice, H. P., 40, 45n39, 46n54, 46n59, 113n30, 116n95

Hacker, P.M.S., 40
hard treatment, 96–97, 112–113n11
harm, 16–18, 28, 37, 39, 41, 64, 69, 70, 80, 82–83, 85, 95, 114–115n48, 126, 131, 132, 154–155n33, 160, 161, 162, 192, 193, 197n26
Hay, Will, 39
healthcare, 40, 76, 87n13, 115n49, 127
Hermogenes, 46n53
Herodotus, 39
Hlava, Jaroslav, 147
hoaxes, 145, 154n30
honor, 20, 179n53

honoraria, 150, 186, 190
honors, 77, 80
Hume, David, 42
incentives, 1, 6, 86, 141–142, 144, 145, 149, 150, 154n29, 154–155n33, 159, 160, 163, 172, 182, 185, 186, 188–191, 196n13, 200, 202, 203n4
"incubation machines," 74n66, 169, 180n61
inequality, 16, 18, 22, 81, 82, 126, 132, 164–165, 175–176n19
inherent limits to markets, 16, 19, 22, 27, 28, 29n2, 41, 119–120, 120–122, 123, 124, 125, 126, 134n7, 135n13, 135n28, 154–155n33
See also, Asymmetry Thesis
intellectual property, 192
interest, charging of, 119
intrinsic value, 15, 25, 56, 63, 98, 101, 114n44–45
instrumental value, 15, 37, 49, 50, 56, 58n11, 62, 66, 67, 73n32, 76, 98, 100, 159

judicial offices, 18, 19, 31–32n57
See also offices
justice, 21, 25–27, 41, 75–79
Just-So story, 184–185

Kant, Immanuel, 24, 119–120, 135n13
Kantian personhood, 130–131
Kerr, Orin S., 143
kidneys, markets in, 3, 16, 18, 40, 126
Koplin, Julian J., 7n11

legal statements, 101, 114n45, 114–115n48
Lessig, Lawrence, 99
Levitt, Steven, 52, 59n27
Lewis, David, 40
libertarian arguments, 12
Lieberman, Hallie, 148
line-standing services, *see* queuing
Lodge, David, 142, 152n5
love, 24, 49, 50, 77, 80–81, 106, 109, 120
Lunt, Dorothy A., 147

MacArthur grant, 191
Maddox, John, 192
Magness, Philip, 142
Maguire, Barry, 97–98, 107, 158n72
Maines, Rachel, 148
Mannoni, Octave, 167
manuscript referees, *see* referees

Marcuse, Herbert, 144, 148, 157n64
market economy, 13, 51, 127–128, 128–129, 133, 134, 202
market inalienability, 16, 121, 122–123, 124, 136–137n53, 154–155n33
market norms, *see* norms, market
markets, noxious, *see* noxious markets
market society, 13, 51, 127–132, 133, 134, 202
market transformation, 122–124
Martin, Laura, 148
martyrdom, 99, 113n28
medical need, 127
Merina, the, 38, 44n23, 148, 165–168, 170, 177n27–28, 178n39, 178n43, 178n47, 178–179n49, 180n66, 202n1
metaphysics, 152n14
misallocation of goods, 37, 69, 79, 127
modal realism, 172
Momoi, Beverly, 79–80, 88n36, 180n64
Monopoly, 122
monopoly, 26

Ng, Yew-Kwang, 164–165, 175–176n19
negligence, 191, 194–195
Nigam, S.P., 147
Nobel Prize, 31–32n57, 80–81, 121, 122, 191
norms, 15, 20–23, 56, 59n43, 63–65, 67, 68, 76, 98–99, 101, 123, 127–128, 129–134, 149–150, 184, 185, 195n1, 195n4, 199; academic, 4, 5, 6, 32n72, 141, 150–151, 158n77, 159–160, 160–161, 170, 172–174, 174n5, 182, 183–185, 186, 189, 190–191, 191–195, 196n9, 196n13, 198n39, 200–202; friendship, 52–55, 131; gift-giving, 55; market, 4, 5, 6, 13, 14, 15, 20, 21, 22, 23, 30n12, 30n21, 51, 56, 57, 61, 62, 63, 66, 67, 68, 70, 71, 73n43–44, 86, 93, 104, 118, 124, 127–128, 129, 131–132, 133, 134, 141, 149, 150, 151, 158n68, 158n73, 158n77, 159–160, 160–161, 162–164, 169, 170, 171, 172, 174, 174n5, 179n50, 180n76, 181n80, 182, 183–185, 186, 188, 189, 190, 192, 193, 196n9, 196n13, 200–202, 203n4; professional, 21–22, 23, 67, 68; semiotic, 97
noxious markets, 16–18, 80, 169
Nozick, Robert, 113n30, 114n43, 114n47

offices, 18–19, 26, 31–32n57, 76–77, 78, 87n16

ontological limits to markets, 77–78, 80–81, 106–107, 120–122, 123, 124
opportunity costs, 39, 64, 72n26, 85
organs, markets in, 39, 72n26, 126, 131
See also kidneys, markets in
Pateman, Carole, 44n9
paternalism, 23, 82, 129
Patriotta, Gerardo, 144
peer review, 1–2, 93, 144, 152n11, 158n72, 196n10
penalties, 96–97, 112–113n11, 189
Pennyfeather, Paul, 100, 113–114n33, 114n40, 114n42
performative demonstration, 200
performative utterances, 40
philosophy of language, 40, 203n3
Piglet, 146
plagiarism, 6, 145, 175–176n19, 182, 191–195, 197n34–35, 197–198n37; self, *see* duplicate publication
Plato, 46n53
pluralistic theory of value, 20, 63, 128
political influence, purchase of, 132
See also votes, markets in
Pooh, *see* Winnie-the-Pooh
Popeye, 148
Preceding Sentence Club, The, 135n19
See also, Second Preceding Sentence Club, The, preferences, 37, 38, 50, 52–54, 82, 106, 109, 116n80, 116n91, 131–132
principle of charity, 42, 84, 50, 173
prizes, 77, 80, 121, 122
See also Nobel Prize
See also Pulitzer Prize
promissory obligation, 29n1, 42
prostitution, 2, 16, 23, 31n33, 34n122, 44n9, 62, 67–68, 70, 74n51, 75, 76, 81–82, 88n57, 89n67, 136–137n53, 165, 168, 179n50
See also sex
Pulitzer Prize, 77–78
Pullum, Geoffrey K., 148
punishment, 96–97, 112n8, 112–113n11
See also death penalty
See also hard treatment
Putnam, Hilary, 40

queuing, 12–14, 117n98, 125
Quine, W. V. O., 40, 45n41

Radin, Margaret Jane, 27, 30n24, 34n126, 45n36, 73n43, 82, 88n57, 130–131, 136–137n53, 179n55

refereeing, *see* referees
referees, 2, 6, 7n14, 142–145, 154n29, 159, 173, 182–185, 188, 189, 196n10, 200; as bounty hunters, 186–188, 200
references, 6, 7, 143–144, 146–147, 154n33, 160, 161, 163–164, 173, 175n13, 183, 185, 186–188, 194, 201
See also citation, absent
regulative ideal of government, 18, 19, 31n53
reproductive labor, 16, 22, 30n31, 44n9, 81–83, 88n57
See also, surrogacy
republican ideal of government, 18, 19, 31n53, 31–32n57
Research Assessment Exercise, 196n9, 202
retroactive law, 97
rights, 12, 24, 33n96, 37, 41, 62, 69, 82, 95, 102, 105, 115n52, 153n20, 162
ritual action, 40, 165
Ritzer, George, 30n24, 154–155n33, 180n71
Rosamond, Ben, 192
Rubik's Cube, 164–165, 170, 180n79
Rushton, Martin, 147–148

Sakalava, the, 166, 167, 168, 178n3
Sandel, Michael J., 2, 5, 11, 12–15, 19, 30n12, 30n17–18, 30n21, 30n23, 30n24, 40, 43, 48–57, 58n10–11, 58n15, 58n17, 59n27, 59n29, 59n34, 60n45, 60n46, 71, 71–72n6, 86, 88n33, 111–112n2, 118, 121, 128, 130, 191
Satz, Debra, 2, 5, 11–12, 15–19, 20, 31n33, 31n39, 31n46, 31n53, 31n55, 40, 43, 44n9, 51, 57n9, 75, 79–80, 80–81, 81–83, 86, 87n20, 88n32, 88n36, 88n57, 89n77, 112n2, 117n98, 118, 126, 135n33, 136–137n53, 169, 180n64
Schatzberg, Eric, 148
scholarshit, 144, 148, 151, 183, 195
Second Preceding Sentence Club, The, 122
See also, Preceding Sentence Club, The
secret ballot, 125
Segar, E., 148, 157n56
semiotic arguments, 2, 3, 4, 15, 35–43, 43n3, 44n9, 45n39, 46n64, 47n67, 71–72n6, 74n72, 80–81, 81–83, 83–84, 88n41, 93, 94–95, 95–96, 97, 99, 103, 105, 106, 107, 110, 111, 111n1, 111–112n2, 112n3, 115n72, 118, 148, 165; attributed to Anderson, 5, 45n41, 62–63, 66–71, 72n14, 74n51; attributed to Archard, 5, 27, 46n49, 83, 89n72, 153n18; attributed to Pateman, 44n9; attributed to Sandel, 15, 49–53, 55–57, 58n17, 71–72n6; attributed to Satz, 5, 79–80, 88n57; attributed to Walzer, 5, 26, 75–79, 155n34; contingent, 40–42, 59n29, 85, 95; essentialist, 15, 27, 36–39, 39–40, 41, 42, 43, 43n3, 45n41, 46n54–55, 49–53, 55–57, 62–63, 63–64, 66–71, 75–79, 88n57, 89n73, 95, 96, 102, 103, 110, 170, 180n73, 199–200; impure, 89n83; putatively in democratic theory, 44n6, 155n36
semiotic essentialism, 36, 40, 45n41, 46n53–54, 56, 63–64, 66, 67, 71, 85, 153n18, 170, 180n73
See also, semiotic arguments, essentialist
sex, 3, 19, 20–23, 25, 30n26, 32n80, 40, 61, 62–63, 66–71, 73n43, 73n45, 74n49, 76, 81–83, 84, 95, 98, 105, 106, 107, 109, 116n76, 116n84, 122, 124, 125, 128, 136–137n53, 158n77, 160, 165–168, 170, 177n27–28, 178n36, 178n47, 179n50, 179n53
See also prostitution
sex therapy, *see* sex
Shakespeare in the Park, 12–14
Sidelsky, Edward, 154–155n33
Sidelsky, Robert, 30n24, 154–155n33
Simmel, Georg, 46n54, 59n36, 59–60n43, 178–179n49
simony, 29, 75, 76
Singer, Peter, 27
Skorupski, John, 40
slavery, voluntary, 19, 24–25, 33n96, 44n9
Snapper. John W., 192, 197n26
social utility, 12–14, 57, 58n15
socially constructed goods, 80, 125
solidarity, 28, 84, 167
Sparks, Jacob, 95, 105, 106–107, 107–110, 112n3, 113n16, 116n80, 116n91, 116n94, 116n97
speaking engagements, 6, 153n27, 172, 190
sphere differentiation, 20–23, 26, 62–63, 70, 72n12, 75–79, 93, 98, 128, 134, 141, 154–155n33, 158n77, 195
sphere segregation, 21, 101, 158n77
Stanford University, 79, 180n64
status, social, 19, 22, 39, 44n9, 65, 68, 81, 121, 167
Stoebenau, Kirsten, 166, 178n39
Suárez, Francisco, 29, 119

sugar babies, 179n53
sugar daddies, 179n53
Sunstein, Cass R., 98–99, 101, 113–114n33, 114n44–45
surrogacy, 19, 20, 23–25, 33n100, 61, 63, 66, 71, 74n66, 81, 98, 169, 180n61
surrogate motherhood, *see* surrogacy
surrogate pregnancy, *see* surrogacy
Sutton, Mike, 148

taboo, 51
Tandroy, the, 166, 168, 178n36, 179n53
Telephone, child's game, 146
terrorism, financial speculation on, 49–50, 50–51, 58n11, 60n45
  See also, bets
thick concepts, 64, 65
Titmuss, Richard, 27, 34n118, 83
toxicity, 161, 174n5-6

universal commodification, 66, 130, 136n53, 179n55
Uplavici, O., 147
utilitarian arguments, 12

vaccination, 161
vagueness, 161

Vane-Trumpington, Digby, 100
voice, 21, 23, 149, 150, 158n73, 173
votes, 3, 18, 19, 22, 32n58, 98, 102, 107–109, 116n87, 125–126, 132, 153n20
  See also gift, votes as a
  See also political influence, purchase of
votes, markets in, *see* votes
vulnerability, 16, 126

Waldfogel, Joel, 51, 59n27, 59n29
Walzer, Michael, 2, 5, 11, 25–27, 30n23, 33n102, 34n103, 40, 43, 59n29, 75–79, 80, 86, 87n5, 87n7-8, 87n13, 87n16, 88n33, 89n77, 111–112n2, 118, 128, 136n39, 155n34
Waugh, Evelyn, 100
weak agency, 16, 126
Winnie-the-Pooh, 146–147
Wittgenstein, Ludwig, 40
woozle, academic, 58n17, 147–148, 150, 153n17, 156n44, 173, 180n70, 182, 188, 194, 199–200, 202; animal, 146

Yale University, 153n13
Yosemite, 14–15, 30n12, 56–57

Zelizer, Viviana A., 165, 177n30